GLOUCESTER MASSACHUSETTS

ROCKPORT PUBLISHERS

Type Style Finder

The Busy Designer's Guide to Choosing Type

Written and compiled by
Timothy Samara

Acknowledgments

Producing this book required rigorous attention to detail on the part of contributors and editorial staff alike to overcome a host of potential pitfalls. My sincere appreciation to the team at Rockport Publishers, and in particular Kristin, Regina, Rochelle, and Cora. Their diligence and commitment to quality are what make books like this possible.

I would also like to extend my appreciation to the type houses who lent their fonts for this publication—The Chank Company, Device, Garage Fonts, MVB Fonts, Nick's Fonts, and T.26—especially to Rian Hughes of Device and Nick Curtis of Nick's Fonts, who produced their specimens for me.

And last, but certainly not least, I would like to offer my profound thanks to Linotype for generously supplying half the specimens included in this book. A tremendous amount of my time and effort was greatly reduced through the work of Otmar Hoefer and his colleagues in Linotype's marketing department, who created and organized this important contribution from one of the most highly respected—and historically important—type foundries. Linotype's stewardship of typeface design and distribution is exemplified by the quality of the faces they catalogue and continue to produce.

This book is dedicated to Sean, my parents and friends, and my students. Ever onward.

First published in the United States of America by
Rockport Publishers, a member of
Quayside Publishing Group
33 Commercial Street
Gloucester, Massachusetts 01930-5089
Telephone: (978) 282-9590
Fax: (978) 283-2742
www.rockpub.com

Cover and Book Design Timothy Samara
*This book was typeset using the sans-serif family
Tabula and the serif family Slimbach.*

Library of Congress Cataloging-in-Publication Data
Samara, Timothy.
——Type style finder : the busy designer's guide to
choosing type / Timothy Samara.
——p.——cm.
——Includes index.
——ISBN 1-59253-190-3 (vinyl)
—1. Type and type-founding. 2. Graphic design
(Typography) I. Title.
—Z250.S164 2006
—686.2'24—dc22   2005018146
                                                        CIP

ISBN 1-59253-190-3

10 9 8 7 6 5 4 3 2 1

Printed in China

Contents

A Type and Color Primer

Sumerian cuneiform Impressed in clay: 1600 B.C.

The Origins of Type: An Abridged History

Our modern conception of type comes to us after a 4,000-year trek through Mesopotamia, Egypt, Greece, and the Italian peninsula, and finally into western Europe. The Roman alphabet, codified during the second and first centuries B.C. and initially inscribed with a chisel, derives from Greek lapidary (stone-carved) writing, evolved over millennia from characters developed by the Sumerians, Etruscans, and Phoenicians. Besides introducing additional characters, the Romans simplified the structure of existing characters; retaining a single thickness in the character strokes. Eventually, scribes began to plan inscriptions by painting on the stones before carving. The square-cut reed pens and brushes they used left contrasting marks, and the resulting thick and thin strokes (shading), along with serifs, would profoundly influence letterform construction for the next 2,000 years.

Greek lapidary capitals Carved in stone, 500 B.C.

The quadrant-proportioned, so-called "square capitals" of the first century A.D. mark the beginning of modern writing, no longer reserved for Imperial documents alone. Further simplified shapes called majuscules and minuscules, popularized after Rome's fall in 476 A.D., would later become the modern lower-case, during the Medieval period (500–1300 A.D.). Charlemagne, the Frankish conqueror who united much of feudal Europe during the eighth century, is often credited with standardizing the writing of minuscules and majuscules across his empire. With the eventual disintegration of Charlemagne's empire in the 900s, however, a shift toward more regional scripts of varying roundness and contrast—the Gothic Textura and Fraktur—held sway until the fourteenth century, when Renaissance humanists rediscovered Carolingian scripts and took them as their model for developing new alphabets.

Roman lapidary capitals First century A.D.

Coincidentally, the thirteenth and fourteenth centuries also marked the introduction of wood-block printing and papermaking to Europe from the East. Eventually, a quest for quicker production methods was undertaken. Most historical evidence credits a German inventor, Johannes Gutenberg, with adapting several technologies to create a system of reusable, durable, and extraordinarily precise letters in metal and transferring their image onto paper at a remarkable speed. His first project, a Bible set with moveable type, was printed in 1455.

Written Roman capitals Second century A.D.

Roman cursive capitals Fourth century A.D.

The subsequent evolution of printing technology encouraged dramatic exploration of design ideas, and printers refined new approaches to the alphabet over the course of the next few centuries. Within a period of 500 years, the design of letters underwent a radical shift in form, progressing beyond the Carolingian-inspired, brushlike organic strokes of oldstyle toward more rational drawings that were increasingly precise, sharper in detail, bolder, simpler, and increasingly more uniform in proportion. By the early twentieth century, a new form— the sans serif—had become common, symbolic of corporate identities and the emerging International Style of typographic design. The stylistic neutrality of these sans-serif forms spoke to the idea of a universal visual language. In 1952, the Swiss type foundry Haas released Helvetica, a sans-serif family with an extraordinarily large lowercase and an optical uniformity among the letters that is rivaled only by Univers, released by Monotype in 1958. Strikingly, these modern forms retain evidence of their origin in the brush some 2,000 years ago.

Now well into the early phase of a technological revolution, designers have become comfortable manipulating existing forms, as well as constructing new ones when needed—a process made possible by the personal computer and resulting in intuitively designed faces that challenge notions of proper construction and legibility. As font designer Zuzanna Licko of Émigré, one of the pioneering digital type houses of the early 1990s, has said, the legibility of typefaces changes over time through use. Complicated textura forms, for example, were considered quite legible in the fifteenth century but today are seen as hard to read.

Whatever the form, typefaces carry messages above and beyond the words that they spell out—emotional responses or associations that viewers make in response to a typeface's formal details. To a large degree, this response is subjective and based on the viewer's personal experience and cultural background. Some designers say that this variable makes the choice of typeface irrelevant—that it is what the designer does with the typeface's size and arrangement in a composition that imparts communication. But in the sense that designers often speak to very targeted audiences, the choice of typeface as part of the communication can be an effective part of resonating with a particular group. So long as the designer can understand appreciate the formal, visual characteristics of a typeface's strokes and details that contribute to such associations, he or she can make intelligent decisions about finding the right type style for the job at hand.

Roman cursive miniscule Fifth century A.D.

Carolingian half-uncials 700–800 A.D.

Carolingian majuscule and miniscule 750–800 A.D.

Gothic textura writing 1250–1300 A.D.

Printed textura type 1450–1500 A.D.

Alphabet Structure and Variation

The twenty-six letters in the English alphabet are interrelated. Drawn with a minimum of strokes, each archetypal form is as different as possible from all the others. Some forms—E, F, H, I, J, L, and T, for example—are related visually and historically, but while they are similar in that they are composed only of horizontal and vertical strokes, they also are different enough to be easily distinguished.

The letterforms in all typefaces vary from their archetypes in only six aspects: case, weight, contrast, width, posture, and style. Type designers—referring to historical models—subtly alter and combine the variables in these six aspects to create individual type styles that, though appearing remarkably different, all convey the same information about the letterforms in the alphabet. Different approaches to the drawing of typefaces have evolved, become popular, or been discarded over time, and as a result, the formal aspects of particular typefaces often carry associations with specific periods in history, cultural movements, or geographic location—some faces feel "modern" or "classical," others feel "French" or "English." More important, the drawing of a typeface often exhibits a particular kind of rhythm, or cadence, and provides distinct physical presence in a design that may connote feelings—fast or slow, aggressive or elegant, cheap or reliable. It's important to consider that not all viewers will perceive the same associations in a given typeface; the designer must therefore carefully evaluate his or her typeface selection in the context of the audience for a particular piece. Additionally, mixing typefaces that are incongruous—for example, using an archaic Roman capital in a flyer promoting an electronica concert—will often add surprising layers of communication to the overall message.

Further, the drawing characteristics of typefaces affect their functional qualities, making some more legible at certain sizes or affected by color in particular ways. Recognizing and understanding the six fundamental aspects of alphabet variation is an important first step in being able to select and combine appropriate typefaces for a job.

Letterform Anatomy
The strokes of letters share a terminology codified among scribes and typesetters for 2,000 years. These terms are among those in standard usage among type designers.

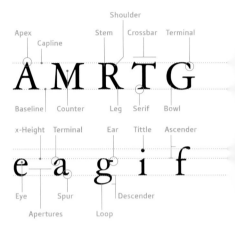

The most subtle alteration of even one variable of a letter's archetypal structure—and more so in combination—results in typefaces of dramatically different appearance. The essential characteristics of the base structure, so long as they remain intact, allow these variations in form to be perceived and understood without difficulty. In the example below, an overlay of various uppercase A's reveals the infinite possibilities within the archetype: two diagonals, meeting at an apex, joined by a horizontal stroke.

Three letters shown in uppercase (left) and lowercase (right)

Case Every letter in the Western alphabet occurs in a large form—the capitals, or uppercase—and a small, more casual form—lowercase. The uppercase requires added space between letters to permit easier reading. The lowercase is more varied and more quickly recognized in text.

Aa Gg Mm

Light	Medium	Bold	Black

Weight The overall thickness of the strokes, relative to the height of the uppercase, may change. Light, regular, bold, and black weights—increasing in stroke thickness—for a single type style define a type family. Variation in weight helps add visual contrast, as well as helps distinguish between informational components within a hierarchy.

Uniform Strokes	Slight Contrast and Modulation	High Contrast	Extreme Contrast

Contrast The strokes within the letters of a typeface may be uniform in weight or may vary significantly; the more they do so, the more contrast the face is said to exhibit. Contrast within a stroke—such asflaring from thin to thick—is called *modulation*; the rate at which this occurs is referred to as the typeface's *ductus*.

Extra Condensed	Condensed	Regular	Extended *or* Expanded

M M M M

Width The proportional width of the letters in a typeface is based on the width of the uppercase M. Faces that are narrower are said to be condensed, while wider ones are said to be extended or expanded.

Three uppercase letters in roman and corresponding italic

Posture Roman letters are those whose vertical axis is 90° to the baseline—they stand upright. Italic letters, developed by humanist scholars during the Renaissance, slant 12–15° to the right, mimicking the slant of handwriting.

AA GG MM

Style in a historical progression, archaic to contemporary | Style in terms of decorative quality

| Serif | Serif | Sans Serif | Neutral | Stylized |
| Archaic | Transitional | Modern | | |

Style This term is used to describe 1) the two major classes of type—*serif* (having little feet at the ends of the strokes) and *sans serif* (having no such feet); 2) the historical period in which the typeface was drawn; and 3) the relative neutrality or decorative quality of a typeface. Typefaces that are neutral are closest to the basic structure, while those with exaggerated characteristics are said to be stylized, idiosyncratic, or decorative.

Typeface Classification

Classifying type into groups can help highlight the differences among styles, organizing them in a general way and further helping to select an appropriate typeface for a particular project. Sometimes the historical or cultural context of a particular style adds relevant communication to a typographic design. In other instances, selecting a historical style that is anachronistic to the project's context will add a layer of meaning that is appropriate.

Classification is by no means easy, however. Type designers have traditionally used older forms as a basis for exploration, and so even centuries ago, classifying a typeface was difficult—historical references that became the basis of the design process introduced a certain amount of stylistic overlap from period to period. With an even greater archive of typographic evolution on hand today, contemporary type designers often mix and match qualities from a number of periods to produce hybrids of classification. The typeface Optima, for example, drawn by Hermann Zapf in the 1950s, is a sans serif face that exhibits modulation that could have been derived from a brush, as well as structural details that are often seen in oldstyle serif faces.

A number of systems for classifying type have been developed over the past several decades. Nowadays, as then, classifications change, but a few basic categories remain constant. Knowing what differences to look for—and where those differences come from—is a good start to evaluating type styles to carry specific kinds of messages.

Stroke Terminals and Spurs

Apertures

Serif Shapes

Joint Variation

Axis and Spine

Beaks

Ductus and Modulation

Branch Variation and Counter Shapes

The Differences in the Details

The formal characteristics of every typeface—the degree of contrast in the strokes, the relative height of the lowercase, the shapes of terminals and serifs, the overall width and rhythm of strokes and counters, and so on—vary considerably from one to the next. Sometimes these differences appear quite small, but their overall effect is a change in presence that, though potentially subtle, affects the typeface's feeling and therefore the associations it may evoke in an audience. Being able to locate details within different faces for comparison, as well as understanding how those details affect thevisual rhythm and feeling of the face, are important skills to master. Some important structural details to consider are highlighted in the collage above; comparison of the letters among the classified styles, opposite, will reveal further distinctions.

A E M F S B K O G R Y
a e m f s b k o g r y

Oldstyle Characterized by organic contrast of weight in the strokes—from brush or pen drawing; an angled, or oblique, axis in the curved forms; and a notably small x-height defining the lowercase letters. The terminals are pear shaped and the apertures in the lowercase letters are small.

A E M F S B K O G R Y
a e m f s b k o g r y

Transitional These types show an evolution in structure. Stroke contrast is greatly increased and more rationally applied—its rhythm is greatly pronounced. The x-height of the lowercase is larger; the axis is more upright; and the serifs are sharper and more defined, their brackets curving quickly into the stems.

A E M F S B K O G R Y
a e m f s b k o g r y

Modern Stroke contrast is extreme—the thin strokes are reduced to hairlines and the thick strokes made bolder. The axis of the curved forms is completely upright, and the brackets connecting the serifs to the stems have been removed, creating a stark and elegant juncture. The serifs in a number of the lowercase characters have become completely rounded, reflecting the logic of contrast and circularity.

A E M F S B K O G R Y
a e m f s b k o g r y

Sans Serif These typefaces are an outgrowth of "display types" of the nineteenth century, designed to be bold and stripped of nonessential details. They are defined by a lack of serifs; the terminals end sharply without adornment. Their stroke weight is uniform, and their axis is completely upright. Sans-serif types set tighter in text and are legible at small sizes; during the past fifty years, they have become acceptable for extended reading.

A E M F S B K O G R Y
a e m f s b k o g r y

Slab Serif Another outgrowth of display types, slab serif faces hybridize the bold presentation of a sans-serif and the horizontal stress of a serif face, characterized by an overall consistency in stroke weight. The serifs are the same weight as the stems, hence "slabs;" the body of the slab serif is often wider than what is considered normal.

Graphic These typefaces are the experimental, decorative, children of the display types. Their visual qualities are expressive but not conducive to reading in a long text. This category of faces includes specimens such as script faces, fancy and complex faces inspired by handwriting, and idiosyncratic faces that are illustrative or conceptual.

Choosing the Right Face: Visual Associations

Selecting a typeface for its feeling or mood is a tricky endeavor that often comes down to a designer's gut reaction to the rhythm or shapes inherent in a particular style. Some typefaces, for example, feel fast or slow, heavy or light, and these qualities can be quickly attributed to the interplay of counterspaces, stroke weights and contrasts, joints, and so on. A great many typefaces also conjure associations with cultural motifs because of their common use in advertising or other pop-culture venues for specific kinds of subject matter: gothic blackletters or textura faces, for instance, commonly evoke horror or fantasy because they are tied to certain historical time periods and because they have been used widely in posters and advertising for movies and books in this genre.

However, the intrinsic drawing of a typeface may involve shapes that can be read as other shapes that are found in our environments. Sinewy, curved shoulders that seem to sprout from the vertical stems of letters, or leafy terminals, allude clearly to natural forms such as plants or animals. When thinking about choosing an appropriate typeface, it is helpful to look at the images that accompany the text, or to think about objects or places related to the subject matter of the text, as inspiration.

The geometric, linear texture of this architectural façade is complemented by the rigid quality of the sans serif.

The rounded forms and sinewy modulation of this italic serif echo the organic quality of the figure. A bolder version alludes to the figure's muscularity.

A stylized serif with graphic details closely resembles the branching, twisting forms of the tree branches.

Repetitive, industrial forms with linear character and rapid alternation of positive and negative space have a rhythm similar to the condensed sans serif.

Combining Type Styles: The Basics

The conventional wisdom for mixing typefaces is to select two type families for a given job. Context, however, plays an important role in deciding whether or not to adhere to such a limitation. The complexity of the information being presented affects the decision to combine typefaces, as does the overall neutrality, consistency, and expressiveness. If a job requires seven or eight typefaces, so be it—but choose wisely.

Contrast among juxtaposed typefaces is critical. The only reason to change a typeface is to gain an effect of contrast, so the contrast achieved by the combination should be clearly recognizable—otherwise, why bother? Opposing the extremes of weight (light against bold), of width (regular against condensed or expanded), or style (neutral sans serif against slab serif or script), is a natural starting point. But somewhere in the mix, even among extremes of this nature, there must be some formal relationship between the selected fonts to enrich their visual dialogue. Choosing a sans serif and a serif that are about the same weight or width, for example, creates a tension of similarity and difference that can be quite sophisticated. Selecting two serif faces that are similar in weight, but very different in width or contrast, achieves a similar tension. Sometimes this choice is functional: for example, if the difference between the face selected for text and its bold counterpart in the same family is not particularly pronounced (meaning that the use of the bold doesn't achieve the desired emphasis), a similarly shaped bold style may be substituted. Generally, it is unwise to combine two faces of a similar style unless the difference is pronounced enough for the average reader to notice.

The historical quality of typefaces may also play a role in how they are selected and combined. Since the average reader usually associates certain qualities with a given typeface because of its classical or modern drawing qualities, mixing typefaces from related—or dramatically different—periods may help generate additional messages. A Roman capital, such as Trajan, in combination with a geometric sans serif, such as Futura, may not only present a great deal of contrasting typographic color but may also allude to a historical association: old and new, continuum, evolution, innovation, and so on. In this particular case, both Trajan and Futura are based on Roman geometric proportion, despite being separated by 2,000 years of history.

A
each **incidence** requires

B
each **incidence** requires

The bold weight (A) of this text face isn't much different from the regular weight; therefore, a bold face from an alternate yet similar family (B) may be substituted. Note the similarity of the details between the two faces.

A
MABDRO aefgo

B
MABDRO aefgo

When mixing typefaces, select counterparts with enough contrast—but be aware of their potential similarities as well. In this example, the serif (A) and the sans serif (B) are radically different in stroke contrast and detail, but their construction is similarly geometric.

lorem ipsum dolor 123 sit amet
consectitur 478 adipscing eram

1,205.17	1,205.17
4,493.35	4,493.35
716.04	716.04

Nonlining numerals are more consistent with the lowercase in running text; lining numerals are stylistically simpler and therefore should be used to set tabulated figures for greater clarity. When mixing numerals from different typefaces, check for similarities in their weight and width.

form FOLLOWS **function**

Combining a variety of type styles is a sure way to increase the typographic color of a layout. Using different widths, weights, and historical styles together creates a poetic, expressive collage of rhythm, light, and dark.

Fundamentals of Color

A composition in black and white may exhibit dynamic typographic color—contrast in scale, gray value, and spacing. What happens when type isn't black? Coloring type elements adds dimension, expression, and informational clarity.

A single color is defined by four essential qualities: hue, saturation, value, and temperature. Hue is the identity of a color—red, violet, orange, yellow, and the like. Saturation describes its intensity—whether the color is vibrant or dull. A color's value is the aspect most closely related to typographic color—its darkness or lightness. Temperature is a subjective, experiential quality. A warm color, such as red or orange, reminds us of heat; a cool color, such as green or blue, reminds us of "cold" objects, such as plants or water. The perception of these color characteristics is relative, changing as different colors interact. The perception of hue is the most absolute: a color is seen either as blue or green. However, if two similar blues are placed next to each other, one will be perceived as being more red, while the other will be perceived as being more green. A color's value, temperature, and saturation will also appear to change when brought into context with another color. A blue may appear dark against a white field but may appear light against a black field.

Color Models and Relationships

Since the seventeenth century, artists and scientists have been creating visual models for describing color relationships. Of these, the most common is the color wheel, developed by Albert Munsell, a British painter and scientist. Munsell's color wheel is a circular representation of hue (the differences in wavelength that distinguish blue from yellow from red) modified along two axes that describe the color's value (its darkness or lightness) and saturation (its relative brilliance). A color model helps a designer see these relationships for planning color ideas.

A color model for refracted light, however, is different from a color model for substances that are mixed, such as paints or inks. Because the former involves splitting waves from pure light (which contains all colors and appears white) and the latter involves mixing chemical pigments to create other colors (combining from pure to black), each medium has its own type of color model. A color model for light is said to be subtractive, while a color model for ink is said to be additive.

Hue

Saturation

Value

Temperature

The intrinsic attributes of color are hue, saturation, value, and temperature. Each attribute affects the same color in different ways. Darkening the color tends to decrease its intensity, as does making it lighter. Changing the color's temperature affects its relative hue—as it gets cooler, it becomes more of a violet; as it gets warmer, it appears orange.

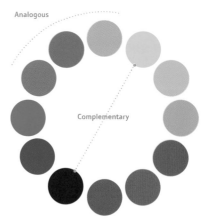

Analogous

Complementary

Relationships between colors are defined by their relative position on the Munsell color wheel (above). Colors that appear next to each other in sequence are called analogous; colors situated opposite each other are called complementary.

The Psychology of Color

The emotional component of color is connected to human experience at an instinctual and biological level. Colors of varying wavelengths have different effects on the autonomic nervous system. Warmer colors, such as reds and yellows, have long wavelengths, so more energy is needed to process them as they enter the eye and brain. The accompanying rise in energy level and metabolic rate translates as arousal. Conversely, the shorter wavelengths of cooler colors—blue, green, and violet—require far less energy to process, resulting in the slowing of our metabolic rate and a soothing, calming effect.

The psychological properties of color are also highly dependent on a viewer's culture and personal experience. Many cultures equate red with feelings of hunger, anger, or energy because red is closely associated with meat, blood, heat, and violence. Vegetarians, by contrast, may associate the color green with hunger. In Western cultures, which are predominantly Christian, black is associated with death and mourning, but Hindus associate death with the color white. Christians, for their part, associate white with purity or cleanliness. In Western civilization, violet has long signified authority and luxury. Most cultures associate blue with water or life and often perceive it as spiritual or contemplative. Because of these types of color symbolism, selecting a color for specific words in a composition can add meaning by linking its associations to the verbal message.

Red This vibrant color is among the most noticeable. Red stimulates the autonomic nervous system to the highest degree, invoking the "fight or flight" adrenaline response, causing us to salivate with hunger, or causing us to feel impulsive. Red evokes feelings of passion and arousal.

Blue The power of blue to calm and create a sense of protection or safety results from its short wavelength; its association with the ocean and sky account for its perception as solid and dependable. Statistically, blue is the best-liked of all the colors.

Yellow Associated with the sun and warmth, yellow stimulates a sense of happiness. It appears to advance spatially in relation to other colors and also helps to enliven surrounding colors. Yellow encourages clear thinking and memory retention. A brighter, greener yellow can cause anxiety; deeper yellows evoke wealth.

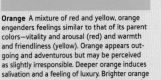

Green With the shortest wavelength, green is the most relaxing color of the spectrum. Its association with nature and vegetation makes it feel safe. The brighter the green, the more youthful and energetic. Deeper greens suggest reliable economic growth. More neutral greens, such as olive, evoke earthiness. However, green, in the right context, can connote illness or decay.

Orange A mixture of red and yellow, orange engenders feelings similar to that of its parent colors—vitality and arousal (red) and warmth and friendliness (yellow). Orange appears outgoing and adventurous but may be perceived as slightly irresponsible. Deeper orange induces salivation and a feeling of luxury. Brighter orange connotes health, freshness, quality, and strength. As orange becomes more neutral, its activity decreases, but it retains a certain sophistication, becoming exotic.

Violet Violet is sometimes perceived as compromising—but also as mysterious and elusive. The value and hue of violet greatly affect its communication: deep violets, approaching black, connote death; pale, cooler violets, such as lavender, are dreamy and nostalgic; red-hued violets, such as fuchsia, are dramatic and energetic; plumlike hues are magical.

Brown The association of brown with earth and wood creates a sense of comfort and safety. The solidity of the color, because of its organic connotation, evokes feelings of timelessness and lasting value. Brown's natural qualities are perceived as rugged, ecological, and hard-working; its earthy connection connotes trustworthiness and durability.

Gray The ultimate neutral, gray may be perceived as noncommittal, but can be formal, dignified, and authoritative. Lacking the emotion that chroma carries, it may seem aloof or suggest untouchable wealth. Gray may be associated with technology, especially when presented as silver. It suggests precision, control, competence, sophistication, and industry.

Black Unknowable and extreme, black is the strongest color in the visible spectrum. Its density and contrast are dominant, but it seems neither to recede nor to advance in space. Its indeterminate quality reminds viewers of nothingness, outer space, and, in Western culture, death. Its mystery is perceived as formal and exclusive, suggesting authority, superiority, and dignity.

White In a subtractive color model, white represents the presence of all color wavelengths; in an additive model, it is the absence of color. Both of these models help form the basis for white's authoritative, pure, and all-encompassing power. As the mixture of all colors of light, it connotes spiritual wholeness and power. Around areas of color activity in a composition—especially around black, its ultimate contrast—white appears restful, stately, and pure.

Interactions of Type and Color

Color exhibits a number of spatial properties in addition to its psychological aspects and thus has a profound effect on composition and legibility when applied to type. Cool colors appear to recede, whereas warm colors appear to advance. Of the primary colors, blue appears to recede and yellow to advance, but red appears to sit statically at a middle depth within space. A color appears darker the less there is of it. A large rectangle and a narrow line of the same color, for example, will appear to have different values if set against a white background: the color in the rectangle will appear lighter than it does in the line, because the line is surrounded by much brighter white space. A designer must pay careful attention to the relative values of colors and their effect on legibility, especially in instances in which a colored background interacts with colored type. As their values approach each other, the contrast between type and background diminishes, and the type becomes less legible. It is important to maintain considerable contrast between the type color and the background color so that the type remains visible.

The application of color to a typographic composition has an immediate effect on hierarchy. The intrinsic value relationships of typographic color in a hierarchy may be exaggerated, and therefore clarified, through the application of chromatic color. For example, if information at the top of a hierarchy is set in a deep, vibrant orange-red, while the secondary information is set in a cool gray, the two levels of the hierarchy will be visually separated to a much greater degree. The application of color to the ground within a composition can further enhance the hierarchy. Type in one color, set on a field of another color, will either join closely with the field or separate from it aggressively, depending on the relationship between the two colors. If the colors of type and background are related, the two elements will occupy a similar spatial depth. If they are complementary, they will be forced apart. Color may also be used to link related informational components within a hierarchy. In an event poster, for example, all the information related to the time and place of the event may be assigned a particular color, related to that assigned to the title of the event, but contrasting supporting text. The color relationship of the title and location components creates a meaningful link for the viewer.

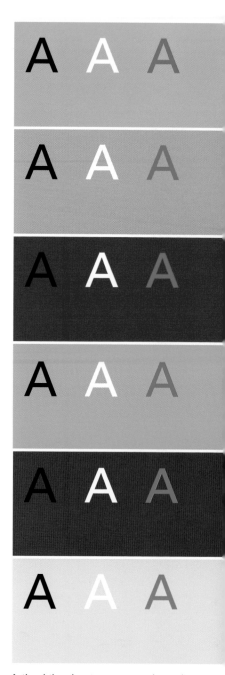

As the relative values, temperatures, and saturation of type and background change, so do their apparent spatial relationships—along with legibility. Contrast in hue and temperature help create clear separation, as does a strong contrast in value. As the value of a background's color comes closer to that of the type on top, there is a loss of separation and, therefore, legibility—especially when complements interact.

D   T

Anzeigen Grotesk
Sans Serif | Bold Weight |
Uniform Strokes | Condensed |

Linotype Library GmbH
www.linotype.com
info@linotype.com
+49 (0) 6172 484.418

The Type Style Finder

While some claim that it's not so much which typeface is chosen as how the type is arranged that really matters, the undeniable fact is that typefaces—by virtue of their abstract shapes and details—carry some messaging with them. The concepts or moods they convey may vary among audiences, but part of a designer's task is to target his or her audience as directly as possible and thus understand how the forms of given type styles might resonate better with them.

Following are forty-three type style categories, sorted by mood, concept, time frame, and age group. At the beginning of each category is a design project that exemplifies the category, along with a brief overview of the characteristics that create an appropriate association in type. Specimens related to a given category are each shown in their full alphabet and as a line sample. Rounding out each category is a color palette that may further help direct decisions during the design process. A process color formula—given as percentage builds of cyan, magenta, yellow, and black—is provided for each swatch in the palette.

Though these categories are by no means exhaustive, they offer an introduction to looking at formal qualities in type and color so that designers may more thoroughly consider the typefaces they select to get their jobs done.

Each featured typeface is presented with an informational caption like the one above that includes the font's name and a summary of its specific attributes. The name of the font's distributor follows, supported by website address and useful contact information.

Small icons appear in yellow squares above the typeface name, noting that face's appropriateness for certain uses:

D **Display** The typeface is best used for titling, short headlines, and similar applications at large sizes.

T **Text** The typeface is usable at small sizes for extended reading.

t **Decorative Text** Use of the typeface is best limited to subtitles, subheads, introductory paragraphs or pull-quotes. Consider carefully when using these faces at sizes under 14 points and for text longer than 100 words.

A complete contrast to the idea of "dynamic," tranquility is serene and slow, almost static—think warm milk or the gentle lap of waves on a beach. Tranquility is nonconfrontational and restful, inviting the viewer to ponder, to daydream, lulling them into a relaxed state of ease. Far from dull or boring, tranquil typefaces and colors seduce with a kind of rich smoothness and integrated form.

Tranquil

Considering typefaces in an effort to produce a restful state is a difficult affair, as type, in its linear, rhythmic quality, is predominantly active. While it often comes down to countering this surface activity by tinting the type to a lighter density, or spacing the type more loosely to create a slower reading rhythm, there are a selection of typefaces that, in their inherent form, are far more tranquil than others. These include semibold or even heavy script faces with an extremely low x-height—in which the up-and-down motion of the strokes is reduced in favor of a sloping, side-ways motion—as well as moderately extended sans-serif faces with sloping shoulders, more elliptical bowls, and open apertures. Too extended, and the stylized quality of the horizontal movement becomes self-conscious and extreme, decreasing the tranquil aspect of the face. Serif faces with slightly extended proportions, low contrast, and slow ductus are also rela-tively inactive, producing a gentle motion through a line of text.

Magazine Cover
top, and detail, bottom

Time, Inc.
Martyn Thompson,
photographer
New York City *USA*

A a B b C c D d E e F f G g H h I i J j K k L l M m
N n O o P p Q q R r S s T t U u V v W w X x Y y
Z z 0 1 2 3 4 5 6 7 8 9 ! ? @ # $ % & * ( ) { } : ; " "
The quick brown fox jumps over the lazy dog.

ITC Bookman® Light
Serif | Moderate Contrast |
Slightly Extended |

Linotype Library GmbH
www.linotype.com
info@linotype.com
+49 (0) 6172 484.418

A a B b C c D d E e F f G g H h I i J j K k L l M m
N n O o P p Q q R r S s T t U u V v W w X x Y y
Z z 0 1 2 3 4 5 6 7 8 9 ! ? & @ # $ % * : ; "
The quick brown fox jumps over the lazy dog.

JY Raj
Stylized Sans Serif | Slightly
Extended | Medium Weight |

JY&A Fonts *Distributor*
www.jyanet.com/fonts

A a B b C c D d E e F f G g H h I i J j K k L l M m N n
O o P p Q q R r S s T t U u V v W w X x Y y Z z 0 1
2 3 4 5 6 7 8 9 ! ? @ # $ % & * ( ) { } : ; " "
The quick brown fox jumps over the lazy dog.

Cisalpin™ Std Regular
Sans Serif | Medium Weight |
Large x-Height |
Abrupt Terminals |

Linotype Library GmbH
www.linotype.com
info@linotype.com
+49 (0) 6172 484.418

A a B b C c D d E e F f G g H h I i J j K k L l M m
N n O o P p Q q R r S s T t U u V v W w X x Y y
Z z 0 1 2 3 4 5 6 7 8 9 ! ? & @ # $ % * : ; "
The quick brown fox jumps over the lazy dog.

Sauna Roman
Sans Serif–Serif Hybrid |
Soft Terminals |
Lighter Medium Weight |

Underware
www.underware.nl
info@underware.nl
31 (0)70.42.78.117

A a B b C c D d E e F f G g H h I i J j K k L l M m N n
O o P p Q q R r S s T t U u V v W w X x Y y Z z 0 1 2 3
4 5 6 7 8 9 ! ? @ # $ % & * ( ) { } : ; " "
The quick brown fox jumps over the lazy dog.

Bodebeck™
Serif | Light Weight | Slight
Contrast | Slightly Condensed

Linotype Library GmbH
www.linotype.com
info@linotype.com
+49 (0) 6172 484.418

A a B b C c D d E e F f G g H h I i J j K k L l M m N n
O o P p Q q R r S s T t U u V v W w X x Y y Z z 0 1 2
3 4 5 6 7 8 9 ! ? & @ # $ % * : ; "
The quick brown fox jumps over the lazy dog.

JY Koliba Ultra Light
Sans Serif | Uniform Strokes |
Moderately Extended |

JY&A Fonts
www.jyanet.com/fonts

A a B b C c D d E e F f G g H h I i J j K k L l M m
N n O o P p Q q R r S s T t U u V v W w X x Y y
Z z 0 1 2 3 4 5 6 7 8 9 ! ? @ # $ % & * ( ) { } : ; " "
The quick brown fox jumps over the lazy dog.

D T

Breughel™ Regular
Serif | Medium Weight |
Modulated Strokes |

Linotype Library GmbH
www.linotype.com
info@linotype.com
+49 (0) 6172 484.418

**A a B b C c D d E e F f G g H h I i J j K k L l M m
N n O o P p Q q R r S s T t U u V v W w X x Y y
Z z 0 1 2 3 4 5 6 7 8 9 ! ? @ # $ % & * ( ) { } : ; " "
The quick brown fox jumps over the lazy dog.**

D T

ITC Souvenir® Medium
Serif | Bolder Medium Weight |
Notable Contrast | Very Fluid
Ductus | Soft Terminals |

Linotype Library GmbH
www.linotype.com
info@linotype.com
+49 (0) 6172 484.418

A a B b C c D d E e F f G g H h I i J j K k L l M m N n O o
P p Q q R r S s T t U u V v W w X x Y y Z z 0 1 2 3 4 5
6 7 8 9 ! ? @ # $ % & * ( ) { } : ; " "
The quick brown fox jumps over the lazy dog.

D T

Cronos™ Pro Regular
Sans Serif | Medium Weight |
Slight Contrast |
Canted Terminals |

Linotype Library GmbH
www.linotype.com
info@linotype.com
+49 (0) 6172 484.418

A a B b C c D d E e F f G g H h I i J j K k L l M m
N n O o P p Q q R r S s T t U u V v W w X x Y y Z z
0 1 2 3 4 5 6 7 8 9 ! ? @ # $ % & * ( ) { } : ; " "
The quick brown fox jumps over the lazy dog.

D T

Diverda™ Serif Std Regular
Slab Serif | Medium Weight |
Slight Contrast |

Linotype Library GmbH
www.linotype.com
info@linotype.com
+49 (0) 6172 484.418

A a B b C c D d E e F f G g H h I i J j K k L l M m
N n O o P p Q q R r S s T t U u V v W w X x Y y
Z z 0 1 2 3 4 5 6 7 8 9 ! ? @ # $ % & * ( ) { } : ; " "
The quick brown fox jumps over the lazy dog.

D T

Figural™ Book
Serif | Lighter Medium Weight |
Slight Modulation |

Linotype Library GmbH
www.linotype.com
info@linotype.com
+49 (0) 6172 484.418

A a B b C c D d E e F f G g H h I i J j K k L l M m N n
O o P p Q q R r S s T t U u V v W w X x Y y Z z 0 1 2 3
4 5 6 7 8 9 ! ? @ # $ % & * ( ) { } : ; " "
The quick brown fox jumps over the lazy dog.

D T

ITC Legacy® Sans Book
Sans Serif | Lighter Medium
Weight | Slight Contrast |

Linotype Library GmbH
www.linotype.com
info@linotype.com
+49 (0) 6172 484.418

A a B b C c D d E e F f G g H h I i J j K k L l M m
N n O o P p Q q R r S s T t U u V v W w X x Y y
Z z 0 1 2 3 4 5 6 7 8 9 ! ? @ # $ % & * ( ) { } : ; " "
The quick brown fox jumps over the lazy dog.

D **T**

Noa™ Std Regular
Sans Serif | Medium Weight |
Pronounced Horizontal
Emphasis | Large x-Height |

Linotype Library GmbH
www.linotype.com
info@linotype.com
+49 (0) 6172 484.418

A a B b C c D d E e F f G g H h I i J j K k L l M m N n
O o P p Q q R r S s T t U u V v W w X x Y y Z z 0 1
2 3 4 5 6 7 8 9 ! ? @ # $ % & * ( ) { } : ; " "
The quick brown fox jumps over the lazy dog.

D **T**

Optima™ Nova Regular
Sans Serif | Heavier Medium
Weight | Notable Contrast |
Modulation

Linotype Library GmbH
www.linotype.com
info@linotype.com
+49 (0) 6172 484.418

A a B b C c D d E e F f G g H h I i J j K k L l M m
N n O o P p Q q R r S s T t U u V v W w X x Y y
Z z 0 1 2 3 4 5 6 7 8 9 ! ? @ # $ % & * ( ) { } : ; " "
The quick brown fox jumps over the lazy dog.

D **T**

Sabon™ Roman
Serif | Medium Weight |
Fluid Ductus |

Linotype Library GmbH
www.linotype.com
info@linotype.com
+49 (0) 6172 484.418

A a B b C c D d E e F f G g H h I i J j K k L l M m N n
O o P p Q q R r S s T t U u V v W w X x Y y Z z 0 1 2 3
4 5 6 7 8 9 ! ? @ # $ % & * ( ) { } : ; " "
The quick brown fox jumps over the lazy dog.

D **T**

Linotype Brewery™ Light
Sans Serif | Very Light Weight |
Little Contrast |
Slight Modulation |

Linotype Library GmbH
www.linotype.com
info@linotype.com
+49 (0) 6172 484.418

A a B b C c D d E e F f G g H h I i J j K k L l M m
N n O o P p Q q R r S s T t U u V v W w X x Y y
Z z 0 1 2 3 4 5 6 7 8 9 ! ? @ # $ % & * ( ) { } : ; " "
The quick brown fox jumps over the lazy dog.

D **T**

ITC Stone® Informal Medium
Serif | Bolder Medium Weight |
Noticeable Contrast |
Fluid Ductus | Soft Terminals |

Linotype Library GmbH
www.linotype.com
info@linotype.com
+49 (0) 6172 484.418

A a B b C c D d E e F f G g H h I i J j K k L l M m N n
O o P p Q q R r S s T t U u V v W w X x Y y Z z 0 1
2 3 4 5 6 7 8 9 ! ? @ # $ % & * ( ) { } : ; " "
The quick brown fox jumps over the lazy dog.

D **T**

Titus
Serif | Light Weight | Moderate
Contrast | Curved Terminals |

Linotype library gmbh
www.linotype.com
info@linotype.com
+49 (0) 6172 484.418

A a B b C c D d E e F f G g H h I i J j K k L l M m N n
O o P p Q q R r S s T t U u V v W w X x Y y Z z 0 1 2 3
4 5 6 7 8 9 ! ? @ # $ % & * ( ) { } : ; " "
The quick brown fox jumps over the lazy dog.

D T

Trade Gothic™ Light
Sans Serif | Uniform Strokes |
Slightly Condensed |
Noticeably Open Counters |

Linotype Library GmbH
www.linotype.com
info@linotype.com
+49 (0) 6172 484.418

A a B b C c D d E e F f G g H h I i J j K k L l
M m N n O o P p Q q R r S s T t U u V v W w
X x Y y Z z 0 1 2 3 4 5 6 7 8 9 ! ? @ # $ %
& * ( ) { } : ; " "
The quick brown fox jumps over the lazy dog.

D t

Univers™ 53 Extended
Sans Serif | Uniform Weight |
Moderately Extended |

Linotype Library GmbH
www.linotype.com
info@linotype.com
+49 (0) 6172 484.418

A a B b C c D d E e F f G g H h I i J j K k L l M m
N n O o P p Q q R r S s T t U u V v W w X x Y y Z z
0 1 2 3 4 5 6 7 8 9 ! ? @ # $ % & * ( ) { } : ; " "
The quick brown fox jumps over the lazy dog.

D T

Utopia™ Regular
Serif | Medium Weight | Fluid Ductus

Linotype Library GmbH
www.linotype.com
info@linotype.com
+49 (0) 6172 484.418

A a B b C c D d E e F f G g H h I i J j
K k L l M m N n O o P p Q q R r S s
T t U u V v W w X x Y y Z z 0 1 2 3 4 5
6 7 8 9 ! ? @ # $ % & * ( ) { } : ; " "
The quick brown fox jumps over the lazy dog.

D t

Maximus™
Serif | Notable Contrast |
Extended

Linotype Library GmbH
www.linotype.com
info@linotype.com
+49 (0) 6172 484.418

A a B b C c D d E e F f G g H h I i J j K k L l M m
N n O o P p Q q R r S s T t U u V v W w X x Y y Z z
0 1 2 3 4 5 6 7 8 9 ! ? @ # $ % & * ( ) { } : ; " "
The quick brown fox jumps over the lazy dog.

D T

ITC New Baskerville® Roman
Serif | Medium Weight |
Fluid Ductus |

Linotype Library GmbH
www.linotype.com
info@linotype.com
+49 (0) 6172 484.418

A a B b C c D d E e F f G g H h I i J j K k L l M m
N n O o P p Q q R r S s T t U u V v W w X x Y y Z z
0 1 2 3 4 5 6 7 8 9 ! ? & @ # $ % * : ; "
The quick brown fox jumps over the lazy dog.

D T

Defused Regular
Sans Serif | Medium Weight |
Rounded Terminals |

T.26 Digital Type Foundry
www.t26.com
info@t26.com
888.T26.FONT

Tranquil Color

Hues with short wavelengths, such as blue, blue-violet, and blue-green, enter the eye easily and require little energy to process in the brain, resulting in a physical response—a decrease in metabolic rate. Adjusting this narrow spectrum through value and saturation—both lightening slightly and decreasing brilliance—creates a partial palette of cool, soothing, yet not particularly refreshing, colors. Warm colors in a medium-to-lighter value range, also neutral, connote comfort and safety, especially as they move away from the arousing red and yellow range toward brown. Lighter, warm grays are particularly relaxing and offer the added indeterminate quality of that neutrality as an invitation to thoughtfulness. When using colors in combination, a serene quality is imparted by keeping the values of adjacent colors similar, so their edges appear to soften. If these colors are also analogous, or closer in hue—rather than complementary—the activity of their relationship is further reduced.

Sample Color Combinations

28 C	
13 M	
0 Y	
0 K	

30 C	
22 M	
5 Y	
0 K	

43 C	
0 M	
10 Y	
0 K	

82 C	
48 M	
0 Y	
0 K	

6 C	
13 M	
0 Y	
14 K	

86 C	
70 M	
0 Y	
0 K	

16 C	
19 M	
30 Y	
0 K	

0 C	
6 M	
6 Y	
20 K	

56 C	
65 M	
0 Y	
0 K	

55 C	
5 M	
15 Y	
17 K	

Engaging, outgoing, adventurous, and easy to get along with—the qualities that we look for in people we'd like to be our friends are the same qualities that exemplify friendly design, typography, and color. Fonts that are casual and unpretentious, hues that come right out and say hi, combinations of typeface and color that make us feel good and help us through a layout are friends, indeed.

Friendly

In terms of type, friendly faces are just like friendly faces in a design studio: open, smiling, ready to work and to have fun doing it. Large x-heights and counters, open apertures, a minimum of details—but unexpected ones here and there—create welcome legibility and entry into text, as well as some fun at larger sizes where an unusually loopy bowl, an unusually small tittle, or a sprightly spur may add a little adventure to the line. Generally, typefaces with roundness in the bowls and shoulders, generous ductus in the branches, and soft terminals—sometimes even perkily condensed—feel accessible and easy to use. Pronounced openness in the apertures (lowercase e and a), flare in the legs or tail (uppercase R and Q, lowercase k), and large eyes (lowercase e and g, uppercase B) add to the welcoming quality that is transmitted as a byproduct of legibility. Sometimes, an aperture or counter may have a sort of "smiling" effect, or an unexpected lift in a crossbar that seems genuine and approachable. Curly graphic inclusions, decorative abstract elements, and handmade qualities all qualify as friendly.

Font Catalog Cover
top, and detail, bottom

Underware
Akiem Helmling
Amsterdam *Netherlands*

AaBbCcDdEeFfGgHhIiJjKkLlMm NnOoPpQqRrSsTtUuVvWwXxYy Zz0123456789!?@#$%&*(){}:;" "
The quick brown fox jumps over the lazy dog.

D   t

Immi™ 505
Sans Serif | Medium Weight | Modulated Strokes | Moderately Extended |

Linotype Library GmbH
www.linotype.com
info@linotype.com
+49 (0) 6172 484.418

AaBbCcDdEeFfGgHhIiJjKkLlMmNnOoPp QqRrSsTtUuVvWwXxYyZz 0123456789 !?&☼$:;" "

The quick brown fox jumps over the lazy dog.

D

P22 Ohley
Graphic-Script Hybrid | Light Weight |

P22 Type Foundry
www.p22.com
p22@p22.com
800.p22.5080

AaBbCcDdEeFfGgHhIiJjKkLlMm NnOoPpQqRrSsTtUuVvWwXxYyZz 0123456789!?&@#$%*:;"

The quick brown fox jumps over the lazy dog.

D

Quimby Mayoral
Script | Light Weight |

The Chank Company
www.chank.com
friendlyfolks@chank.com
877.GO.CHANK

AaBbCcDdEeFfGgHhIiJjKkLlMmNn OoPpQqRrSsTtUuVvWwXxYyZz012 3456789!?&@#$%*:;"

The quick brown fox jumps over the lazy dog.

D

Swingdancer
Script–Sans Serif Hybrid | Medium Weight | Condensed |

The Chank Company
www.chank.com
friendlyfolks@chank.com
877.GO.CHANK

AABBCCDDEEFFGGHHIIJJKKLL MMNNOODDQRRSSTTUUVVWW XXYYZZ0123456789!?&Fi%*()[]:;

THE QUICK BROWN FOX JUMPS OVER THE LAZY DOG.

D

Snoodle Toons
Stylized Sans Serif | Medium Weight | Caps and Alternates |

Nick's Fonts
www.nicksfonts.com

AaBbCcDdEeFfGgHhIiJjKkLl MmNnOoPpQqRrSsTtUuVvWw XxYyZz0123456789!?&@#$%*:;

The quick brown fox jumps over the lazy Dog.

D

Kaixo Regular
Script–Sans Serif Hybrid | Medium Weight |

T.26 Digital Type Foundry
www.t26.com
info@t26.com
888.T26.FONT

A a B b C c D d E e F f G g H h I i J j K k L l M m N n
O o P p Q q R r S s T t U u V v W w X x Y y Z z 0 1 2
3 4 5 6 7 8 9 ! ? & @ $: ;

The quick brown fox jumps over the lazy dog.

P22 Preissig Lino
Stylized Serif |
Medium Weight |

P22 Type Foundry
www.p22.com
p22@p22.com
800.p22.5080

A a B b C c D d E e F f G g H h I i J j K K L l M m
N n O o P p Q q R r S S T t U u V v W w X x Y y Z z
0 1 2 3 4 5 6 7 8 9 ! ? ¢ @ # $ % * : ; "

The quick brown fox jumps over the lazy dog.

Chub
Stylized Sans Serif |
Bold Weight |

The Chank Company
www.chank.com
friendlyfolks@chank.com
877.GO.CHANK

A a B b C c D d E e F f G g H h I i J j K k L l
M m N n O o P p Q q R r S s T t U u V v W w X x
Y y Z z 0 1 2 3 4 5 6 7 8 9 ! ? & @ # $ % * : ; "

The quick brown fox jumps over the lazy dog.

MVB Fantabular Bold
Slab Serif | Medium Width |
Uniform Strokes |

MVB Fonts
www.mvbfonts.com
info@mvbfonts.com
510.525.4288

A a B b C c D d E e F f G g H h I i J j K k L l M m
N n O o P p Q q R r S s T t U u V v W w X x Y y Z z
0 1 2 3 4 5 6 7 8 9 ! ? & @ # $ % * : ; "

The quick brown fox jumps over the lazy dog.

Sauna Black Italic
Script–Serif–Sans Serif
Hybrid | Moderate Posture |

Underware
www.underware.nl
info@underware.nl
31 (0)70.42.78.117

A a B b C c D d E e F f G g H h I i J j K k L l M m
N n O o P p Q q R r S s T t U u V v W w X x Y y Z z
0 1 2 3 4 5 6 7 8 9 ! ? & @ # $ % * : ; "

The quick brown fox jumps over the lazy dog.

Espresso Regular
Stylized Serif | Medium Weight |
Erratic Posture and Height |

T.26 Digital Type Foundry
www.t26.com
info@t26.com
888.T26.FONT

A a B b C c D d E e F f G g H h I i J j K k L l M m
N n O o P p Q q R r S s T t U u V v W w X x Y y
Z z 0 1 2 3 4 5 6 7 8 9 ! ? & @ # $ % * : ; "

The quick brown fox jumps over the lazy dog.

P22 Tulda Regular
Graphic | Extra Light Weight |
Open Face |

P22 Type Foundry
www.p22.com
p22@p22.com
800.P22.5080

ℛa Bb Cc Dd Ee Ff Gg Hh Ii Jj Kk Ll Mm Nn Oo Pp Qq Rr Ss Tt Uu Vv Ww Xx Yy Zz 0123456 789!?&@÷$%:;"*

The quick brown fox jumps over the lazy dog.

D

Santanera Chachacha
Script–Sans Serif Hybrid | Medium Weight | Condensed |

T.26 Digital Type Foundry
www.t26.com
info@t26.com
888.T26.FONT

Oo Bb Cc Dd Ee Ff Gg Hh Ii Jj Kk Ll Mm Nn Oo Pp Qq Rr Ss Tt Uu Vv Ww Xx Yy Zz 0123456789!?&@*$%*:;"

The quick brown fox jumps over the lazy dog.

D **t**

Sister Medium
Stylized Sans Serif | Medium Weight | Condensed |

T.26 Digital Type Foundry
www.t26.com
info@t26.com
888.T26.FONT

A a B b C c D d E e F f G g H h I i J j K k L l M m N n O o P p Q q R r S s T t U u V v W w X x Y y Z z 0 1 2 3 4 5 6 7 8 9 ! ? @ # $ % & * ( ) { } : ; " "

The quick brown fox jumps over the lazy dog.

D **T**

Metrolite #2™
Sans Serif | Light Weight | Open Counters |

Linotype Library GmbH
www.linotype.com
info@linotype.com
+49 (0) 6172 484.418

AaBbCcDDEeFfGgHhIiJjKkLlMm NNOoPPQqRRSStTUuVvWwXxYyZz 0123456789!?&@#$%*:;"

The quick brown fox jumps over the lazy dog.

D

Corndog Clean
Stylized Sans Serif | Condensed | Medium Weight | Erratic Proportions |

The Chank Company
www.chank.com
friendlyfolks@chank.com
877.GO.CHANK

AaBbCcDdEeFfGgHhIiJjKkLlMmNnOo PpQqRrSsTtUuVvWwXxYyZz01234567 89!?@#$%&(){}:;" "*

The quick brown fox jumps over the lazy dog.

D **t**

Matthia™
Sans Serif–Script Hybrid | Light Weight | Moderately Condensed

Linotype Library GmbH
www.linotype.com
info@linotype.com
+49 (0) 6172 484.418

AaBbCcDdEeFfGgHhIiJjKkLlMmNnOo PpQqRrSsTtUuVvWwXxYyZzOI23 456789!?&@#$%:;"*

The quick brown fox jumps over the lazy dog.

D

Bon Guia
Graphic–Script–Sans Serif Hybrid | Extra Condensed |

T.26 Digital Type Foundry
www.t26.com
info@t26.com
888.T26.FONT

A a B b C c D d E e F f G g H h I i J j K k L l M m N n O o P p Q q R r S s T t U u V v W w X x Y y Z z 0 1 2 3 4 5 6 7 8 9 ! ? @ # $ % & * ( ) { } : ; " "

The quick brown fox jumps over the lazy dog.

D T

Stymie Medium
Slab Serif | Light Weight | Uniform Strokes

Linotype Library GmbH
www.linotype.com
info@linotype.com
+49 (0) 6172 484.418

A a B b C c D d E e F f G g H h I i J j K k L l M m N n O o P p Q q R r S s T t U u V v W w X x Y y Z z 0 1 2 3 4 5 6 7 8 9 ! ? @ # $ % & * ( ) { } : ; " "

The quick brown fox jumps over the lazy dog.

D *t*

ITC Souvenir® Bold
Serif | Heavier Bold Weight | Noticeable Contrast |

Linotype Library GmbH
www.linotype.com
info@linotype.com
+49 (0) 6172 484.418

A a B b C c D d E e F f G g H h I i J j K k L l M m N n O o P p Q q R r S s T t U u V v W w X x Y y Z z 0 1 2 3 4 5 6 7 8 9 ! ? @ # $ % & * ( ) { } : ; " "

The quick brown fox jumps over the lazy dog.

D T

Linotype Syntax™ Letter
Modified Serif | Lighter Medium Weight | Slightly Condensed

Linotype Library GmbH
www.linotype.com
info@linotype.com
+49 (0) 6172 484.418

A a B b C c D d E e F f G g H h I i J j K k L l M m N n O o P p Q q R r S s T t U u V v W w X x Y y Z z 0 1 2 3 4 5 6 7 8 9 ! ? @ # $ % & * ( ) { } : ; " "

The quick brown fox jumps over the lazy dog.

D

Nevison Casual
Script San Serif | Light Weight | Erratic Width |

Linotype Library GmbH
www.linotype.com
info@linotype.com
+49 (0) 6172 484.418

A a B b C c D d E e F f G g H h I i J j K k L l M m N n O o P p Q q R r S s T t U u V v W w X x Y y Z z 0 1 2 3 4 5 6 7 8 9 ! ? $ % & * ( ) : ; " "

The quick brown fox jumps over the lazy dog.

D

Vario™ Std Regular
Sans Serif | Bold Weight | Modulation | Brush Details |

Linotype Library GmbH
www.linotype.com
info@linotype.com
+49 (0) 6172 484.418

A a B b C c D d E e F f G g H h I i J j K k L l M m N n O o P p Q q R r S s T t U u V v W w X x Y y Z z 0 1 2 3 4 5 6 7 8 9 ! ? @ # $ % & * ( ) { } : ; " "

The quick brown fox jumps over the lazy dog.

D *t*

Veronika™ Std Regular
Modified Serif | Lighter Medium Weight | Slightly Condensed |

Linotype Library GmbH
www.linotype.com
info@linotype.com
+49 (0) 6172 484.418

Friendly Color

As a general rule, if it's orange, it's friendly—a saturated, slightly redder orange, as opposed to the spicier, more sophisticated orange that becomes a little too earthy or sophisticated to be truly friendly. Sweet colors, such as reds with a hint of violet in them (think a cherry lollipop) or apple-y greens are also friendly and help cool and refresh the heat of orange. Golden yellow, approaching orange in character but not quite there, is sunny but has the adventurous overtone of orange. Slightly desaturated colors in this range can also be friendly and somewhat more relaxing than the brighter, more brilliant versions of the same colors. Placing a more saturated and less saturated version of the same hue—or a slightly analogous hue—may be perceived as friendly because of the close chromatic relationship. Light, warm hues, even pastels, are softer versions of "friendly."

Sample Color Combinations

C	M	Y	K
0	72	79	0
0	52	100	0
12	100	43	0
0	100	30	0
0	26	100	0
58	0	100	0
0	27	45	0
10	48	0	0
22	0	40	0
40	0	20	0

Time to laugh out loud! Humor is a tremendously effective device for engaging an audience and bringing them a little relief from their workaday experience. Whether cute and quirky or campy and irreverent, type and color that laugh with you are fun and frivolous. In the context of a serious or potentially dry subject, a little humor goes a long way in helping get the message across in a memorable manner.

Comical

There's no end to the fun that can be had with typefaces and color. So many recent experimental faces are funny to look at that it's hard to pin down what captures the comical in an alphabet. Most often, it has to do with decorative qualities—curlicue serifs, playful ascenders and descenders, bulbous strokes, or graphic inclusions. Depending on context, it may involve typefaces that call to mind campy time periods (think 1950s or 1960s suburbia) or that make jokes (a neoclassical serif with incorrect proportions, constructed of chunky dots). Typefaces with reverse italic posture, or posture changes between the letters of the alphabet, are bouncy and dance like clowns. Very short lowercase letters in a face with tall ascenders and deep descenders are funny, as are exceptionally small or overly large details such as tittles and swashes. Sometimes, a bold face with stroke contrast, in which the counterspaces defy the outer contours of the letters, will have a quirky, irreverent quality—somewhat like a stand-up comic delivering un-comfortable material that still makes us laugh. Pictorial typefaces, in which letters or parts of letters are made of recognizable objects, can be very funny. Outline types, brush-written sans serifs, and sans serifs with rounded terminals evoke comic books and newspaper funnies.

Type Specimen
top, and detail, bottom

P22 Type Foundry
Richard Kegler, art director
Colin Kahn, designer
Buffalo [NY] *USA*

AaBbCcDdEeFFGgHhIiJjKKLlMmNnOo
PpQqRrSsTtUuVvWwXxYyZzO12345
6789!?&A%*()[]:;""©¥$

The quick brown fox jumps over the lazy dog.

D

Hardy Har Har
Graphic–Sans Serif Hybrid |
Bold Weight |

Nick's Fonts
www.nicksfonts.com

AABBCCDDEEFFGGHHIiIJjKKLL
MMNNO©PPQQRR2STtUUVVWW
XXYYZZO123456789!?*and* *at* #$%*:;"

THE QUICK BROWN FOX JUMPS ©VER +HE LAZY D©G.

D

Chicken Parts
Graphic–Sans Serif Hybrid |
Contrasting Weights |

Garage Fonts Type Foundry
www.garagefonts.com
info@garagefonts.com
800.681.9375

AaBbCcDdEeFfGgHhIiJjKkLlMmNn
OoPpQqRrSsTtUuVvWwXxYyZz1
234567 89!?⊕♯%&*()::""

The quick brown fox jumps over the lazy dog.

D

Scruff™
Graphic | Erratic Weight |
Erratic Posture | Stroke
Distortion | Abstract Details

Linotype Library GmbH
www.linotype.com
info@linotype.com
+49 (0) 6172 484.418

AaBbCcDdEeFfGgHhIiJjKkLlMm
NnOoPpQqRrSsTtUuVvWwXxYyZz
0123456789!?&@#$%*:;"

The quick brown fox jumps over the lazy dog.

D

Eatwell Chubby
Sans Serif | Bold Weight |

The Chank Company
www.chank.com
friendlyfolks@chank.com
877.GO.CHANK

AaBb(c)dEeFfGgHhIiJjKkLlMm
NnO©oPpQqLSsItUuVvWwXxYy
Zz0123456789!?@#$%&*{}:;""

The quick brown fox jumps over the lazy dog.

D

P22 Bagaglio Flat
Graphic | Condensed |
Erratic Weights and Height |

P22 Type Foundry
www.p22.com
p22@p22.com
800.P22.5080

AaBbCcDdEeFfGgHhIiJjKkLlMm
NnOoPpQqRrSsTtUuVvWwXxYy
Zz0123456789!?&@#$%*:;"

The quick brown fox jumps over the lazy dog.

D

Rancho Bold
Stylized Sans Serif | Medium
Weight |

T.26 Digital Type Foundry
www.t26.com
info@t26.com
888.T26.FONT

AaBb CcDd Ee Ff Gg Hh Ii Jj Kk Ll M m
Nn Oo Pp Qq Rr Ss Tt Uu Vv Ww Xx Yy Zz 0
1 2 3 4 5 6 7 8 9 ! ? & @ $: ; " "

The quick brown fox jumps over the lazy dog.

D

P22 Bramble Wild
Serif-Script Hybrid | Light Weight | Swash Details |

P22 Type Foundry
www.p22.com
p22@p22.com
800.P22.5080

AaBbCcDdEeFfGgHhIiJjKkLLMm
NnOoPpQqRrSsTtUuVvWwX*Yy
Zz0123456789!?@#$%&*(){}:;
" "

The quick brown fox jumps over the lazy dog.

D

F2F Tagliatelle Sugo™
Sans Serif | Erratic Contrast | Heavy Weight |

Linotype Library GmbH
www.linotype.com
info@linotype.com
+49 (0) 6172 484.418

AaBbCcDd EeFf Gg Hh Ii Jj Kk Ll MmNn
OoPp Qq Rr Ss Tt Uu Vv WwXx Yy Zz 012
3456789!? & @ $:;" "

The quick brown fox jumps over the lazy dog.

D *t*

P22 Prehistoric Pen
Stylized Sans Serif | Medium Weight |

P22 Type Foundry
www.p22.com
p22@p22.com
800.P22.5080

AaBbCcDd EeFf Gg HhIi JjKk Ll Mm
Nn Oo Pp Qq Rr Ss Tt UuVv Ww Xx Yy
Zz 0123456789!? & @ $:; " "

The quick brown fox jumps over the lazy dog.

D *t*

P22 Rakugaki Latin
Stylized Sans Serif | Bold Weight |

P22 Type Foundry
www.p22.com
p22@p22.com
800.P22.5080

AaBbCcDdEeFfGgHhiiJjKkL1
MmNnOoPpQqRrSsTtUuVvWw
XxYyZz0123456789!?&@#$%.*:;"

The quick brown fox jumps over the lazy dog.

D

Buckethead
Stylized Serif | Bold Weight |

The Chank Company
www.chank.com
friendlyfolks@chank.com
877.GO.CHANK

AaBbCcDdEeFfGgHhItJjKkLlMm
NnOoPpQqRrSsTtUuVvWwXxYy
Zz0123456789!?&@#$%*:;"

The quick brown fox jumps over the lazy dog.

D

Drunk Cowboy
Modified Slab Serif | Condensed |

The Chank Company
www.chank.com
friendlyfolks@chank.com
877.GO.CHANK

AaBbCcDdEeFfGgHhIiJjKkLlMmNnOoPp
QqRrSsTtUuVvWwXxYyZz0123456789!?
@ND$%&*()[]:;""
THE QUICK BROWN FOX JUMPS OVER THE LAZY DOG.

D

Metropol Noir
Stylized Sans Serif | Caps and
Alternates | Bold Weight |

Device
www.devicefonts.co.uk
44 (0) 7979.602.272
rianhughes@aol.com

AaBbCcDdEeFfGgHhIiJjKkLlMmNnOoPp
QqRrSsTtUuVvWwXxYyZz0123456789!?
@N?$%&*(){}:;""
The quick brown fox jumps over the lazy dog.

D

Foonky Heavy
Stylized Sans Serif |
Extra Bold Weight |

Device
www.devicefonts.co.uk
rianhughes@aol.com
44 (0) 7979.602.272

AaBbCcDdEeFfGgHhIiJjKkLlMmNnOoPp
QqRrSsTtUuVvWwXxYyZz0123456789!?
@#$%&*(){}:;""
The quick brown fox jumps over the lazy dog.

D

Cantaloupe
Stylized Sans Serif | Erratic
Counters | Bold Weight |

Device
www.devicefonts.co.uk
rianhughes@aol.com
44 (0) 7979.602.272

AaBbCcDdEeFfGgHhIiJjKkLlMmNn
OoPpQqRrSsTtUuVvWwXxYyZz01
23456789!?@*$%*★:;"
THE QUICK BROWN FOX JUMPS OVER THE LAZY DOG.

D

Bric a Brac
Graphic | Condensed |
Caps with Alternates |

The Chank Company
www.chank.com
friendlyfolks@chank.com
877.GO.CHANK

AaBbCcDdEeFfGgHhIiJjKkLlMmNnOo
PpQqRrSsTtUuVvWwXxYyZz012345
6789!?$%&*():;" "
The quick brown fox jumps over the lazy dog.

D

Gill Kayo Condensed™
Sans Serif | Black Weight |
Condensed |

Linotype Library GmbH
www.linotype.com
info@linotype.com
+49 (0) 6172 484.418

AaBbCcDdEeFfGgHhIiJjKkLlMmNn
OoPpQqRrSsTtUuVvWwXxYyZz0123
456789!?@$%&*()dk:;" "
The quick brown fox jumps over the lazy dog.

D

Jokerman™
Graphic Sans Serif |
Abstract Details |
Moderately Condensed |

Linotype Library GmbH
www.linotype.com
info@linotype.com
+49 (0) 6172 484.418

A a B b C c D d E e F f G g H h I i J j K k L l M m N n O o P p Q q R r S s T t U u V v W w X x Y y Z z 0 1 2 3 4 5 6 7 8 9 ! ? @ # $ % & * ( ) { } : ; " "

The quick brown fox jumps over the lazy dog.

A a B b C c D d E e F f G g H h I i J j K K L l M N N N O O P p Q q R r S s T t U u V v V w X X Y Y Z Z 0 1 2 3 4 5 6 7 8 9 ! ? @ # $ % & * ( ) { } : ; " "

The quick brown fox jumps over the lazy dog.

Postino™
Slab Serif | Bold Weight | Extended | Flared Strokes |

Linotype Library GmbH
www.linotype.com
info@linotype.com
+49 (0) 6172 484.418

ITC Schizoid™
Graphic | Erratic Weight and Contrast | Moderately Condensed |

Linotype Library GmbH
www.linotype.com
info@linotype.com
+49 (0) 6172 484.418

A a B b C c D d E e F f G g H h I i J j K K L l M m N n O o P p Q q R r S s T t U u V v W w X x Y y Z z 0 1 2 3 4 5 6 7 8 9 ! ? @ # $ % & * ( ) { } : ; " "

The quick brown fox jumps over the lazy dog.

ITC Snap™
Modified Wedge Serif | Black Weight | Erratic Counters |

Linotype Library GmbH
www.linotype.com
info@linotype.com
+49 (0) 6172 484.418

A a B b C c D d E e F f G g H h I i J j K k L l M m N n O o P p 2 q R r S s T t U u V v W w X x Y y Z z 0 1 2 3 4 5 6 7 8 9 ! ? @ # $ % & * ( ) { } : ; " "

The quick brown fox jumps over the lazy dog.

ITC Tapioca™
Graphic Sans Serif | Light Weight | Textured Strokes | Erratic Posture

Linotype Library GmbH
www.linotype.com
info@linotype.com
+49 (0) 6172 484.418

A a B b C c D d E e F f G g H h I i J j K k L l M m N n O o P p Q q R r S s T t U u V v W w X x Y y Z z 0 1 2 3 4 5 6 7 8 9 ! ? & @ # $ % * : ; "

The quick brown fox jumps over the lazy dog.

Couchlover
Modified Modern Serif | Medium Weight |

The Chank Company
www.chank.com
friendlyfolks@chank.com
877.GO.CHANK

A a B B C C D D E e F F G G H h i i J J K K L L M M N n O O P P Q q R R S S T T U U V v W W X X Y Y Z z 0 1 2 3 4 5 6 7 8 9 ! ? & @ # $ % * : ; "

The quick brown fox jumps over the lazy dog.

Dirt Devil
Graphic Sans Serif | Erratic Weight | Mixed Case Alternates |

T.26 Digital Type Foundry
www.t26.com
info@t26.com
888.T26.FONT

Comical Color

With its connotations of childishness, games, and friendliness, comical color is bright and somewhat naïve. Bright pink, orange, and violet together bring a circuslike quality to the palette, as well as pink's soft energy, orange's adventurous spirit, and bright violet's compromising nature. Golden and lemon yellow appear for added warmth, and a slightly more yellow version of Kelly green acts as a foil to reddish hues. Although deep tones of blue and violet should be avoided in light of their somber, more restful, and sophisticated messages, a saturated cyan, especially in close proximity to its complement, yellow-orange, can be quite funny. Saturated primaries in combination with small amounts of black bring out an association with comic books.

Sample Color Combinations

0 C
80 M
7 Y
0 K

30 C
90 M
0 Y
0 K

0 C
67 M
100 Y
0 K

0 C
28 M
100 Y
0 K

5 C
5 M
100 Y
0 K

34 C
0 M
100 Y
0 K

100 C
0 M
6 Y
0 K

100 C
36 M
0 Y
0 K

0 C
100 M
72 Y
0 K

46 C
96 M
0 Y
0 K

Romance, with its related connotations of passion, glamour, and
elegance, is all about curves and tactility. Typefaces that offer tense,
exaggerated details, such as long, bulbous serifs, heavier weights,
sinewy spines and junctures, and rounded terminals give viewers
something to "grab on to" like a lover or a rich cloth. Similarly,
romantic color is equally tactile and sensuous, seductive and deep.

Romantic

The perception of romance in type can derive from a number of characteristics. Most often, these are weight and width proportions that push or
pull the eye teasingly around the forms. Slightly condensed, as well as
extended, styles—in medium to bolder weights—provide a sense of body
or girth, of corpulence. The rounder the curves, or the slower the transi-
tions between thicks and thins or between curves and stems, the more
romantic the letters will seem. Typefaces with a great deal of modulation—
a noticeable flare from mid-stem to terminal, for instance—appear to
move in a seductive and sensuous rhythm. Scripts bring more elegant,
cultured romanticism to the fore, edging toward glamour and delicacy.
Typefaces with flourishes, decorative serifs, and exaggerated bowls, leg
shapes, or eyes may lend a sense of nostalgia or charm to their overall
romantic presentation.

Collateral *details*

Mires
Gale Spitzley
San Diego [CA] *USA*

A a B b C c D d E e F f G g H h I i J j K k L l
M m N n O o P p Q q R r S s T t U u V v W w
X x Y y Z z 0 1 2 3 4 5 6 7 8 9 ! ? & @ # $ % * : ; ”

The quick brown fox jumps over the lazy dog.

D T

Belen Regular
Serif | Medium Weight |

T.26 Digital Type Foundry
www.t26.com
info@t26.com
888.T26.FONT

*A a B b C c D d E e F f G g H h I i J j K k L l M m N n O o
P p Q q R r S s T t U u V v W w X x Y y Z z 0 1 2 3 4 5 6 7 8 9 : :*

The quick brown fox jumps over the lazy dog.

D

P22 Dearest Swash
Stylized Swash-Cap Script | Light Weight |

P22 Type Foundry
www.p22.com
p22@p22.com
800.P22.5080

**A a B b C c D d E e F f G g H h I i J j K k L l
M m N n O o P p Q q R r S s T t U u V v W w
X x Y y Z z 0 1 2 3 4 5 6 7 8 9 ! ? & @ # $ % * : ; ”**

The quick brown fox jumps over the lazy dog.

D ℓ

Denim Medium
Serif | Bold Medium Weight | Textured Contour |

T.26 Digital Type Foundry
www.t26.com
info@t26.com
888.T26.FONT

*A a B b C c D d E e F f G g H h I i J j K k L l M m N n O o P p Q q R r S s
T t U u V v W w X x Y y Z z 0 1 2 3 4 5 6 7 8 9 ! ? @ # & : ; " "*

The quick brown fox jumps over the lazy dog.

D

P22 Hopper Edward
Stylized Script | Lighter Medium Weight | Little Contrast |

P22 Type Foundry
www.p22.com
p22@p22.com
800.P22.5080

A a B b C c D d E e F f G g H h I i J j K k L l M m N n O o
P p Q q R r S s T t U u V v W w X x Y y Z z 0 1 2 3 4 5 6 7
8 9 ! ? @ # $ % ð * ( ) { } : ; " ”

The quick brown fox jumps over the lazy dog.

D T

Boberia™ Light
Serif | Pronounced Contrast | Condensed |

Linotype Library GmbH
www.linotype.com
info@linotype.com
+49 (0) 6172 484.418

*A a B b C c D d E e F f G g H h I i J j K k L l
M m N n O o P p Q q R r S s T t U u V v W w X x
Y y Z z 0 1 2 3 4 5 6 7 8 9 ! ? & @ $: ; " "*

The quick brown fox jumps over the lazy dog.

D

P22 Monet Regular
Stylized Script | Pronounced Contrast |

P22 Type Foundry
www.p22.com
p22@p22.com
800.P22.5080

A a B b C c D d E e F f G g H h I i J j K k L l M m
N n O o P p Q q R r S s T t U u V v W w X x Y y
Z z O I 2 3 4 5 6 7 8 9 ! ? & @ # $ % * : ; "

The quick brown fox jumps over the lazy dog.

D T

MVB Sirenne Text OsF
Serif | Medium Weight |

MVB Fonts
www.mvbfonts.com
info@mvbfonts.com
510.525.4288

A a B b C c D d E e F f G g H h I i J j K k L l M m
N n O o P p Q q R r S s T t U u V v W w X x Y y Z z
0 1 2 3 4 5 6 7 8 9 ! ? & @ # $ % * : : "

The quick brown fox jumps over the lazy dog.

D t

Hegemonic
Stylized Serif–Script Hybrid |
Slight Italic Posture |
Condensed | Swash Details |

Garage Fonts Type Foundry
www.garagefonts.com
info@garagefonts.com
800.681.9375

A a B b C c D d E e F f G g H h I i J j K k L l
M m N n O o P p Q q R r S s T t U u V v W w
X x Y y Z z 0 1 2 3 4 5 6 7 8 9 ! ? & @ # $ % * : ; "

The quick brown fox jumps over the lazy dog.

D

Gourmet Bold
Script-Serif Hybrid |
Moderate Italic Posture |

T.26 Digital Type Foundry
www.t26.com
info@t26.com
888.T26.FONT

A B C D E F G H I J K L M N O P Q R S T U V W
X Y Z

THE QUICK BROWN FOX JUMPS OVER THE LAZY DOG

D

Linotype Venezia™ Initiale
Serif | Light Weight | Contrast |
Inline Detail | All Uppercase |
Lacking Numerals |

Linotype Library GmbH
www.linotype.com
info@linotype.com
+49 (0) 6172 484.418

A a B b C c D d E e F f G g H h I i J j K k L l M m
N n O o P p Q q R r S s T t U u V v W w X x Y y Z z
0 1 2 3 4 5 6 7 8 9 ! ? & @ # $ % * : ;

The quick brown fox jumps over the lazy dog.

D t

Julie Book
Script–Sans Serif Hybrid |
Condensed |

T.26 Digital Type Foundry
www.t26.com
info@t26.com
888.T26.FONT

A a B b C c D d E e F f G g H h I i J j K k L l
M m N n O o P p Q q R r S s T t U u V v W w
X x Y y Z z 0 1 2 3 4 5 6 7 8 9 ! ? & @ # $ % *

The quick brown fox jumps over the lazy dog.

D

Uniglow 50 Cursive
Script–Sans Serif Hybrid |
Moderately Extended |

T.26 Digital Type Foundry
www.t26.com
info@t26.com
888.T26.FONT

*Aa Bb Cc Dd Ee Ff Gg Hh Ii Jj Kk Ll Mm Nn Oo Pp Qq Rr Ss Tt Uu Vv Ww Xx Yy Zz 0 1 2 3 4 5 6 7 8 9 ! ? &@ # $ % * : ; "*

The quick brown fox jumps over the lazy dog.

D

P22 Imperial Script
Script | Moderate Contrast |
Lighter Medium Weight |

P22 Type Foundry
www.p22.com
p22@p22.com
800.P22.5080

A a B b C c D d E e F f G g H h I i J j K k L l M m N n O o P p Q q R r S s T t U u V v W w X x Y y Z z 0 1 2 3 4 5 6 7 8 9 ! ? & @ # $ % * : ; "

The quick brown fox jumps over the lazy dog.

D

Zephyr Regular
Stylized Serifs | Semi-Swash
Caps | Medium Weight |

P22 Type Foundry
www.p22.com
p22@p22.com
800.P22.5080

A a B b C c D d E e F f G g H h I i J j K k L l M m N n O o P p Q q R r S s T t U u V v W w X x Y y Z z 0 1 2 3 4 5 6 7 8 9 ! ? @ # $ % & * ( ) { } : ; " "

The quick brown fox jumps over the lazy dog.

D T

Baskerville™ Regular
Serif | Medium Weight |
Noticeable Contrast |
Slightly Abrupt Ductus |

Linotype Library GmbH
www.linotype.com
info@linotype.com
+49 (0) 6172 484.418

A a B b C c D d E e F f G g H h I i J j K k L l M m N n O o P p Q q R r S s T t U u V v W w X x Y y Z z 0 1 2 3 4 5 6 7 8 9 ! ? $ % & * ( ) : ; " "

The quick brown fox jumps over the lazy dog.

D t

Papyrus™ Regular
Sans Serif | Lighter Medium
Weight | Textured Modulation |
Pronounced Ascenders and
Descenders |

Linotype Library GmbH
www.linotype.com
info@linotype.com
+49 (0) 6172 484.418

*Aa Bb Cc Dd Ee Ff Gg Hh Ii Jj Kk Ll Mm Nn Oo Pp Qq Rr Ss Tt Uu Vv Ww Xx Yy Zz 0 1 2 3 4 5 6 7 8 9 ! ? d $ % & * ( ) p x : ; " "*

The quick brown fox jumps over the lazy dog.

D t

Gravura™
Script | Light Weight |
Slight Contrast | Swash Caps |

Linotype Library GmbH
www.linotype.com
info@linotype.com
+49 (0) 6172 484.418

A a B b C c D d E e F f G g H h I i J j K k L l M m N n O o P p Q q R r S s T t U u V v W w X x Y y Z z 0 1 2 3 4 5 6 7 8 9 ! ? @ # $ % & * ( ) { } : ;

The quick brown fox jumps over the lazy dog.

D T

Hadriano™ Light
Serif | Medium Weight |
Stylized Terminals |

Linotype Library GmbH
www.linotype.com
info@linotype.com
+49 (0) 6172 484.418

AaBbCcDdEeFfGgHhIiJjKkLlMmNn Oo Pp Qg Rr Ss Tt Uu Vv Ww Xx Yy Zz 0123456 789 !? & © fi % :; ( ) ≠ $ " "

The quick brown fox jumps over the lazy dog.

D

Bayern Handschrift
Script | Medium Weight |

Nick's Fonts
www.nicksfonts.com

*AaBbCcDdEeFfGgHhIiJjKkLlMmNnOo Pp Qq Rr Ss Tt Uu Vv Ww Xx Yy Zz 0123456789 !? @ #$%& * ( ) { } :; " "*

The quick brown fox jumps over the lazy dog.

D *t*

LinoScript™
*Script | Medium Weight |
Noticeable Contrast | Upright
Posture | Slightly Condensed |*

Linotype Library GmbH
www.linotype.com
info@linotype.com
+49 (0) 6172 484.418

AaBbCcDdEeFfGgHhIiJjKkLlMmNnOoPpQq RrSsTtUuVvWwXxYyZz0123456789!?@#$% &*(){}:;""

The quick brown fox jumps over the lazy dog.

D *t*

ITC Silvermoon™
*Script-Sans Serif | Ultra Light
Weight | Ultra Condensed |
Loop Details |*

Linotype Library GmbH
www.linotype.com
info@linotype.com
+49 (0) 6172 484.418

AaBbCcDdEeFfGgHhIiJjKkLlMmNn OoPpQqRrSsTtUuVvWwXxYyZz012 3456789!?@#&:;" "

The quick brown fox jumps over the lazy dog.

D *t*

P22 Dyrynk Italic
*Serif | Condensed | Light
Weight | Noticeable Contrast |
Moderate Posture |*

P22 Type Foundry
www.p22.com
p22@p22.com
800.P22.5080

AaBbCcDdEeFfGgHhIiJjKkLlMm NnOoPpQqRrSsTtUuVvWwXxYyZz 0123456789!?@#$%&(){}:;" "*

The quick brown fox jumps over the lazy dog.

D *t*

ITC Isadora™ Roman
*Script | Pronounced Contrast |
Looped Joints |
Dual-Stroke Capitals |*

Linotype Library GmbH
www.linotype.com
info@linotype.com
+49 (0) 6172 484.418

AaBbCcDdEeFfGgHhIiJjKkLlMmNn OoPpQqRrSsTtUuVvWwXxYyZz0123 456789!?@#$%&(){}:;" "*

The quick brown fox jumps over the lazy dog.

D *t*

Varius™ 2 Std Italic
*Serif | Medium Weight | Erratic
Ductus | Slightly Condensed |*

Linotype Library GmbH
www.linotype.com
info@linotype.com
+49 (0) 6172 484.418

Romantic Color

Dark and deeply saturated colors—especially those along the red and violet range of the color wheel—suggest passion and sensuous romance. Influenced by blue, violet conveys a sense of blood and passion but is languorous and restive. These deep colors, sometimes called jewel tones, help romanticize cooler colors (such as blue-green) or neutrals (such as rich, umber brown) as foils. Black, though usually associated with death or power, can help intensify the romantic qualities of jewel tones when used as a backdrop. Red, of course, is arousing, and speaks of passion and love—especially when it is hot (beginning to approach a deep orange) and slightly desaturated. Pale versions of these colors, such as lavender, pink, and peach, offer a refreshing, dreamy romanticism and may be perceived as youthful and charming.

Sample Color Combinations

69 C	
100 M	
0 Y	
0 K	

15 C	
85 M	
100 Y	
65 K	

12 C	
100 M	
95 Y	
40 K	

46 C	
100 M	
0 Y	
48 K	

83 C	
100 M	
0 Y	
25 K	

20 C	
20 M	
20 Y	
100 K	

0 C	
90 M	
100 Y	
20 K	

0 C	
43 M	
32 Y	
0 K	

37 C	
42 M	
0 Y	
0 K	

0 C	
45 M	
0 Y	
0 K	

Like a good friend whose advice, though sometimes challenging, is direct and sincere, honest-feeling typography and color eschew artifice and contrivance. When design is honest—authentic, reliable in its clarity—it transmits messages easily and with an offhand ease, resulting from the confidence that it's telling the truth and doing its job.

Honest

Honest-feeling typefaces tend to be primarily neutral in their style. Sans serifs, in general, convey a sense of honesty because of their neutral character—but handle them with care. Too austere a sans serif, and the viewer—especially if younger and less mainstream—is apt to associate them with corporate culture, immediately distrusting the communication and considering it slick or potentially false. Sans serifs whose proportions vary a little more and whose details are a little quirky, such as Gill Sans, may have a more honest feeling than a squared-off, rigorously proportioned face such as Univers. Perpendicular cutoffs of terminals connote a certain kind of directness, as does a generally medium or regular width. If the sans serif's terminals are slightly rounded, or its x-heights slightly smaller, a viewer may sense an innocent naïveté, possibly because of the childlike quality that these details impart. Neutral serifs with slightly exaggerated ductus and soft terminals will also feel as though they have some character while retaining the straightforward quality of their conventional structure. Oddly enough, some typefaces that are highly stylized may come across as honest in feeling, especially faces whose strokes are drawn to resemble brush strokes, or whose counters or widths seem to change irregularly—as though the typeface is so honest it's letting the viewer see it for what it is.

Print Collateral Promotion
top, and detail, bottom

Motive Design Research
Michael Connors, Kari Strand,
Peter Anderson, Tom Connors
Seattle *USA*

A a B b C c D d E e F f G g H h I i J j K k L l M m
N n O o P p Q q R r S s T t U u V v W w X x Y y
Z z 0 1 2 3 4 5 6 7 8 9 ! ? & @ # $ % * : ; "
The quick brown fox jumps over the lazy dog.

D *t*

7 Seconds Regular
*Stylized Sans Serif | Slightly
Erratic Posture Changes |
Light Weight |*

T.26 Digital Type Foundry
www.t26.com
info@t26.com
888.T26.FONT

A a B b C c D d E e F f G g H h I i J j K k L l M m
N n O o P p Q q R r S s T t U u V v W w X x Y y Z z
0 1 2 3 4 5 6 7 8 9 ! ? @ # $ % & * ( ) { } : ; " "
The quick brown fox jumps over the lazy dog.

D T

Avenir™ 55 Roman
*Sans Serif | Medium Weight |
Uniform Strokes |*

Linotype Library GmbH
www.linotype.com
info@linotype.com
+49 (0) 6172 484.418

A a B b C c D d E e F f G g H h I i J j K k L l M m N n
O o P p Q q R r S s T t U u V v W w X x Y y Z z 0 1
2 3 4 5 6 7 8 9 ! ? @ # $ % & * ( ) { } : ; " "
The quick brown fox jumps over the lazy dog.

D T

VectoraTM 55 Roman
*Sans Serif | Condensed |
Extremely Large x-Height |*

Linotype Library GmbH
www.linotype.com
info@linotype.com
+49 (0) 6172 484.418

A a B b C c D d E e F f G g H h I i J j K k L l M m
N n O o P p Q q R r S s T t U u V v W w X x Y y Z z
0 1 2 3 4 5 6 7 8 9 ! ? & @ # $ % * : ; "
The quick brown fox jumps over the lazy dog.

D *t*

MVB Calliope
*Stylized Sans Serif |
Italic Posture |*

MVB Fonts
www.mvbfonts.com
info@mvbfonts.com
510.525.4288

A a B b C c D d E e F f G g H h I i J j K k L l M m
N n O o P p Q q R r S s T t U u V v W w X x Y y
Z z 0 1 2 3 4 5 6 7 8 9 ! ? & @ # $ % * : ; "
The quick brown fox jumps over the lazy dog.

D T

Auto 1 Light
*Sans Serif | Uniform Weight |
Abrupt Joints |*

Underware
www.underware.nl
info@underware.nl
31 (0)70.42.78.117

A a B b C c D d E e F f G g H h I i J j K k L l
M m N n O o P p Q q R r S s T t U u V v U w w
X x y y Z z 0 1 2 3 4 5 6 7 8 9 ! ? & @ # $ % * : ; "
The quick brown fox jumps over the lazy dog.

D

Naomi
*Stylized Sans Serif |
Moderately Extended |*

Garage Fonts Type Foundry
www.garagefonts.com
info@garagefonts.com
800.681.9375

A a B b C c D d E e F f G g H h I i J j K k L l M m N n
O o P p Q q R r S s T t U u V v W w X x Y y Z z 0 1 2
3 4 5 6 7 8 9 ! ? & @ # $ % * : ; "

The quick brown fox jumps over the lazy dog.

Revalo Modern Bold
Sans Serif | Condensed | Medium Weight |

T.26 Digital Type Foundry
www.t26.com
info@t26.com
888.T26.FONT

A a B b C c D d E e F f G g H h I i J j K k L l M m N n O o
P p Q q R r S s T t U u V v W w X x Y y Z z 0 1 2 3 4 5 6 7
8 9 ! ? & @ # $ % * : ; "

The quick brown fox jumps over the lazy dog.

Vinyl Regular
Sans Serif | Condensed | Medium Weight |

T.26 Digital Type Foundry
www.t26.com
info@t26.com
888.T26.FONT

Aa Bb Cc Dd Ee Ff Gg Hh Ii Jj Kk Ll Mm Nn
Oo Pp Qq Rr Ss Tt Uu Vv Ww Xx Yy Zz 0 1 2
3 4 5 6 7 8 9 &?! $ € ß

The quick brown fox jumps over the lazy dog.

Adrianna Extended Light
Sans Serif | Uniform Weight |

The Chank Company
www.chank.com
friendlyfolks@chank.com
877.GO.CHANK

A a B b C c D d E e F f G g H h I i J j K k L l M m N n
O o P p Q q R r S s T t U u V v W w X x Y y Z z 0 1 2 3
4 5 6 7 8 9 ! ? & @ # $ % * : ; "

The quick brown fox jumps over the lazy dog.

Aaux Office Bold
Slab Serif | Uniform Weight | Condensed |

T.26 Digital Type Foundry
www.t26.com
info@t26.com
888.T26.FONT

A a B b C c D d E e F f G g H h I i J j K k L l M m N n O o
P p Q q R r S s T t U u V v W w X x Y y Z z 0 1 2 3 4 5
6 7 8 9 ! ? @ # & : ; " "

The quick brown fox jumps over the lazy dog.

P22 Hiromina Latin
Stylized Sans Serif | Ultra Light Weight |

P22 Type Foundry
www.p22.com
p22@p22.com
800.P22.5080

A a B b C c D d E e F f G g H h I i J j K k L l M m N n O o
P p Q q R r S s T t U u V v W w X x Y y Z z 0 1 2 3 4 5 6
7 8 9 ! ? & @ # $ % * : ; "

The quick brown fox jumps over the lazy dog.

P22 Stanyan Regular
Serif | Condensed | Medium Weight |

P22 Type Foundry
www.p22.com
p22@p22.com
800.P22.5080

Honest Color

Somewhat related to the ideas of reliability and trustworthiness, honesty in color makes use of blue as a primary component in its palette. The particular shade of blue is important: it must be devoid of red, a medium or lighter value, and brilliant in saturation—in short, a "pure" blue, akin to the base primary component of refracted light. Blue that clearly has no violet overtone prevents it from feeling compromising. Too dark, such as navy, and it takes on an authoritarian quality, although still "dependable" in nature. A medium to light value suggests a certain kind of comfort, and a more satu-rated blue with these characteristics avoids the ambiguity that might be associated with smokier, less saturated versions. Similarly, pure, less "mixed" colors—the secondary colors orange and green, as well as brighter violets toward the red end of the spectrum—reinforce the reliability of blue, add their own respective notes of openness, safety, and energy, and act as a foil for blue's calming quality. A slightly greener blue introduces the safe and clean quality of that color. Rounding out the palette, a rich, woody brown also feels sincere.

Sample Color Combinations

>	100 C
	25 M
	0 Y
	0 K

>	82 C
	10 M
	0 Y
	0 K

>	55 C
	0 M
	0 Y
	0 K

>	57 C
	0 M
	10 Y
	0 K

>	76 C
	0 M
	78 Y
	0 K

>	0 C
	66 M
	100 Y
	0 K

>	26 C
	100 M
	0 Y
	0 K

>	85 C
	13 M
	24 Y
	0 K

>	50 C
	80 M
	95 Y
	20 K

>	100 C
	40 M
	0 Y
	31 K

Motion, power, action! The Italian Futurists of the early twentieth century were after it, in painting, design, and architecture. Dynamism is embodied in things that move and vibrate, whether people or machines, animation or typography. Dynamic color is similarly aggressive and adventurous but sometimes complex and charismatic, as well as forceful.

Dynamic

A very rhythmic interplay of positive (stroke) and negative (counter) within a typeface, as well as an actively geometric construction, conveys a dynamic sense of energy. As the counters and strokes of a typeface approach each other in optical similarity, their alternation in groupings makes them active and vibratory. Often, bold condensed faces exhibit this characteristic to the greatest degree; while many are designed to alleviate this quality so as to enhance their use in text, some exaggerate it. Sharp, angular terminals, especially at the apex of the letter A and the junctures of the diagonal strokes in M, Z, K, and N; very circular bowls and lobes in O, P, R, and D; and the contrasting square proportions of H and X; the active geometry in these proportions creates energy as well. The italic versions of typefaces, overall, imply speed and emphasis through their slant. Using italic as the basis for text, with Roman (upright) for emphasis, is an interesting reversal of the conventional treatment for running text; the unexpected, overall forward motion will certainly be perceived as dynamic.

Collateral Pages
top, and detail, bottom

Starshot
Lars Harmsen, Claudia Klein,
Tina Weisser
Munich *Germany*

aabbccddeEFFGGHHIiJJKKLLMmnn
OoPPQQQRRSSTTUUVVWwXXYYZZ012
3456789!?&⊖#$%*::"

THE QUICK bROWN FOX JUMPS OVER THE LAZY dOG.

D

Hijack
Stylized Sans Serif |
Erratic Baseline |

Garage Fonts Type Foundry
www.garagefonts.com
info@garagefonts.com
800.681.9375

AaBbCcDdEeFfGgHhIiJjKkLlMmNn
OoPpQqRrSsTtUuVvWwXxYyZz012345
6789!?G@ſ:;""

The quick brown fox jumps over the lazy dog.

D *t*

P22 Pooper Black
Script–Sans Serif Hybrid |
Pronounced Contrast |
Acute Posture |

P22 Type Foundry
www.p22.com
p22@p22.com
800.P22.5080

AABB CCDD EE FF GG HH Ii JJ KK LL
MM NN OO PP QQ RRSS TT VV VV WW
XX YY ZZ 0123456789!?&⊘$::

THE QUICK BROWN FOX JUMPS OVER THE LAZY DOG.

D

P22 Vienna Black
Stylized Sans Serif |
Caps and Alternates |

P22 Type Foundry
www.p22.com
p22@p22.com
800.P22.5080

AaBbCcDdEeFfGgHhIiJjKkLlMmNn
OoPpQqRrSsTtUuVvWwXxYyZz0123
456789!?@#$%&*(){}:;" "

The quick brown fox jumps over the lazy dog.

D *t*

Strayhorn™ Bold
Sans Serif | Pronounced
Contrast | Abrupt Ductus |
Pronounced Modulation |

Linotype Library GmbH
www.linotype.com
info@linotype.com
+49 (0) 6172 484.418

AaBbCcddEeFFGghhiijJkkLL
MmnnOoPPQQRRSSttUUVVWw
XxYyZz@123456789!?&@#$%"\""

the quick brown fox jumps over the lazy dog.

D

Cappuccino Bold
Graphic | Medium Weight |

Garage Fonts Type Foundry
www.garagefonts.com
info@garagefonts.com
800.681.9375

AaBbCcDdEeFfGgHhIiJjKKLLmmnn
OoPpQqRrSsTtUuVuWwXxYyZz0123
456789!?&@#$%*:;"

The quick brown fox jumps over the lazy dog.

D

Getback Normal
Sans Serif | Condensed |
Bolder Medium Weight |

Garage Fonts Type Foundry
www.garagefonts.com
info@garagefonts.com
800.681.9375

A a B b C c D d E e F f G g H h I i J j K k L l M m N n
O o P p Q q R r S s T t U u V v W w X x Y y Z z 0 1 2 3
4 5 6 7 8 9 ! ? @ # $ % & * ( ) { } : ; " "
The quick brown fox jumps over the lazy dog.

D *t*

Univers™ 67 Bold
Condensed
*Sans Serif | Bold Weight |
Condensed | Pronounced Stroke
and Counter Alternation*

Linotype Library GmbH
www.linotype.com
info@linotype.com
+49 (0) 6172 484.418

A a B b C c O d E e F f G g H h I i J j K k L l M m
N n O o P p Q q R r S s T t U u V v W w X x Y y Z z
Ø 0 1 2 3 4 5 6 7 8 9 ! ? & @ # $ % * : ; "

The quick brown fox jumps over the lazy dog.

D

Specious
*Stylized Sans Serif |
Pronounced Contrast |
Slight Italic Posture |*

Garage Fonts Type Foundry
www.garagefonts.com
info@garagefonts.com
800.681.9375

A a B b C c O d E e F f G g H h I i J j K k L l M m
N n O o P p Q q R r S s T t U u V v W w X x Y y Z 3
0 1 2 3 4 5 6 7 8 9 ! ? & @ # $ % * : ; "

The quick brown fox jumps over the lazy dog.

D *t*

Juicy Bold
*Script–Sans Serif Hybrid |
Bold Weight |*

T.26 Digital Type Foundry
www.t26.com
info@t26.com
888.T26.FONT

*A a B b C c D d E e F f G g H h I i J j K k L l M m N n B o
P p Q q R r S s T t U u V v W w X x Y y Z z 0 1 2 3 4 5 6 7 8 9 ! !
Ø Ø # $ % * : ;"*

The quick brown fox jumps over the lazy dog.

D

Lassigue d'mato
Graphic | Light Weight |

T.26 Digital Type Foundry
www.t26.com
info@t26.com
888.T26.FONT

A a B b C c D d E e F f G g H h I i J j K k L l
M m N n O o P p Q q R r S s T t U u V v W
w X x Y y Z z 0 1 2 3 4 5 6 7 8 9 ! ? & @ # $ % * : ; "

the quick brown fox jumps over the

D

Sampler Regular
Graphic | Extended |

T.26 Digital Type Foundry
www.t26.com
info@t26.com
888.T26.FONT

A a B b C c D d E e F f G g H h I i J j K k
L l M m N n O o P p Q q R r S s T t U u
V v W w X x Y y Z z 0 1 2 3 4 5 6 7 8 9 !

The quick brown fox jumps over the lazy dog.

D

Trez
*Stylized Sans Serif | Reverse
Oblique | Black Weight |*

T.26 Digital Type Foundry
www.t26.com
info@t26.com
888.T26.FONT

ABCDEFGHIJKLMNOPQRSTUVWXYZ
0123456789!?#$%&*()-():;""

THE QUICK BROWN FOX JUMPS OVER THE LAZY DOG.

D

Jemima Italic
Stylized Sans Serif | Moderate
Posture | Bold Weight |

Device
www.devicefonts.co.uk
rianhughes@aol.com
44 (0) 7979.602.272

AaBbCcDdEeFFGgHhIiJjKkLlMm
NnOoPpQqRrSsTtUuVvWwXxYyZz
0123456789!?$%&*():;""
The quick brown fox jumps over the lazy dog.

D

Arriba™
Graphic Script | Extreme
Contrast | Pronounced Brush
Detail

Linotype Library GmbH
www.linotype.com
info@linotype.com
+49 (0) 6172 484.418

ABCDEFGHIJKLM
NOPQRSTUVWXY
ZO123456789!?@

THE QUICK BROWN FOX JUMPS OVER THE LAZY DOG.

D

ITC Flatiron™
Sans Serif | Medium Weight |
Extremely Extended |

Linotype Library GmbH
www.linotype.com
info@linotype.com
+49 (0) 6172 484.418

AaBbCcDdEeFfGgHhIiJjKkLlMmNnOoPpQq
RrSsTtUuVvWwXxYyZz0123456789!?@#
$%&*(){}:;""
The quick brown fox jumps over the lazy dog.

D

Linotype Gneisenauette™
Script-Sans Serif Hybrid |
Extreme Contrast | Italic Posture |
Ultra Condensed |

Linotype Library GmbH
www.linotype.com
info@linotype.com
+49 (0) 6172 484.418

AaBbCcDdEeFfGgHhIiJjKkLlMmNnOoPpQqRr
SsTtUuVvWwXxYyZz0123456789I?@#$%&*
(){}:;""
The quick brown fox jumps over the lazy dog.

D *t*

ITC Juice™
Serif | Light Weight | Erratic
Contrast and Modulation |
Ultra Condensed | Stem Distortion

Linotype Library GmbH
www.linotype.com
info@linotype.com
+49 (0) 6172 484.418

AaBbCcDdEeFfGgHhIiJjKkLlMm
NnOoPpQqRrSsTtUuVvWwXxYy
ZzO123456789!?&@#$%*:;"

THE QUICK BROWN FOX JUMPS OVER THE LAZY DOG.

D

Roadster
Serif–Sans Serif Hybrid |
Extended | Slight Italic Posture |

The Chank Company
www.chank.com
friendlyfolks@chank.com
877.GO.CHANK

A a B b C c D d E e F f G g H h I i J j K k L l M m N n
O o P p Q q R r S s T t U u V v W w X x Y y Z z 0 1 2 3
4 5 6 7 8 9 ! ? $ % & * ( ) : ; " "

The quick brown fox jumps over the lazy dog.

D

Shatter™
*Graphic Sans Serif | Bold
Weight | Structural Distortion |
Italic Posture |*

Linotype Library GmbH
www.linotype.com
info@linotype.com
+49 (0) 6172 484.418

a a B b c D E c F F c g H I i J j k L l m n o P P q R S t
U U W X Y 0 1 2 3 4 5 6 7 8 9 ! ? and @ # $ z * : ; "

the quick brown fox jumps over the lazy dog.

D

Soopercosmic
*Stylized Sans Serif | Heavy
Bold Weight | Mixed Case with
Alternates | Extra Condensed |*

The Chank Company
www.chank.com
friendlyfolks@chank.com
877.GO.CHANK

A a Ð b C c D d E e F f G ǫ H h I i J j K k L l
Π n N o O o P p Q q R r S s T t U u V v U w
X x Y y Z z 0 1 2 3 4 5 6 7 8 9 ! ? Ⓐ # $ % Ð *
( ) { } : ; " "

The quick brown fox jumps over the lazy doǫ.

D

Linotype Marcu San™
*Sans Serif | Black Weight |
Pronounced Contrast | Stroke
Stylization | Erratic Weight |*

Linotype Library GmbH
www.linotype.com
info@linotype.com
+49 (0) 6172 484.418

A a B b C c D d E e F f G g H h I i J j K k L l M m N n
O o P p Q q R r S s T t U u U v W w X x Y y Z z 0 1 2 3
4 5 6 7 8 9 ! ? @ # $ % & * ( ) { } : ; " "

The quick brown fox jumps over the lazy dog.

D

Einhorn™
*Script-Sans Serif Hybrid |
Black Weight | Pronounced
Contrast | Compressed |*

Linotype Library GmbH
www.linotype.com
info@linotype.com
+49 (0) 6172 484.418

A a B b C c D d E e F f G g H h I i J j K k L l M m N n
O o P p Q q R r S s T t U u V v W w X x Y y Z z 0 1 2 3
4 5 6 7 8 9 ! ? @ # $ % & * ( ) { } : ; " "

The quick brown fox jumps over the lazy dog.

D *t*

Linotype Markin™
*Sans Serif | Bold Weight |
Erratic Posture | Condensed |*

Linotype Library GmbH
www.linotype.com
info@linotype.com
+49 (0) 6172 484.418

A a B b C c D d E e F f G g H h I i J j K k L l M m
N n O o P p Q q R r S s T t U u V v W w X x Y y Z z
0 1 2 3 4 5 6 7 8 9 ! ? & @ # $ % . * : ; "

The quick brown fox jumps over the lazy dog.

D

Dimentia Wide
*Stylized Sans Serif | Extended |
Black Weight |*

T.26 Digital Type Foundry
www.t26.com
info@t26.com
888.T26.FONT

Dynamic Color

Red, red-violet, red-orange… in short, dynamic and red are much the same. Because of red's long wavelengths and the energy it requires for processing, any red derivative will increase metabolism and engage the "fight or flight" mechanism—a mini adrenaline rush—that translates into arousal and a sense of energy. Of the three colors mentioned, though, red-violet, or fuchsia, is the most energetic as opposed to passionate, whereas red-orange is most adventurous in spirit. Pairing these colors with their complements—green, yellow-green, and aqua—intensifies their energies. But "dynamic" can also connote complexity and rich, harmonic relationships, so colors analogous to each of the two members of the complements (adjacent on the color wheel) are added to create more depth in the palette.

Sample Color Combinations

>	0 C
	100 M
	100 Y
	0 K

>	0 C
	83 M
	100 Y
	0 K

>	27 C
	100 M
	0 Y
	0 K

>	91 C
	0 M
	100 Y
	0 K

>	60 C
	0 M
	100 Y
	0 K

>	100 C
	0 M
	40 Y
	0 K

>	100 C
	25 M
	0 Y
	0 K

>	0 C
	28 M
	100 Y
	0 K

>	100 C
	0 M
	0 Y
	0 K

>	0 C
	73 M
	100 Y
	0 K

There are so many ways to be refreshed—a quick dip in a sparkling pool; a brisk jog along a country road; eating a ripe, juicy citrus fruit; seeing an unexpected shape or texture in a dull environment. Typefaces and colors that feel refreshing exude many of these same unexpected qualities. An oldstyle face with unexpected or inventive details may feel refreshing. Sharp, extralight sans serifs bubbling along in a line of text impart energy and bounce. Bright, warm colors and pale, cool colors speak of sunlight, water, breezes and healthy living.

Refreshing

A host of characteristics in typefaces are refreshing in form and rhythm. Condensed faces, especially those lighter in weight, convey energy in their compressed proportions; the lighter such faces, the springier or jauntier they seem. Extra-light sans serifs, in particular, with open counters and crisp, linear movement, will be perceived as energetic and vivacious; their accessible legibility, deriving from a large x-height, adds to their vigor. Typefaces with marked, directional emphasis in the strokes, especially as the strokes branch from junctures, have a slightly syncopated rhythm that creates a sense of energy.

Magazine Page Spread
top, and detail, bottom

***Fast Company* Magazine**
Brad Holland, illustrator
New York City *USA*

A a B b C c D d E e F f G g H h I i J j K k L l M m
N n O o P p Q q R r S s T t U u V v W w X x Y y Z z
0 1 2 3 4 5 6 7 8 9 ! ? & @ # $ % * : ; "

The quick brown fox jumps over the lazy dog.

D T

JY Koliba
Sans Serif | Medium Weight |

JY&A Fonts
www.jyanet.com/fonts

*A a B b C c D d E e F f G g H h I i J j K k L l M m
N n O o P p Q q R r S s T t U u V v W w X x Y y Z z
0 1 2 3 4 5 6 7 8 9 ! ? @ # & :; " "*

The quick brown fox jumps over the lazy dog.

D

P22 Corinthia Regular
Script | Little Contrast |

P22 Type Foundry
www.p22.com
p22@p22.com
800.P22.5080

A a B b C c D d E e F f G g H h I i J j K k L l M m
N n O o P p Q q R r S s T t U u V v W w X x Y y
Z z 0 1 2 3 4 5 6 7 8 9 ! ? @ # & : ; " "

The quick brown fox jumps over the lazy dog.

D T

P22 Dyrynk Roman
*Serif | Condensed |
Light Weight |*

P22 Type Foundry
www.p22.com
p22@p22.com
800.P22.5080

A a B b C c D d E e F f G g H h I i J j K k L l M m N n O o
P p Q q R r S s T t U u V v W w X x Y y Z z 0 1 2 3 4 5 6 7
8 9 ! ? @ # + : ; " "

The quick brown fox jumps over the lazy dog.

D

P22 Hopper Josephine
*Script–Sans Serif Hybrid |
Lighter Medium Weight |*

P22 Type Foundry
www.p22.com
p22@p22.com
800.P22.5080

**A a B b C c D d E e F f G g H h I i J j K k L l M m
N n O o P p Q q R r S s T t U u V v W w X x Y y
Z z 0 1 2 3 4 5 6 7 8 9 ! ? & @ # $ % * : ; "**

The quick brown fox jumps over the lazy dog.

D t

P22 Akebono Regular
*Stylized Sans Serif |
Pronounced Contrast |*

P22 Type Foundry
www.p22.com
p22@p22.com
800.P22.5080

*A a B b C c D d E e F f G g H h I i J j K k L l M m
N n O o P p Q q R r S s T t U u V v W w X x Y y Z z
0 1 2 3 4 5 6 7 8 9 ! ? & @ $: ; " "*

The quick brown fox jumps over the lazy dog.

D

P22 Ruthie
Script | Medium Weight |

P22 Type Foundry
www.p22.com
p22@p22.com
800.P22.5080

A a B b C c D d E e F f G g H h I i J j K k L l M m N n
O o P p Q q R r S s T t U u V v W w X x Y y Z z 0 1 2 3 4
5 6 7 8 9 ! ? & @ # $ % * : ; "

The quick brown fox jumps over the lazy dog.

D · t

JY Integrity Lining
*Serif | Condensed |
Light Weight |*

JY&A Fonts
www.jyanet.com/fonts

A a B b C c D d E e F f G g H h I i J j K k L l
M m N n O o P p Q q R r S s T t U u V v W w
X x Y y Z z 0 1 2 3 4 5 6 7 8 9 ! ? & @ # $ % * : ; "

The quick brown fox jumps over the lazy dog.

D · T

JY Rebeca OSF
*Serif | Moderate Contrast |
Medium Weight |*

JY&A Fonts
www.jyanet.com/fonts

A a B b C c D d E e F f G g H h I i J j K k L l M m N n O o P p
Q q R r S s T t U u V v W w X x Y y Z z 0 1 2 3 4 5 6 7 8 9 ! ?
& @ # $ % * : ; "

The quick brown fox jumps over the lazy dog.

D

MVB Peccadillo 96
*Slab Serif | Uniform Weight |
Extra-Condensed |*

MVB Fonts
www.mvbfonts.com
info@mvbfonts.com
510.525.4288

A a B b C c D d E e F f G g H h I i J j K k L l M m
N n O o P p Q q R r S s T t U u V v W w X x Y y Z z
0 1 2 3 4 5 6 7 8 9 ! ? & @ # $ % * : ; "

The quick brown fox jumps over the lazy dog.

D · T

Auto 1 Italic
*Sans Serif | Slightly Condensed |
Moderate Posture |*

Underware
www.underware.nl
info@underware.nl
31 (0)70.42.78.117

A a B b C c D d E e F f G g H h I i J j K k L l M m
N n O o P p Q q R r S s T t U u V v W w X x Y y Z z
0 1 2 3 4 5 6 7 8 9 ! ? & @ # $ % * : ; "

The quick brown fox jumps over the lazy dog.

D · T

Auto 2 Light Italic
*Semi-Serif | Light Weight |
Moderate Posture |*

Underware
www.underware.nl
info@underware.nl
31 (0)70.42.78.117

A a B b C c D d E e F f G g H h I i J j K k L l M m
N n O o P p Q q R r S s T t U u V v W w X x Y y
Z z 0 1 2 3 4 5 6 7 8 9 ! ? & @ # $ % * : ; "

The quick brown fox jumps over the lazy dog.

D · T

Effectra Thin
*Sans Serif | Condensed |
Medium Weight |*

T.26 Digital Type Foundry
www.t26.com
info@t26.com
888.T26.FONT

Aa Bb Cc Dd Ee Ff Gg Hh Ii Jj Kk Ll Mm
Nn Oo Pp Qq Rr Ss Tt Uu Vv Ww Xx Yy Zz
*0 1 2 3 4 5 6 7 8 9 ! ? & @ # $ % * : ; "*

The quick brown fox jumps over the lazy dog.

October Italic
Serif–Sans Serif Hybrid |
Pronounced Contrast |
Medium Weight |

Garage Fonts Type Foundry
www.garagefonts.com
info@garagefonts.com
800.681.9375

A a B b C c D d E e F f G g H h I i J j K k L l M m
N n O o P p Q q R r S s T t U u V v W w X x Y y Z z
0 1 2 3 4 5 6 7 8 9 ! ? & @ # $ % * : ; "

The quick brown fox jumps over the lazy dog.

District Thin
Sans Serif | Light Weight |

Garage Fonts Type Foundry
www.garagefonts.com
info@garagefonts.com
800.681.9375

A a B b C c D d E e F f G g H h I i J j K k L l M m
N n O o P p Q q R r S s T t U u V v W w X x Y y Z z
0 1 2 3 4 5 6 7 8 9 ! ? & @ # $ % * : ; "

The quick brown fox jumps over the lazy dog.

Epos Ultra Light OsF
Sans Serif | Condensed |

Garage Fonts Type Foundry
www.garagefonts.com
info@garagefonts.com
800.681.9375

A a B b C c D d E e F f G g H h I i J j K k L l M m
N n O o P p Q q R r S s T t U u V v W w X x Y y Z z
0 1 2 3 4 5 6 7 8 9 ! ? & @ # $ % * : ; "

The quick brown fox jumps over the lazy dog.

Metroflex 211 Narrow Light
Sans Serif | Condensed |
Medium Weight |

Garage Fonts Type Foundry
www.garagefonts.com
info@garagefonts.com
800.681.9375

A a B b C c D d E e F f G g H h I i J j K k L l M m
N n O o P p Q q R r S s T t U u V v W w X x Y y Z z
0 1 2 3 4 5 6 7 8 9 ! ? & @ # $ % * : ; "

The quick brown fox jumps over the lazy dog.

Vinyl Inline
Sans Serif | Condensed |
Medium Weight |

T.26 Digital Type Foundry
www.t26.com
info@t26.com
888.T26.FONT

A a B b C c D d E e F f G g H h I i J j K k L l M m
N n O o P p Q q R r S s T t U u V v W w X x Y y
*Z z 0 1 2 3 4 5 6 7 8 9 ! ? & @ # $ % * : ; "*

The quick brown fox jumps over the lazy dog.

Corisande Italic
Stylized Sans Serif |
Moderate Posture |

T.26 Digital Type Foundry
www.t26.com
info@t26.com
888.T26.FONT

A a B b C c D d E e F f G g H h I i J j K k L l M m
N n O o P p Q q R r S s T t U u V v W w X x Y y
Z z 0 1 2 3 4 5 6 7 8 9 ! ? & @ # $ % * : ; "

The quick brown fox jumps over the lazy dog.

D T

Clarice Book
*Serif | Medium Weight |
Noticeable Contrast |
Vestigial Serifs |*

Garage Fonts Type Foundry
www.garagefonts.com
info@garagefonts.com
800.681.9375

A a B b C c D d E e F f G g H h I i J j K k L l M m
N n O o P p Q q R r S s T t U u V v W w X x Y y
Z z 0 1 2 3 4 5 6 7 8 9 ! ? & @ # $ % * : ; "

The quick brown fox jumps over the lazy dog.

D t

Intention Regular
*Sans Serif | Condensed |
Noticeable Contrast |*

T.26 Digital Type Foundry
www.t26.com
info@t26.com
888.T26.FONT

A a B b C c D d E e F f G g H h I i J j K k L l M m
N n O o P p Q q R r S s T t U u V v W w X x Y y
Z z 0 1 2 3 4 5 6 7 8 9 ! ! & @ № $ % * : ; "

The quick brown fox jumps over the lazy dog.

D

Task Open
*Stylized Serif | Inline |
Light Weight |*

T.26 Digital Type Foundry
www.t26.com
info@t26.com
888.T26.FONT

A a B b C c D d E e F f G g H h I i J j K k L l M m N n
O o P p Q q R r S s T t U u V v W w X x Y y Z z
0123456789!?@#$%&*(){}:;""

The quick brown fox jumps over the lazy dog.

D t

Galicia
*Stylized Sans Serif |
Slightly Extended |*

Device
www.devicefonts.co.uk
rianhughes@aol.com
44 (0) 7979.602.272

A a B b C c D d E e F f G g H h I i J j K k L l M m
N n O o P p Q q R r S s T t U u V v W w X x Y y
Z z 0 1 2 3 4 5 6 7 8 9 ! ? @ # $ % & * ( ) { } : ; " "

The quick brown fox jumps over the lazy dog.

D t

Diotima™ Roman OsF
*Serif | Light Weight |
Pronounced Contrast and
Modulation | Sharp Serifs |*

Linotype Library GmbH
www.linotype.com
info@linotype.com
+49 (0) 6172 484.418

A a B b C c D d E e F f G g H h I i J j K k L l M m N n O o P p
Q q R r S s T t U u V v W w X x Y y Z z 0 1 2 3 4 5 6 7 8 9 ! ? @ #
$ % & * ( ) { } : ; " "

The quick brown fox jumps over the lazy dog.

D

Lake Informal™ Roman
*Sans Serif | Light Weight |
Modulation | Italic Posture |
Script Details |*

Linotype Library GmbH
www.linotype.com
info@linotype.com
+49 (0) 6172 484.418

Refreshing Color

Like water, fresh fruit, and lively typefaces, refreshing color exudes a crisp, bright feeling that connotes energy, health, and coolness. Green, teal, and lighter, intense blue hues contribute to the palette's sparkle and cooling splash, while their complements—bright yellow-orange and fuchsia—act as foils, intensifying each side of the palette through chromatic contrast. Unexpected combinations, such as a hot red alongside a more yellow green, supplemented by a cool teal, add freshness and buzz, while analogous combinations of blues and greens create a more subdued, watery experience. Shifting the analogous colors in such a combination apart from each other—a blue toward the more violet end of the spectrum, a green toward the yellow—and balancing them out with a centrally analogous teal, makes for a vivacious tension among the related colors that is none-theless sophisticated in its restraint.

Sample Color Combinations

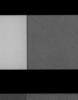

> 80 C
> 0 M
> 100 Y
> 0 K

> 88 C
> 0 M
> 45 Y
> 0 K

> 85 C
> 10 M
> 0 Y
> 0 K

> 60 C
> 6 M
> 0 Y
> 0 K

> 0 C
> 24 M
> 100 Y
> 0 K

> 0 C
> 100 M
> 0 Y
> 0 K

> 81 C
> 36 M
> 0 Y
> 0 K

> 65 C
> 0 M
> 100 Y
> 0 K

> 87 C
> 55 M
> 0 Y
> 0 K

> 0 C
> 88 M
> 71 Y
> 0 K

Communicating a sinister message means evoking associations of horror, black magic, secrecy, or violence. Drawing on historically dangerous time periods or the fantasies of Hollywood as inspiration, sinister messages in type and color create anxiety and induce a quiet terror by playing on our fears and memories of monsters, boogeymen, and dangerous spirits.

Sinister

YOU'RE GONNA WAKE
UP ONE MORNING...

A FILM BY MARK JAY

Quick associations with horror or danger come in typefaces that refer to periods of social upheaval; blackletter gothic typefaces, textura, and other medieval typefaces call to mind the dark, superstitious ancestry of old-world Europe. Even archaic Roman capitals carry a sense of potential terror. Classical serif faces with distorted details or textural degradation are similarly scary. In a more contemporary context, typefaces whose forms have been distorted or whose strokes have details that seem partially destroyed, dirty, slimy, or fractured convey sinister ideas about the under-world. Textural alteration, such as that produced through excessive photocopying or slicing apart, may evoke criminal activity—the notorious ransom note or the obsessive mutilations of a serial killer. Bold sans serifs, for example—usually perceived as strong, objective, and neutral—take on a sinister quality when their contours are ripped or mottled.

Film Title *selected still, top, and detail, bottom*

Crush
Chris Pelling and Carl Rush, design and art direction
Chris Pelling, programming
Brighton *United Kingdom*

aAaRBCcCDdDEeFfGgH∦iijJKKLL
MMNnOOOPoPQorrSstTtUuVV
WeWXxYYZZOO1234567899/?\#$%
&*(){}:;,«"

T∦e quick BrOwn fOx jUMpS OveR t∦e LazY DOg.

D

F2F Entebbe™
*Graphic | Erratic Posture and
Baseline | Mixed Case, Weight |*

Linotype Library GmbH
www.linotype.com
info@linotype.com
+49 (0) 6172 484.418

AaBbCcDdEeFfGgHhIiJjKkLlMmNnOoPp
QqRrSsTtUuVvWwXxYyZz0123456789!?
@N°$%&*(){};;""

The quick brown fox jumps over the lazy dog.

D

Griffin Black
*Stylized Sans Serif |
Black Weight |*

Device
www.devicefonts.co.uk
rianhughes@aol.com
44 (0) 7979.602.272

A a B b C c D d E e F f G g H h I i J j K k L l M m N n
O o P p Q q R r S s T t U u V v W w X x Y y Z z 0 1 2
3 4 5 6 7 8 9 ! ? & @ # $ % * : ; "

The quick brown fox jumps over the lazy dog.

D

Jawbreaker
*Stylized Sans Serif |
Pronounced Modulation |*

The Chank Company
www.chank.com
friendlyfolks@chank.com
877.GO.CHANK

ABCDEFGHIJKLMNOPQRSTUVWXYZ
0123456789!?*✦¡%&✦()[]:;""••

YME QUICK DROWM FOX JUMPS OVER YME LAZY DOG.

D

Mystique Blacque
*Graphic | Caps Only |
Bold Weight |*

Device
www.devicefonts.co.uk
rianhughes@aol.com
44 (0) 7979.602.272

A B C D E F G H I J K L M N O P Q R S T U V
W X Y Z 0 1 2 3 4 5 6 7 8 9 ! ? @ # $ % & * ( ) { }
: ; " "

THE QUICK BROWN FOX JUMPS OVER THE LAZY DOG.

D

Linotype Cerny™
*Graphic Sans Serif |
Black Weight | Texture Details |*

Linotype Library GmbH
www.linotype.com
info@linotype.com
+49 (0) 6172 484.418

A a B b C c D d E e F f G g H h I i J j K k L l M m
N n O o P p Q q R r S s T t U u V v W w X x Y y Z z
0 1 2 3 4 5 6 7 8 9 ! ? & @ # $ % * : ; "

The quick brown fox jumps over the lazy dog.

D

Badoni
*Graphic-Serif Hybrid | Erratic
Baseline | Medium Weight |*

The Chank Company
www.chank.com
friendlyfolks@chank.com
877.GO.CHANK

A B C D E F G H I J K L M N O P Q R S T U
V W X Y Z 0 1 2 3 4 5 6 7 8 9 ! ? @ & : ; " "

D

P22 Fontasaurus Text
Graphic | Medium Weight |

P22 Type Foundry
www.p22.com
p22@p22.com
800.P22.5080

THE QUICK BROWN FOX JUMPS OVER THE LAZY DOG.

A a B b C c D d E e F f G g H h I i J j K k L l M m
N n O o P p Q q R r S s T t U u V v W w X x Y y Z z
0 1 2 3 4 5 6 7 8 9 ! ? & @ # $ % * : ; "

D

Murkshine
*Stylized Serif | Pronounced
Contrast | Bold Weight |*

The Chank Company
www.chank.com
friendlyfolks@chank.com
877.GO.CHANK

The quick brown fox jumps over the lazy dog.

A a B b C c D d E e F f P g H h I i J j K k L l M m
N n O o P p Q q R r S s T t U u V v W w X x Y y Z z
0 1 2 3 4 5 6 7 8 9 ! ? & @ $ % [ ] ( ) * : " "

D

La Danse
*Script | Swash Caps |
Moderate Posture |*

P22 Type Foundry
www.p22.com
p22@p22.com
800.P22.5080

The quick brown fox jumps over the lazy dog.

A a B b C c D d E e F f G g H h I i J j K k L l M m
N n O o P p Q q R r S s T t U u V v W w X x Y y Z z
0 1 2 3 4 5 6 7 8 9 ! ? & @ # $ % * : ; "

D *t*

LTC Pabst Oldstyle
*Serif | Bolder Medium
Weight | Small x-Height |*

P22 Type Foundry
www.p22.com
p22@p22.com
800.P22.5080

The quick brown fox jumps over the lazy dog.

A a B b C c D d E e F f G g H h I i J j K k L l M m
N n O o P p Q q R r S s T t U u V v W w X x Y y Z z
0 1 2 3 4 5 6 7 8 9 ! ? & @ # $ % * : ; "

D

Moonshine
*Stylized Serif | Pronounced
Contrast | Medium Weight |*

The Chank Company
www.chank.com
friendlyfolks@chank.com
877.GO.CHANK

The quick brown fox jumps over the lazy dog.

A a B b C c D d E e F f G g H h I i J j K k L l M m
N n O o P p Q q R r S s T t U u V v W w X x Y y Z z
0 1 2 3 4 5 6 7 8 9 ! ? & @ # $ % * : ; "

D

Superfurniture Studded
*Graphic | Condensed |
Bold Weight |*

T.26 Digital Type Foundry
www.t26.com
info@t26.com
888.T26.FONT

The quick brown fox jumps over the lazy dog.

A a B b C c D d E e F f G g H h I i J j K k L l M m N n
O o P p Q q R r S s T t U u V v W w X x Y y Z z 0 1 2 3
4 5 6 7 8 9 ! ? & @ # $ % * : ; "

The quick brown fox jumps over the lazy dog.

D

Crustier
*Stylized Serif | Pronounced
Contrast | Erratic Baseline |*

The Chank Company
www.chank.com
friendlyfolks@chank.com
877.GO.CHANK

Ạ A a B b C c D d E e F f G G § H h I i J j K k L L I M M m N N n O o o P P p
Q Q q R r S S s T T t U U u V V v W W w X X x Y Y y Z Z z ⊙ 1 2 3 4 5 6 7 8 g ! ?
ⓐ № $ % ū + | | | : ; " "
THE QUICK brown fox jumps over the lazy dog.

D

Pitshanger Initial
*Stylized Wedge Serif | Erratic
Baseline | Medium Weight |*

Device
www.devicefonts.co.uk
rianhughes@aol.com
44 (0) 7979.602.272

A a B b C c D d E e F f G g H h I i J j K k L l M m N n O o
P p Q q R r S s T t U u V v W w X x Y y Z z 0 1 2 3 4 5 6 7
8 9 ! ? @ # $ % & * ( ) { } : ; " "

The quick brown fox jumps over the lazy dog.

D *t*

Caslon Antique
*Serif | Medium Weight |
Graphic Texture | Condensed*

Linotype Library GmbH
www.linotype.com
info@linotype.com
+49 (0) 6172 484.418

A a B b C c D d E e F f G g H h I i J j K k L l M m N n
O o P p Q q R r S s T t U u V v W w X x Y y Z z 0 1
2 3 4 5 6 7 8 9 ! ? @ # $ % & * ( ) [ ] : ; " "

The quick brown fox jumps over the lazy dog.

D *t*

Linotype Fluxus™
*Graphic-Sans Serif Hybrid |
Medium Weight | Erratic
Contrast | Stroke Distortion |*

Linotype Library GmbH
www.linotype.com
info@linotype.com
+49 (0) 6172 484.418

A a B b C c D d E e F f G g H h I i J j K k L l M m
N n O o P p Q q R r S s T t U u V v W w X x Y y
Z z 0 1 2 3 4 5 6 7 8 9 ! ? @ № $ % & * ( ) { } : ; " "

The quick brown fox jumps over the lazy dog.

D

Cutamond™ Basis
*Graphic | Erratic Bold Weight |
Pronounced Contrast |
Structural Distortion |*

Linotype Library GmbH
www.linotype.com
info@linotype.com
+49 (0) 6172 484.418

A a B 6 C c D d E e F f G g H h I i J j K k L l M m
N n O o P p Q q R r S s T t U u V v W w X x Y y Z z
0 1 2 3 4 5 6 7 8 9 ! ? & ● ◆ $ ✖ * : ,

The quick brown fox jumps over the lazy dog.

D

Ammonia
*Graphic | Erratic Baseline |
Bold Weight |*

The Chank Company
www.chank.com
friendlyfolks@chank.com
877.GO.CHANK

A A B B C C D D E E F F G G H H I i J J K K L L M M
N N O O P P Q Q R R S S T T U U V V W W X X Y Y
Z Z 0 1 2 3 4 5 6 7 8 9 ! ? **AND AT NO.** $ % * : ; "

THE QUICK BROWN FOX JUMPS OVER THE LAZY DOG.

D

Cowhied Regular
Graphic Sans Serif | Caps and Alternates | Bold Weight |

Garage Fonts Type Foundry
www.garagefonts.com
info@garagefonts.com
800.681.9375

A a B b C c D d E e F f G g h b l i J j K k L l M m
N n O o P p q q R r S s T ꞇ U u V v W w X x
Y q Z ʒ 0 1 2 3 4 5 b 7 8 q ! ? ʒ #$%*:;"

The quick brown fox jumps over the lazy dog.

D

Prophecy Regular
Archaic–Sans Serif Hybrid | Pronounced Contrast |

T.26 Digital Type Foundry
www.t26.com
info@t26.com
888.T26.FONT

A a B b C c D d E e F f G g H h I i J j K k L l M m N n O o
P p Q q R r S s T t U u V v W w X x Y y Z z 0 1 2 3 4 5 6 7
8 9 ! ? @ $ % & * ( ) 🐈 🐈 : ; " "

The quick brown fox jumps over the lazy dog.

D

Linotype Laika™
Graphic | Bold Weight | Erratic Contrast | Condensed |

Linotype Library GmbH
www.linotype.com
info@linotype.com
+49 (0) 6172 484.418

A a B b C c D d E e F f G g H h I i J j K k L l M m
N n O o P p Q q R r S s T t U u V v W w X x Y y
Z z 0 1 2 3 4 5 6 7 8 9 ! ? @ # $ % & ˘ ( ) { } : :

The quick brown fox jumps over the lazy dog.

D *t*

Linotype Mineru™ Regular
Graphic | Medium Weight | Erratic Contrast | Stroke Distortion |

Linotype Library GmbH
www.linotype.com
info@linotype.com
+49 (0) 6172 484.418

A a B b C c D d E e F f G g H h I i J j K k L l M m N n O o
P p Q q R r S s T t U u V v W w X x Y y Z z 0 1 2 3 4 5
6 7 8 9 ! ? @ # $ % & * ( ) { } : ; " "

The quick brown fox jumps over the lazy dog.

D *t*

Persona™
Graphic Sans Serif | Bold Weight | Erratic Contrast and Posture | Stroke Distortion |

Linotype Library GmbH
www.linotype.com
info@linotype.com
+49 (0) 6172 484.418

A a B b C c D d E e F f G g H h I i J j K k L l M m N n
O O P P Q q R r S s T t U u V V Y Y W w X x Y y Z Z
0 1 2 3 4 5 6 7 8 9 ! ? $ % & * ( ) : ; " "

The quick brown fox jumps over the lazy dog.

D

Spooky™
Graphic Sans Serif | Erratic Weight and Contrast | Stroke Distortion |

Linotype Library GmbH
www.linotype.com
info@linotype.com
+49 (0) 6172 484.418

Sinister Color

Black, of course, is a sinister, terrifying color. Its deep, unknowable space is a metaphor for evil and nothingness; in large quantities, though often sophisticated, it becomes a place of fear: the moonless night, the closed crypt, the back alley. Colors with very deep values, approaching that of black, contribute to a sense that there is little light available and, in combination with black, create an indistinct space. Dark, bloody red, violet, blue-violet, and green allude to violence, magic, decomposition, and reptilian nightmares. Very dark, indeterminate neutrals round out the palette and suggest the earth and stone of graves or the unlit pits of a murderer's lair.

Sample Color Combinations

>	
20 C	
20 M	
20 Y	
100 K	

>	
20 C	
20 M	
20 Y	
80 K	

>	
90 C	
90 M	
0 Y	
70 K	

>	
0 C	
100 M	
0 Y	
80 K	

>	
0 C	
100 M	
90 Y	
65 K	

>	
100 C	
100 M	
65 Y	
0 K	

>	
100 C	
0 M	
100 Y	
77 K	

>	
85 C	
73 M	
85 Y	
0 K	

>	
92 C	
73 M	
96 Y	
10 K	

>	
20 C	
10 M	
15 Y	
72 K	

In the spirit of gaming and athletics, visually communicating the essence of sport means fresh, punchy color and typefaces that feel strong, healthy, and adventurous.

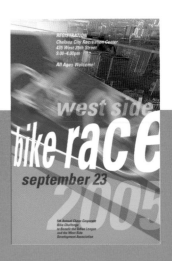

Sporty

Sporty typography calls for bold, simple faces with active rhythm. Sans-serifs with a minimum of detail—bold strokes, perpendicular terminal cutoffs and junctures, and more abrupt ductus between thicks and thins—communicate strength and vigor. Modulation in the strokes of a sans-serif— especially sans serifs that are of regular to slightly condensed width, in which the change in stroke weight enhances tighter counters—creates springiness and syncopated rhythm. Italic versions of these faces, especially those with a deeper, more angled posture, add a measure of speed. Stylized proportions, such as high or low crossbars in characters such as uppercase E, F, and H, and noticeably smaller upper counters, in the lowercase E, for example, induce an exaggerated up-and-down motion across the line. Semibold slab serifs, or serif faces with graphic treatments for the serifs or cross strokes themselves, bring a classical quality to the sporty message, coupled with the geometric simplicity of the slabs or inclusions.Sometimes, faces with true Roman proportion (sans serifs or serifs constructed using square, half-square, and quarter-square widths) or references to Greek lapidary characters (uniform weights, canted stems, and angled terminals) call to mind the pomp of Olympic sports.

Event Poster
top, and detail, bottom

STIM Visual Communication
Timothy Samara
New York City *USA*

A a B b C c D d E e F f G g H h I i J j K k L l M m N n O o P p Q q
R r S s T t U u V v W w X x Y y Z z 0 1 2 3 4 5 6 7 8 9 ! ? @ # $ %
& * ( ) { } : ; " "
The quick brown fox jumps over the lazy dog.

Calcite™ Pro Regular
Sans Serif | Medium Weight |
Italic | Condensed |

Linotype Library GmbH
www.linotype.com
info@linotype.com
+49 (0) 6172 484.418

A a B b C c D d E e F f G g H h I i J j K k L l M m N n O o
P p Q q R r S s T t U u V v W w X x Y y Z z 0 1 2 3 4 5 6 7
8 9 ! ? @ # $ % & * ( ) { } : ; " "
The quick brown fox jumps over the lazy dog.

Conga Brava™ Std Semibold
Slab Serif | Slight Italic Posture |
Modulation |

Linotype Library GmbH
www.linotype.com
info@linotype.com
+49 (0) 6172 484.418

A a B b C c D d E e F f G g H h I i J j K k L l M m N n O o
P p Q q R r S s T t U u V v W w X x Y y Z z 0 1 2 3 4 5
6 7 8 9 ! ? @ # $ % & * ( ) { } : ; " "
The quick brown fox jumps over the lazy dog.

Cronos™ Pro Semibold Italic
Sans Serif | Brush Details |
Uniform Strokes |
Slight Modulation |

Linotype Library GmbH
www.linotype.com
info@linotype.com
+49 (0) 6172 484.418

A a B b C c D d E e F f G g H h I i J j K k L l M m N n
O o P p Q q R r S s T t U u V v W w X x Y y Z z 0 1
2 3 4 5 6 7 8 9 ! ? @ # $ % & * ( ) { } : ; " "
The quick brown fox jumps over the lazy dog.

ITC Franklin Gothic®
Demi Italic
Sans Serif | Bold Weight |
Uniform Strokes |

Linotype Library GmbH
www.linotype.com
info@linotype.com
+49 (0) 6172 484.418

A a B b C c D d E e F f G g H h I i J j K k L l M m N n O o P p Q q
R r S s T t U u V v W w X x Y y Z z 0 1 2 3 4 5 6 7 8 9 ! ? @ #
$ % & * ( ) { } : ; " "
The quick brown fox jumps over the lazy dog.

Futura® Medium Condensed
Oblique
Sans Serif | Medium Weight |
Italic | Condensed

Linotype Library GmbH
www.linotype.com
info@linotype.com
+49 (0) 6172 484.418

A a B b C c D d E e F f G g H h I i J j K k L l M m N n
O o P p Q q R r S s T t U u V v W w X x Y y Z z 0 1
2 3 4 5 6 7 8 9 ! ? @ # $ % & * ( ) { } : ; " "
The quick brown fox jumps over the lazy dog.

Futura® Extra Bold
Condensed
Sans Serif | Black Weight |
Condensed

Linotype Library GmbH
www.linotype.com
info@linotype.com
+49 (0) 6172 484.418

A a B b C c D d E e F f G g H h I i J j K k L l M m N n
O o P p Q q R r S s T t U u V v W w X x Y y Z z 0 1 2 3 4 5
6 7 8 9 ! ? f $ % & * ( ) : ; " "

The quick brown fox jumps over the lazy dog.

D

Laser™ Regular
*Script-Sans Serif Hybrid |
Notable Contrast | Curved
Stems | Brush Details |*

Linotype Library GmbH
www.linotype.com
info@linotype.com
+49 (0) 6172 484.418

A a B b C c D d E e F f G g H h I i J j K k L l M m N n
O o P p Q q R r S s T t U u V v W w X x Y y Z z 0 1 2 3
4 5 6 7 8 9 ! ? @ # $ % & * ( ) { } : ; " "

The quick brown fox jumps over the lazy dog.

D t

Mano™ Regular
*Sans Serif | Medium Weight |
Italic | Slightly Condensed |
Teardrop Bowls |*

Linotype Library GmbH
www.linotype.com
info@linotype.com
+49 (0) 6172 484.418

A a B b C c D d E e F f G g H h I i J j K k L l M m
N n O o P p Q q R r S s T t U u V v W w X x Y y Z z
0 1 2 3 4 5 6 7 8 9 ! ? @ # $ % & * ( ) { } : ; " "

The quick brown fox jumps over the lazy dog.

D t

ITC Mixage® Bold
*Sans Serif | Bold Weight |
Modulation | Abrupt Joints |
Modulation |*

Linotype Library GmbH
www.linotype.com
info@linotype.com
+49 (0) 6172 484.418

A a B b C c D d E e F f G g H h I i J j K k L l M m N n O o
P p Q q R r S s T t U u V v W w X x Y y Z z 0 1 2 3 4 5
6 7 8 9 ! ? @ # $ % & * ( ) { } : ; " "

The quick brown fox jumps over the lazy dog.

D t

**Neue Helvetica™ 77 Bold
Condensed Oblique**
*Sans Serif | Bold Weight | Italic |
Condensed*

Linotype Library GmbH
www.linotype.com
info@linotype.com
+49 (0) 6172 484.418

A a B b C c D d E e F f G g H h I i J j K k L l M m
N n O o P p Q q R r S s T t U u V v W w X x Y y
Z z 0 1 2 3 4 5 6 7 8 9 ! ? @ # $ % & * ( ) { } : ;
" "

The quick brown fox jumps over the lazy dog.

D t

Noa™ Std Bold Oblique
*Sans Serif | Medium Weight |
Condensed | Pronounced
Horizontal Emphasis |*

Linotype Library GmbH
www.linotype.com
info@linotype.com
+49 (0) 6172 484.418

A B C D E F G H I J K L M N O P Q R S T U V W X
Y Z 0 1 2 3 4 5 6 7 8 9 ! ? $ % & * ( ) : ; " "

THE QUICK BROWN FOX JUMPS OVER THE LAZY DOG.

D

Pneuma™
*Graphic | Bold Weight | Texture
Details | Italic Posture |*

Linotype Library GmbH
www.linotype.com
info@linotype.com
+49 (0) 6172 484.418

A a B b C c D d E e F f G g H h I i J j K k L l M m N n O o
P p Q q R r S s T t U u V v W w X x Y y Z z 0 1 2 3 4 5
6 7 8 9 ! ? @ # $ % & * ( ) { } : ; " "
The quick brown fox jumps over the lazy dog.

D **T**

Sassoon® Primary Regular
Sans Serif | Lighter Medium Weight | Slight Italic Posture | Script Terminals |

Linotype Library GmbH
www.linotype.com
info@linotype.com
+49 (0) 6172 484.418

A a B b C c D d E e F f G g H h I i J j K k L l M m
N n O o P p Q q R r S s T t U u V v W w X x Y y Z z
0 1 2 3 4 5 6 7 8 9 ! ? @ # $ % & * [ ] { } : ; " "
The quick brown fox jumps over the lazy dog.

D

Serpentine™ Light Oblique
Sans Serif | Italic Posture | Squared Bowls | Extended |

Linotype Library GmbH
www.linotype.com
info@linotype.com
+49 (0) 6172 484.418

ABCDEFGHIJKLMNOPQRSTUVWX
YZ0123456789!?$%&*():; " "
THE QUICK BROWN FOX JUMPS OVER THE LAZY DOG.

D

Slipstream™
Graphic | Bold Weight | Pronounced Italic Posture |

Linotype Library GmbH
www.linotype.com
info@linotype.com
+49 (0) 6172 484.418

A a B b C c D d E e F f G g H h I i J j K k L l
M m N n O o P p Q q R r S s T t U u V v W w
X x Y y Z z 0 1 2 3 4 5 6 7 8 9 ! ? @ # $ % & * ( )
{ } : ; " "
The quick brown fox jumps over the lazy dog.

D

Sprint™
Sans Serif | Bold Weight | Script Details |

Linotype Library GmbH
www.linotype.com
info@linotype.com
+49 (0) 6172 484.418

A a B b C c D d E e F f G g H h I i J j K k L l M m N n O o P p Q q
R r S s T t U u V v W w X x Y y Z z 0 1 2 3 4 5 6 7 8 9 ! ? @ #
$ % & * ( ) { } : ; " "
The quick brown fox jumps over the lazy dog.

D **t**

Stadion™
Slab Serif-Sans Serif Hybrid | Bold Weight | Condensed

Linotype Library GmbH
www.linotype.com
info@linotype.com
+49 (0) 6172 484.418

A a B b C c D d E e F f G g H h I i J j K k L l M m
N n O o P p Q q R r S s T t U u V v W w X x Y y Z z
0 1 2 3 4 5 6 7 8 9 ! ? @ # $ % & * ( ) { } : ; " "
The quick brown fox jumps over the lazy dog.

D **t**

ITC Stone® Sans Bold Italic
Sans Serif | Slight Modulation | Heavier Bold Weight |

Linotype Library GmbH
www.linotype.com
info@linotype.com
+49 (0) 6172 484.418

A a B b C c D d E e F f G g H h I i J j K k
L l M m N n O o P p Q q R r S s T t U u V v
W w X x Y y Z z 0 1 2 3 4 5 6 7 8 9 ! ? @ s
$ % ¢ K [ ] 8 f : ; " "

The quick brown fox jumps over the lazy dog.

D

Linotype Atomatic™
*Sans Serif | Bold Weight |
Squared Bold | Stylized Joints |
Italic Posture |*

Linotype Library GmbH
www.linotype.com
info@linotype.com
+49 (0) 6172 484.418

A a B b C c D d E e F f G g H h I i J j K k L l M m N n O o P p
Q q R r S s T t U u V v W w X x Y y Z z 0 1 2 3 4 5 6 7 8 9
! ? @ # $ % & * ( ) { } : ; " "

The quick brown fox jumps over the lazy dog.

D

**Tempo Heavy Condensed
Italic**
*Sans Serif | Heavier Bold
Weight | Moderate Posture |*

Linotype Library GmbH
www.linotype.com
info@linotype.com
+49 (0) 6172 484.418

A a B b C c D d E e F f G g H h I i J j K k L l M m N n
O o P p Q q R r S s T t U u V v W w X x Y y Z z 0 1
2 3 4 5 6 7 8 9 ! ? @ # $ % & * ( ) { } : ; " "

The quick brown fox jumps over the lazy dog.

D *t*

**Trade Gothic™ Bold #2
Oblique**
*Sans Serif | Bold Weight | Italic |
Slightly Condensed*

Linotype Library GmbH
www.linotype.com
info@linotype.com
+49 (0) 6172 484.418

A a B b C c D d E e F f G g H h I i J j K k L l M m N n O o
P p Q q R r S s T t U u V v W w X x Y y Z z 0 1 2 3 4 5 6 7
8 9 ! ? @ # $ % & * ( ) { } : ; " "

The quick brown fox jumps over the lazy dog.

D *t*

**Linotype Univers™ 121
Ultra Light Condensed Italic**
*Sans Serif | Ultra Light Weight |
Condensed |*

Linotype Library GmbH
www.linotype.com
info@linotype.com
+49 (0) 6172 484.418

A a B b C c D d E e F f G g H h I i J j K k L l M m N n O o
P p Q q R r S s T t U u V v W w X x Y y Z z 0 1 2 3 4 5
6 7 8 9 ! ? @ # $ % & * ( ) { } : ; " "

The quick brown fox jumps over the lazy dog.

D T

Veto™ Regular
*Sans Serif | Medium Weight |
Sharp Terminals |*

Linotype Library GmbH
www.linotype.com
info@linotype.com
+49 (0) 6172 484.418

A a B b C c D d E e F f G g H h I i J j K k L l M m N n
O o P p Q q R r S s T t U u V v W w X x Y y Z z 0 1 2 3
4 5 6 7 8 9 ! ? @ # $ % & * ( ) { } : ; " "

The quick brown fox jumps over the lazy dog.

D *t*

Linotype Spitz™ Medium
*Sans Serif | Bold Weight |
Condensed | Abrupt Joints |*

Linotype Library GmbH
www.linotype.com
info@linotype.com
+49 (0) 6172 484.418

Sporty Color

The hues of ocean and air, along with those related to team uniforms and sporting equipment, are the basis of the sporty color palette. Strong, slightly violet blue, royal blue, sky blue, aqua, and orange, all at a mid- to light value, are fresh and active; together with hot red, golden yellow, and Kelly green (common in boating sails, jerseys, and playing fields), these colors form analogous relationships that suggest teamwork and harmony. White, additionally, brings openness and suggests boat sails, tennis whites and sneakers, the paulino of bocce, the ice rink, and the regulation markers of various playing courts.

Sample Color Combinations

	C	M	Y	K
❯	100	65	0	0
❯	100	35	0	0
❯	70	10	0	0
❯	87	0	18	0
❯	0	70	100	0
❯	0	84	100	0
❯	0	32	100	0
❯	0	0	0	0
❯	85	0	85	15
❯	48	0	100	0

Fragility—the breakable quality of crystal or glass, the delicate fronds of a leaf, the vaporous nebula of mist—can be both elegant and anxious in its associations. This tension, indeed, is part of what makes fragile objects so interesting. And paradoxically, fragile typefaces can hint at strength, even as they appear to dissolve.

Fragile

When looking for typefaces to represent fragility, the details of their construction must be carefully considered. Since most type is drawn to be as robust as possible, fragility in a type style may depend on lightness in weight; however, it's a brittle quality in the junctures that is crucial, for this will skew the association away from strict elegance or freshness. Abrupt, exceedingly thin junctures against equally thin stems—or against much heavier stems—will cause the strokes to begin to separate optically, making them appear to crack apart at the seams. A bold face with separation between bowl and juncture, or open, almost unbalanced apertures in the lowercase, may also begin to appear fragile. Some typefaces actually separate the strokes from each other, allowing sharp inclusions of counterspace to crack the form. Similarly, heavier, sans-serif forms with linear inclusions or strike-through elements, which damage the intrinsic strength of the forms, may also feel somewhat dissolved. Ethereally light or script faces, especially those without contrast, appear cloudlike and insubstantial.

Book Jacket
top, and detail, bottom

Loewy
Paul Burgess
London *United Kingdom*

ABCDEFGHIJKLMNOPQRSTUV
WXYZ0123456789!?@&$:;
THE QUICK BROWN FOX JUMPS OVER THE LAZY DOG.

D

Laureate Four
Sans Serif | Ultra Light Weight |

T.26 Digital Type Foundry
www.t26.com
info@t26.com
888.T26.FONT

AaBbCcDdEeFfGgHhIiJjKkLlMmNn
OoPpQqRrSsTtUuVvWwXxYyZz01234
56789!?@Nº$%&*{}:;" "

The quick brown fox jumps over the lazy dog.

D *t*

P22 1722 Roman
Graphic Oldstyle Serif |
Textured Contour |
Pronounced Contrast |

P22 Type Foundry
www.p22.com
p22@p22.com
800.P22.5080

AaBbCcDdEeFfGgHhIiJjKkLlMmNn
OoPpQqRrSsTtUuVvWwXxYyZz0123
456789!?@#$%&*(){}:;" "

The quick brown fox jumps over the lazy dog.

D

Neue Helvetica™ 25
Ultra Light
Sans Serif | Uniform Strokes |
Slightly Squared Shoulders |

Linotype Library GmbH
www.linotype.com
info@linotype.com
+49 (0) 6172 484.418

AaBbCcDdEeFfGgHhIiJjKkLlMmN
nOoPpQqRrSsTtUuVvWwXxYyZz
0123456789!?@Nº$%&*(){}:;"

The quick brown fox jumps over the lazy dog.

D *t*

Dynasty Thin
Sans Serif | Light Weight |
Slightly Extended |

Device
www.devicefonts.co.uk
rianhughes@aol.com
44 (0) 7979.602.272

AaBbCcDdEeFfGgHhIiJjKkLlMmN
nOoPpQqRrSsTtUuVvWwXxYyZz
0123456789!?@Nº$%&*(){}:;"""

The quick brown Fox jumps over the lazy dog.

D

Jakita Wide Inline
Stylized Sans Serif | Inline |
Brittle Joints | Extended |

Device
www.devicefonts.co.uk
rianhughes@aol.com
44 (0) 7979.602.272

abcdefghIJKLmnopQRStUu
WXYZ0123456789!?@#$%&*(){}:;""

the quick brown Fox Jumps over the Lazy dog.

D

Camellia™
Sans Serif | Very Light
Weight | Lowercase |
Exaggerated Proportions |

Linotype Library GmbH
www.linotype.com
info@linotype.com
+49 (0) 6172 484.418

abcdefghijklmnopqrstuvwxyz
0123456789!?@#$%&*(){}:;`´

the quick brown fox jumps over the lazy dog.

D

Cirkulus™
*Sans Serif | Ultra Light
Weight | Uniform Strokes |
False Joints |*

Linotype Library GmbH
www.linotype.com
info@linotype.com
+49 (0) 6172 484.418

A a B b C c D d E e F f G g H h I i J j K k L l M m N n O o
P p Q q R r S s T t U u V v W w X x Y y Z z 0 1 2 3 4 5
6 7 8 9 ! ? @ # $ % & * ( ) { } : ; " "
The quick brown fox jumps over the lazy dog.

D T

Cronos™ Pro Light
*Sans Serif | Light Weight |
Slight Contrast | Brush Details |*

Linotype Library GmbH
www.linotype.com
info@linotype.com
+49 (0) 6172 484.418

A a B b C c D d E e F f G g H h I i J j K k L l M m N n
O o P p Q q R r S s T t U u V v W w X x Y y Z z 0 1
2 3 4 5 6 7 8 9 ! ? @ # $ % & * ( ) { } : ; " "
The quick brown fox jumps over the lazy dog.

D

ITC Cyberkugel™
*Graphic Script | Erratic
Light Weight | Condensed |
Sharp Joints |*

Linotype Library GmbH
www.linotype.com
info@linotype.com
+49 (0) 6172 484.418

A a B b C c D d E e F f G g H h I i J j K k L l M m N n
O o P p Q q R r S s T t U u V v W w X x Y y Z z 0 1 2 3
4 5 6 7 8 9 ! ? @ # $ % & * ( ) { } : ; " "
The quick brown fox jumps over the lazy dog.

D

F2F Allineato™
*Graphic | Erratic Contours |
Light Weight |
Stroke Distortion |*

Linotype Library GmbH
www.linotype.com
info@linotype.com
+49 (0) 6172 484.418

A a B b C c D d E e F f G g H h I i J j K k L l M m N n O o
P p Q q R r S s T t U u V v W w X x Y y Z z 0 1 2 3 4 5 6 7
8 9 ! ? @ # $ % & * ( ) { } : ; " "
The quick brown fox jumps over the lazy dog.

D t

Horatio Light
*Sans Serif | Uniform Strokes |
Slightly Condensed | Open Bowls*

Linotype Library GmbH
www.linotype.com
info@linotype.com
+49 (0) 6172 484.418

A a B b C c D d E e F f G g H h I i J j K k L l M m
N n O o P p Q q R r S s T t U u V v W w X x Y y
Z z 0 1 2 3 4 5 6 7 8 9 ! ? @ # $ % & * ( ) { } : ; " "
The quick brown fox jumps over the lazy dog.

D t

ITC Mithras™ Roman
*Serif | Light Weight | Textured
Modulation | Sharp Serifs*

Linotype Library GmbH
www.linotype.com
info@linotype.com
+49 (0) 6172 484.418

A a B b C c D d E e F f G g H h I i J j K k L l M m N n
O o P p Q q R r S s T t U u V v W w X x Y y Z z 0 1 2 3
4 5 6 7 8 9 ! ? @ # $ % & * ( ) | | : ; " "
The quick brown fox jumps over the lazy dog.

D T

ITC Mixage® Book
Sans Serif | Light Weight |
Slight Modulation |

Linotype Library GmbH
www.linotype.com
info@linotype.com
+49 (0) 6172 484.418

A a B b C c D d E e F f G g H h I i J j K k L l M m N n
O o P p Q q R r S s T t U u V v W w X x Y y Z z o 1
2 3 4 5 6 7 8 9 ! ? @ # $ % & * ( ) { } : ; " "
The quick brown fox jumps over the lazy dog.

D T

Noa™ Std Light
Sans Serif | Slight Contrast |
Pronounced Horizontal
Emphasis |

Linotype Library GmbH
www.linotype.com
info@linotype.com
+49 (0) 6172 484.418

A a B b C c D d E e F f G g H h I i J j K k L l M m
N n O o P p Q q R r S s T t U u V v W w X x Y y Z z
0 1 2 3 4 5 6 7 8 9 ! ? Ɛ ℮ ⓐ # $ % * : ; "
The quick brown fox jumps over the lazy dog.

D

Sensuell Thin
Sans Serif | Ultra Light
Weight | Extended |

The Chank Company
www.chank.com
friendlyfolks@chank.com
877.GO.CHANK

A a B b C c D d E e F f G g H h I i J j K k L l M m N n O o
P p Q q R r S s T t U u V v W w X x Y y Z z 0 1 2 3 4 5 6 7
8 9 ! ? @ # $ % & * ( ) { } : ; " "
The quick brown fox jumps over the lazy dog.

D *t*

Nueva™ Std Light
Serif | Light Weight | Notable
Modulation | Notable Upper
Emphasis | Reverse Oblique Axis

Linotype Library GmbH
www.linotype.com
info@linotype.com
+49 (0) 6172 484.418

A a B b C c D d E e F f G g H h I i J j K k L l M m N n O o
P p Q q R r S s T t U u V v W w X x Y y Z z 0 1 2 3 4 5 6 7
8 9 ! ? @ # $ % & * ( ) { } : ; " "
The quick brown fox jumps over the lazy dog.

D

Linotype Puritas™ Light
Sans Serif | Noticeable
Modulation | Slight Upper
Emphasis |

Linotype Library GmbH
www.linotype.com
info@linotype.com
+49 (0) 6172 484.418

A a B b C c D d E e F f G g H h I i J j K k L l M m N n
O o P p Q q R r S s T t U u V v W w X x Y y Z z 0 1 2 3
4 5 6 7 8 9 ! ? @ # $ % & * ( ) { } : ; " "
The quick brown fox jumps over the lazy dog.

D T

ITC Quorum® Light
Serif | Little Contrast | Slightly
Condensed |

Linotype Library GmbH
www.linotype.com
info@linotype.com
+49 (0) 6172 484.418

A B C D E F G H I J K L M N O P Q R S
T U V W X Y Z @ ! 1 2 3 4 5 6 7 8 9 ! ? & . : ; " "

THE QUICK BROWN FOX JUMPS OVER THE LAZY DOG.

D

Linotype Silver™
Graphic | Light Weight |
Uppercase |

Linotype Library GmbH
www.linotype.com
info@linotype.com
+49 (0) 6172 484.418

A B C D E F G H I J K L M N O P Q R S T U V W
X Y Z 0 1 2 3 4 5 6 7 8 9 ! ? & ( ) : ; " "

THE QUICK BROWN FOX JUMPS OVER THE LAZY DOG.

D

Linotype Startec™
Graphic Sans Serif | Light
Weight | Inline Detail |

Linotype Library GmbH
www.linotype.com
info@linotype.com
+49 (0) 6172 484.418

A a B b C c D d E e F f G g H h I i J j K k L l M m N n
O o P p Q q R r S s T t U u V v W w X x Y y Z z 0 1
2 3 4 5 6 7 8 9 ! ? @ # $ % & * ( ) { } : ; " "
The quick brown fox jumps over the lazy dog.

D *t*

Titus
Serif | Lighter Medium
Weight | Slight Modulation |

Linotype Library GmbH
www.linotype.com
info@linotype.com
+49 (0) 6172 484.418

A a B b C c D d E e F f G g H h I i J j K k L l M m N n O o
P p Q q R r S s T t U u V v W w X x Y y Z z 0 1 2 3 4 5
6 7 8 9 ! ? @ # $ % & + ( ) { } : ; " "
The quick brown fox jumps over the lazy dog.

D *t*

Venus® Mager
Sans Serif | Light Weight |
Slightly Condensed

Linotype Library GmbH
www.linotype.com
info@linotype.com
+49 (0) 6172 484.418

A B C D E F G H I J K L M N O P Q R S T U V W
X Y Z 0 1 2 3 4 5 6 7 8 9 ! ? $ % & * ( ) [ ] : ; " "

THE QUICK BROWN FOX JUMPS OVER THE LAZY DOG.

D

Linotype Schachtelhalm™
Graphic Sans Serif |
Light Weight | Abstract Details |

Linotype Library GmbH
www.linotype.com
info@linotype.com
+49 (0) 6172 484.418

A a B b C c D d E e F f G g H h I i J j K k L l M m N n O o
P p Q q R r S s T t U u V v W w X x Y y Z z 0 1 2 3 4 5 6 7
8 9 ! ? @ # $ % & * ( ) { } : ; " "
The quick brown fox jumps over the lazy dog.

D *t*

ITC Woodland™ Light
Sans Serif | Light Weight |
Modulation |

Linotype Library GmbH
www.linotype.com
info@linotype.com
+49 (0) 6172 484.418

Fragile Color

Pale colors, in general, feel weaker and more ethereal than those
with deeper value, and the colder these pale tones are, the more
fragile they will seem. Very cold yellow—one that begins to approach
green, but isn't quite there yet—as well as icy blues, blue violets,
and aqua, also form the basis of the fragile palette. Similarly, a cold,
light gray will feel somewhat brittle and ethereal. In combination,
some distance between these hues on the color wheel is helpful in
achieving a sense of fragility; a cold yellow and a light, icy blue
(toward the green end of the spectrum), for example, are almost
analogous—but just off enough to create some separation anxiety.

Sample Color Combinations

10 C	
0 M	
0 Y	
0 K	

7 C
0 M
54 Y
0 K

13 C
5 M
0 Y
0 K

32 C
2 M
5 Y
0 K

8 C
0 M
0 Y
8 K

0 C
0 M
0 Y
5 K

6 C
2 M
13 Y
0 K

24 C
0 M
0 Y
0 K

0 C
0 M
6 Y
5 K

12 C
0 M
8 Y
0 K

Disturbed, aggressive, obsessive, hallucinatory—these qualities define psychosis, a mental state not quite in touch with reality. Type and color that exemplify this psychological disconnect show disturbance through visual relationships that are anything but normal.

Psychotic

Designers looking to express a psychotic mood through type can find this quality in faces that have structural disconnects or treatments that disturb their basic structures—unexpected changes in stroke weight or direction within characters, inclusions of counterspace that break across strokes, or jagged edges and abrupt joints that appear disconnected or fractured. These qualities are enhanced in bolder weight faces, especially italics. Faces that show disconnects in style—hybrid serif/sans-serif forms, serif faces with unrelated or exaggerated formal details, or faces incorporating condensed, extended, and italic structural attributes convey a sense of disconnection. Typefaces with harsh, included treatments—textural breaks or distortion—may also communicate a psychotic mood, along with those that appear to have been cut, spliced, scratched, and so on.

Catalog Cover
top, and detail, bottom

MAGMA [Büro fur Gestaltung]
Sandra Augstein, Lars Harmsen,
Boris Kahl
Karlsruhe *Germany*

*A B C D E F G H I J K L M N O P Q R S T U V W X Y Z 0 1 2 3 4 5 6 7 8 9 ! ? @ # $ % & * ( ) { } : ; " "*

THE QUICK BROWN FOX JUMPS OVER THE LAZY DOG.

D ITC Atmosphere™
*Graphic | Bold Weight |
Slight Italic Posture |*

Linotype Library GmbH
www.linotype.com
info@linotype.com
+49 (0) 6172 484.418

A a B b C c D d E e F f G g H h I i J j K k L l M m N n O o P p Q q R r S s T t U u V v W w X x Y y Z z 0 1 2 3 4 5 6 7 8 9 ! ? a $ % & * ( ) : ; " "

The quick brown fox jumps over the lazy dog.

D Bergell™
*Graphic Script | Light Erratic
Weight | Upright Posture |*

Linotype Library GmbH
www.linotype.com
info@linotype.com
+49 (0) 6172 484.418

A a B b C c D d E e F f G g H h I i J j K k L l M m N n O o P p Q q R r S s T t U u V v W w X x Y y Z z 0 1 2 3 4 5 6 7 8 9 ! ? @ # $ % & * ( ) : ; " "

The quick brown fox jumps over the lazy dog.

D **t** Bonray™ Regular
*Graphic Serif | Bold Weight |
Broken Strokes |
Structural Distortion |*

Linotype Library GmbH
www.linotype.com
info@linotype.com
+49 (0) 6172 484.418

A a B b C c D d E e F f G g H h I i J j K k L l M m N n O o P p Q q R r S s T t U u V v W w X x Y y Z z 0 1 2 3 4 5 6 7 8 9 ! ? ♡ ⌐ $ % & * ( ) # ☞ : ; " "

The quick brown fox jumps over the lazy dog.

D Chiller™
*Graphic | Erratic Weight and
Posture | Slightly Condensed |*

Linotype Library GmbH
www.linotype.com
info@linotype.com
+49 (0) 6172 484.418

A a B b C c D d E e F f G g H h I i J j K k L l M m N n O o P p Q q R r S s T t U u V v W w X x Y y Z z 0 1 2 3 4 5 6 7 8 9 ! ? @ # $ % & * ( ) : ; " "

The quick brown fox jumps over the lazy dog.

D F2F Prototipa Multipla™
*Graphic | Erratic Weight |
Textural Presentation |*

Linotype Library GmbH
www.linotype.com
info@linotype.com
+49 (0) 6172 484.418

A a B b C c D d E e F f G g H h I i J j K k L l M m N n O o P p Q q R r S s T t U u V v W w X x Y y Z z 0 1 2 3 4 5 6 7 8 9 ! ? @ # $ % & * ( ) { } : ; " "

The quick brown fox jumps over the lazy dog.

D Linotype Mega™ Out
*Graphic Sans Serif | Black
Weight | Contour Distortion |
Slightly Condensed |*

Linotype Library GmbH
www.linotype.com
info@linotype.com
+49 (0) 6172 484.418

AaBbCcDdEeFfGgHhIiJjKkLlMmNn
OoPpQqRrSsTtUuVvWwXxYyZz0123
456789!?@#$%&*(){}:;""
The quick brown fox jumps over the lazy dog.

D

F2F Shakkarakk™
*Graphic | Bold Weight |
Stroke Distortion |*

Linotype Library GmbH
www.linotype.com
info@linotype.com
+49 (0) 6172 484.418

AaBbCcDdEeFfGgHhIiJjKk
LlMmNnOoPpQqRrSsTtUu
VvWwXxYyZz0123456789
!?&():;""
The quick brown fox jumps over the lazy dog.

D

F2F Twins™
*Graphic | Heavier Bold Weight |
Erratic Posture | Erratic Body
Height |*

Linotype Library GmbH
www.linotype.com
info@linotype.com
+49 (0) 6172 484.418

AaBbCcDdEeFfGgHhIiJjKkLl
MmNnOoPpQqRrSsTtUuVvWw
XxYyZz0123456789!?&():;""
THE QUICK BROWN FOS JUMPS OVER THE LAZY DOG.

D

P22 Ed Rogers Duplex
*Graphic | Erratic Posture |
Pronounced Contrast |*

P22 Type Foundry
www.p22.com
p22@p22.com
800.P22.5080

AaBbCcDdEeFfGgHhIiJjKkLlMm
NnOoPpQqRrSsTtUuVvWwXxYyZz
0123456789!?&*(){}:;""
The quick brown fox jumps over the lazy dog.

D

Schwennel™ Lila
*Graphic | Erratic Weight |
Broken Strokes |
Stroke Distortion |*

Linotype Library GmbH
www.linotype.com
info@linotype.com
+49 (0) 6172 484.418

AABBCCDDEEFFGGHHIIJJKKLLMMNN
OOPPQQRRSSTTUUVVWWXXYYZZ0123
456789!?$%&*():;""
THE QUICK BROWN FOX JUMPS OVER THE LAZY DOG.

D

Linotype Not Painted™
*Graphic | Medium Weight |
Surprinted Characters |*

Linotype Library GmbH
www.linotype.com
info@linotype.com
+49 (0) 6172 484.418

AaBbCcDdEeFfGgHhIiJjKkLlMm
NnOoPpQqRrSsTtUuVvWwXxYyZz
0123456789!?@#$%&*'){}:;""
The quick brown fox jumps over the lazy dog.

D

Schwennel™ Negro
*Graphic | Erratic Weight |
Broken Strokes |
Stroke Distortion |*

Linotype Library GmbH
www.linotype.com
info@linotype.com
+49 (0) 6172 484.418

A a B b C c D d E e F f G g H h I i J j K k L l M m N n O o P p Q q
R r S s T t U u V v W w X x Y y Z z 0 1 2 3 4 5 6 7 8 9 ! ? @ # $ %
& * ( ) { } : ; " "
The quick brown fox jumps over the lazy dog.

D t

ITC Outback™
Sans Serif | Bold Weight |
Condensed | Textured Contour |

Linotype Library GmbH
www.linotype.com
info@linotype.com
+49 (0) 6172 484.418

A a B b C c D d E e F f G g H h I i J j K k L l M m N n O o
P p Q q R r S s T t U u V v W w X x Y y Z z 0 1 2 3 4 5 6 7 8 9
! ? j C $ % & * ( ) O 2 : ; " "
The quick brown fox jumps over the lazy dog.

D t

Pink™
Sans Serif | Light Weight |
Structural Distortion |
Modulation |

Linotype Library GmbH
www.linotype.com
info@linotype.com
+49 (0) 6172 484.418

A a B b C c D d E e F f G g H h I i J j K k L l
M m N n O o P p Q q R r S s T t U u V v W w X x
Y y Z z 0 1 2 3 4 5 6 7 8 9 ! ? @ $ % & * ( ) : ;
The quick brown fox jumps over the lazy dog.

D

Hot Plate™ Std 2
Graphic | Mixed Style, Case,
and Weight | Abstract Details |

Linotype Library GmbH
www.linotype.com
info@linotype.com
+49 (0) 6172 484.418

A a B b C c D d E e F f G g H h I i J j K k L l
M m N n O o P p Q q R r S s T t U u V v W w X x
Y y Z z 0 1 2 3 4 5 6 7 8 9 ! ? @ $ % & * ( ) : ;
The quick brown fox jumps over the lazy dog.

D

Hot Plate™ Std 4
Graphic | Mixed Style, Case,
and Weight | Abstract Details |

Linotype Library GmbH
www.linotype.com
info@linotype.com
+49 (0) 6172 484.418

A a B b C c D d E e F f G g H h I i J j K k L l M m N n
O o P p Q q R r S s T t U u V v W w X x Y y Z z 0 1
2 3 4 5 6 7 8 9 ! ? @ # $ % & * ( ) { } : ; " "
The quick brown fox jumps over the lazy dog.

D

Quake™
Graphic Serif | Medium Weight |
Stroke Distortion |

Linotype Library GmbH
www.linotype.com
info@linotype.com
+49 (0) 6172 484.418

A a B b C c D d E e F f G g H h I i J j K k L l M m N n O o P p Q q R r S s T t
U u V v W w X x Y y Z z 0 1 2 3 4 5 6 7 8 9 ! ? @ # $ % & * ( ) { } : ; " "

The quick brown fox jumps over the lazy dog.

D

ITC Pious Henry™
Sans Serif | Light Weight |
Ultra Condensed | Erratic
Posture and Body Height |

Linotype Library GmbH
www.linotype.com
info@linotype.com
+49 (0) 6172 484.418

AaBbCcDdEeFfGgHhIiJjKkLlMm
NnOoPpQqRrSsTtUuVvWwXxYyZz
0123456789!?@"$%&:;""
The quick brown fox jumps over the lazy dog.

D

Linotype Seven™
*Graphic | Bold Weight |
Brush Detail |*

Linotype Library GmbH
www.linotype.com
info@linotype.com
+49 (0) 6172 484.418

ABCDEFGHIJKLMNOPQ
RSTUVWXYZ012345678
9!?A#$%&*[]{}:;""

THE QUICK BROWN FOX JUMPS OVER THE LAZY DOG.

D

Linotype Sjablony™
*Graphic | Bold Weight |
Broken Joints |*

Linotype Library GmbH
www.linotype.com
info@linotype.com
+49 (0) 6172 484.418

AaBbCcDdEeFfGgHhIiJjKkLlMm
NnOoPpQqRrSsTtUuVvWwXxYy
Zz0123456789!?@#$%&*(){};""
The quick brown fox jumps over the lazy dog.

D *t*

ITC Temble™
*Graphic Serif | Erratic Weight |
Stroke Distortion | Sharp Serifs |*

Linotype Library GmbH
www.linotype.com
info@linotype.com
+49 (0) 6172 484.418

AaBbCcDdEeFfGgHhIiJjKkLlMm
NnOoPpQqRrSsTtUuVvWwXxYy
Zz0123456789!?s@#$%*:;"

THE QUICK BROWN FOX JUMPS OVER THE LAZY DOG.

D

Glue Regular
*Graphic | Mixed Case, Weight,
and Heights | Textural Details |*

T.26 Digital Type Foundry
www.t26.com
info@t26.com
888.T26.FONT

AaBbCcDdEeFfGgHhIiJjKkLlMm
NnOoPpQqRrSsTtUuVvWwXxYy
Zz0123456789!?&@#$%*:;"
The quick brown fox jumps over the lazy dog.

D

Havoc
*Graphic | Bold Weight |
Erratic Baseline and Posture |
Textural Details |*

T.26 Digital Type Foundry
www.t26.com
info@t26.com
888.T26.FONT

AaBbCcDdEeFfGgHhIiJjKkLlMm
NnOoPpPpQqRrSsTtUuVvWwXxYyZz
0123456789!?&@#$%*:;"
The quick brown fox jumps over the lazy dog.

D

Helter Skelter
*Graphic | Light Weight |
Overall Italic Posture |
Textural Details |*

T.26 Digital Type Foundry
www.t26.com
info@t26.com
888.T26.FONT

Psychotic Color

Extremely vivid colors in unusual, generally complementary, combinations—red-orange with acid green, bright purple with sickly olive ochre, deep blue-violet with acid lemon yellow—may pair with very cold gray to convey the emotional disconnect of this mental state. Psychotic color often has more to do with the quantity of such colors—using them in an overwhelming volume—than with their specific hue identities. Red is a mainstay of most aggressive color schemes because of its ability to arouse and to evoke violence; heating red with a touch of yellow, toward the orange but still clearly red, enhances its aggressive nature. Treating supersaturated colors with fluorescent ink will augment their psychotic quality.

Sample Color Combinations

0 C	83 M	100 Y	0 K
20 C	0 M	100 Y	0 K
28 C	100 M	0 Y	0 K
0 C	5 M	100 Y	42 K
0 C	100 M	91 Y	5 K
0 C	90 M	100 Y	0 K
100 C	85 M	0 Y	50 K
8 C	0 M	100 Y	0 K
10 C	0 M	0 Y	25 K
0 C	100 M	40 Y	0 K

The sense of "foreign" exotic implies depends, of course, on context; exotic in France is not the same as exotic in the United States (where, in some places, "French" itself may qualify as "exotic"). Specific allusions to locale, therefore, are meaningless without a specific audience in mind. But notions of outlandishness, curious or bizarre qualities, or even glamour—perhaps a somewhat outdated interpretation—all are conveyed by unusual shapes, proportions, and odd color combinations.

Exotic

Graphic and experimental typefaces are most often immediately associated with the exotic; they often try, purposely, to flout convention. Typefaces with extreme exaggerations of width, posture, or weight—and sometimes all three—as well as proportional discontinuity among characters or counterspaces, typify exotic typefaces. Added to these structural extremes may be graphical substitutions of abstract shapes, curls, dots, and so on, for the expected stems, diagonals, and cross-strokes of a classical face. Alternatively, strange size changes between letters within the alphabet, tilting off-baseline in straight setting, bleeding, burn marks, extra limbs, and illustrative or abstract inclusions—all these stylistic possibilities may characterize a typeface as exotic. If the type becomes difficult to read because of these formal alterations, chances are it's an exotic face.

Event Poster
top, and detail, bottom

Joe Miller's Company
Santa Clara [CA] *USA*

AaBb Cc Dd Ee Ff Gg Hh Ii Jj Kk Ll Mm
Nn Oo Pp Qq Rr Ss Tt Uu Vv Ww Xx Yy
Zz ⊙ 1 2 3 4 5 6 7 8 9 ! ? ʊ @ $:; " ʾ

The quick brown fox jumps over the lazy dog.

D

P22 Catalan
*Graphic | Pronounced
Contrast | Erratic Baseline |*

P22 Type Foundry
www.p22.com
p22@p22.com
800.P22.5080

Aa Bb Cc Dd Ee Ff Gg Hh Ii Jj Kk Ll Mm Nn Oo
Pp Qq Rr Ss Tt Uu Vv Ww Xx Yy Zz 0 1 2 3 4 5 6 7
8 9 ! ? @ # $ % & * ( ) { } : ; " "

The quick brown fox jumps over the lazy dog.

D

Linotype Albafire™ Regular
*Graphic | Bold Weight |
Abstract Details |*

Linotype Library GmbH
www.linotype.com
info@linotype.com
+49 (0) 6172 484.418

Aa Bb Cc Dd Ee Ff Gg Hh Ii Jj Kk Ll Mm Nn
Oo Pp Qq Rr Ss Tt Uu Vv Ww Xx Yy Zz 01
2 3 4 5 6 7 8 9 ! ? ∩ ∩ $ % & * ( ) : ; " "

The quick brown fox jumps over the lazy dog.

D

Cult™
*Graphic Sans Serif | Light
Weight | Erratic Widths |
Heavy Joints |*

Linotype Library GmbH
www.linotype.com
info@linotype.com
+49 (0) 6172 484.418

AaBbCcDdEeFfGgHhIiJjKkLlMmNn
OoPpQqRrSsTtUuVvWwXxYyZz0123
456789!?●_$%&*():;""

The quick brown fox jumps over the lazy dog.

D

F2F Mekkaso Tomanik™
*Graphic | Light Weight |
Textural Details |*

Linotype Library GmbH
www.linotype.com
info@linotype.com
+49 (0) 6172 484.418

AaBbCcDdEeFfGgHhIiJjKkLlMmNnOo
PpQqRrSsTtUuVvWwXxYzZ0123456789!?@
#$%&*[]{}:;""

the quick brown fox jumps over the lazy dog.

D

Fusaka™
*Graphic | Medium Weight |
Glyphic Detail |*

Linotype Library GmbH
www.linotype.com
info@linotype.com
+49 (0) 6172 484.418

AaBbCcDdEeFfGgHhIiJjKkLlMmNn
OoPpQqRrSsTtUuVvWwXxYyZz0123
456789!?⛤☺$%&*()✳☯:;""

The quick brown fox jumps over the lazy dog.

D *t*

Hollyweird™
*Graphic | Medium Weight |
Script Detail | Moderate
Contrast | Erratic Posture |*

Linotype Library GmbH
www.linotype.com
info@linotype.com
+49 (0) 6172 484.418

A a B b C c D d E e F f G g H h I i J j K k L l M m
N n O o P p Q q R r S s T t U u V v W w X x Y y
Z z 0 1 2 3 4 5 6 7 8 9 ! ? ? $ % & * ( ) : ; " "
The quick brown fox jumps over the lazy dog.

D

Jazz™
Graphic | Black Weight |
Pronounced Contrast |
Inline Detail |

Linotype Library GmbH
www.linotype.com
info@linotype.com
+49 (0) 6172 484.418

A A B B C C D D E E F F G G H H I I J J K K L L M M N N
O O P P Q Q R R S S T T U U V V W W X X Y Y Z Z 0 1 2 3
4 5 6 7 8 9 ! ? ? $ % & * ( ) { } : ; " "
THE QUICK BROWN FOX JUMPS OVER THE LAZY DOG.

D

Juniper™
Serif | Bold Weight |
Pronounced Contrast |
Condensed |
Flared Strokes |

Linotype Library GmbH
www.linotype.com
info@linotype.com
+49 (0) 6172 484.418

A a B b C c D d E e F O G H O I i J K K L l
M N O P Q R S T TH U V
W X Y Z 0 1 2 3 4 5 6 7 8 9 ! ? $ %
THE QUICK BROWN FOX JUMPS OVER THE LAZY DOG.

D

Shaman™
Graphic | Bold Weight |
Inline and Illustrative Detail |

Linotype Library GmbH
www.linotype.com
info@linotype.com
+49 (0) 6172 484.418

A a B b C c D d E e F f G g H h I i J j K h L l M m N n O o P p
Q q R r S s T t U u V v W w X x Y y Z z 0 1 2 3 4 5 6 7 8 9
! ? @ # $ % & * ( ) { } : ; " "
The quick brown fox jumps over the lazy dog.

D

Linotype Sunburst™
East Heavy
Graphic Serif | Bold Weight |
Angled Bowls and Joints |
Slight Italic Posture |

Linotype Library GmbH
www.linotype.com
info@linotype.com
+49 (0) 6172 484.418

A A B B C C D D E E F F G G H H I I J J K K L L M M D N O O P P Q Q R R
S S T T U U V V W W X X Y Y Z Z 0 1 2 3 4 5 6 7 8 9 ! ? @ # $ % & * ( )
{ } : ; " "
THE QUICK BROWN FOX JUMPS OVER THE LAZY DOG.

D

ITC Cherie™
Sans Serif | Light Weight |
Pronounced Upper Emphasis |
Alternate Capitals |

Linotype Library GmbH
www.linotype.com
info@linotype.com
+49 (0) 6172 484.418

A a B b C c D d E e F f G g H h I i J j K k L l M m N n
O o P p Q q R r S s T t U u V v W w X x Y y Z z 0 1
2 3 4 5 6 7 8 9 ! ? @ # $ % & * ( ) { } : ; " "
The quick brown fox jumps over the lazy dog.

D

Linotype Sicula™ Regular
Graphic | Erratic Weight |
Pronounced Contrast | Structural
Distortion | Script Details |

Linotype Library GmbH
www.linotype.com
info@linotype.com
+49 (0) 6172 484.418

Exotic Color

Color that can be considered exotic is difficult to pin down. Since "exotic" connotes something unknown or foreign, and most colors carry associations that are familiar, attempting to represent the alien and outlandish can be challenging. Often, designers resort to jarring combinations, such as a hot orange and a supersaturated pink; but these are not exotic so much as electric. Another relatively weak color concept is to use earthy tones that evoke the designer's sense of the so-called "Third World" of preindustrial nations—terra cotta, deep ochre, olive, and deep rose. These colors are a good base for the palette, but what becomes unusual enough to represent exotic are combinations of them in almost unrelated ways: a pale cyan, an electric violet, and a muddy, olive brown, for example. Complementary combinations, such as violet and yellow, allude to the idea of foreignness in their chromatic opposition—as do orange and blue, red and green.

0 C	
79 M	
100 Y	
0 K	

10 C	
100 M	
0 Y	
0 K	

0 C	
68 M	
79 Y	
22 K	

0 C	
41 M	
85 Y	
34 K	

65 C	
100 M	
0 Y	
0 K	

34 C	
0 M	
5 Y	
0 K	

80 C	
80 M	
100 Y	
0 K	

100 C	
40 M	
0 Y	
60 K	

43 C	
15 M	
100 Y	
71 K	

0 C	
65 M	
0 Y	
75 K	

Sample Color Combinations

Immediate, instinctive, and visceral energy mark the visual qualities associated with intuition—the indescribable "gut feeling" of invention. Typography that embodies the intuitive is free and unstudied; color that evokes this mood is light and energetic.

Intuitive

Most typefaces that appear hand-drawn with a brush, pen, or rough tools will convey the sense of intuition, especially if the characters are italic and have the uneven, unrefined qualities of such tools. The character proportions in such faces tend not to be uniform, creating a syncopated, unstudied rhythm in setting that makes them feel undesigned—as though they were laid down without planning. The gestural freedom within the strokes of faces that appear hand-drawn—in which the terminals of characters are extended, similar to those in scripts or swashes—further contributes to the intuitive feeling of these faces. In this sense, italic serif faces often feel intuitive, deriving their base forms from handwriting. Serif text faces without particularly pronounced details or stroke modulation, as well as sans serifs with abrupt joints, lighter overall weights, and some modulation— but with very quick ductus—also feel intuitive and immediate. The more refined the face, the less intuitive or immediate it feels. Bolder weight, condensed, italic faces—especially sans-serif versions—convey a sense of the visceral because of the rapid alternation of stroke and counter, enhanced by the italic slant.

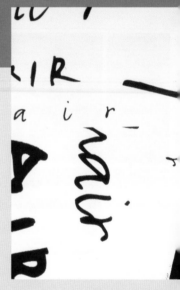

Catalog Section Divider
top, and detail, bottom

Voice
Scott Carslake and Anthony De Leo, design and typography
David Solm, Oz, photography
Adelaide *Australia*

A a B b C c D d E e F f G g H h i i J j k k L L
m m N n ⊙ o o p p q q R r S s T t u u v W w
X x y y Z z 0 1 2 3 4 5 6 7 8 9 ! ? ⓒ @ # $ % * : ; "

The quick brown fox jumps over the lazy dog.

D

Voiture Plat
Graphic | Erratic Weight |
Erratic Baseline |

T.26 Digital Type Foundry
www.t26.com
info@t26.com
888.T26.FONT

A a B b C c D d E e F f G g H h I i J j K k
L l M m N n O o P p Q q R r S s T t U u
V v W w X x Y y Z z 0 1 2 3 4 5 6 7 8 9 ! ?
@ # $ % & * ( ) { } : ; "

The quick brown fox jumps over the lazy dog.

D

Linotype Elisa™ Regular
Script | Light Weight | Italic
Posture | Pen Details |

Linotype Library GmbH
www.linotype.com
info@linotype.com
+49 (0) 6172 484.418

A a B b C c D d E e F f G g H h I i J j K K L L
M M N n O o o p p q q R r S s T t U u V v W w
X x Y y Z z 0 1 2 3 4 5 6 7 8 9 ! ? & @ # $ %

The quick brown fox jumps over the lazy dog.

D

Flurry Normal
Graphic | Light Weight |

Garage Fonts Type Foundry
www.garagefonts.com
info@garagefonts.com
800.681.9375

A A B B C C D D E E F F G G H H I I J J K K L L M M
N N O O P P Q Q R R S S T T J U U V V W W X X Y Y Z Z O
1 2 3 4 5 6 7 8 9 ! ? & @ $: ; " "

THE QUICK BROWN FOX JUMPS OVER THE LAZY DOG.

D

P22 Ed Rogers Regular
Graphic | Erratic Weight |
Erratic Posture |

P22 Type Foundry
www.p22.com
p22@p22.com
800.P22.5080

A A B B C (D D E E F F G G H I I J J K K L L
M M N N O O P P Q Q R R S S T T U U V V
W W X X Y Y Z Z 0 1 2 3 4 5 6 7 8 9 ! ? @ # $ %
& * ( ) { } : ; " "

THE QUICK BROWN FOX JUMPS OVER THE LAZY DOG.

D **t**

ITC Underscript™
Sans Serif | Bold Weight |
Varied Widths | Alternate
Capitals | Rounded Terminals

Linotype Library GmbH
www.linotype.com
info@linotype.com
+49 (0) 6172 484.418

A a B b C c D d E e F f G g H h I i J j K k L l M m
N n O o P p Q q R r S s T t U u V v W w X x Y y Z z
0 1 2 3 4 5 6 7 8 9 ! ? & @ # $ % * : ; "

The quick brown fox jumps over the lazy dog.

D

MVB Emmascript
Script | Erratic Baseline |
Medium Weight |

MVB Fonts
www.mvbfonts.com
info@mvbfonts.com
510.525.4288

Aa Bb Cc Dd Ee ff Gg Hh Ii Jj Kk Ll Mm Nn Oo Pp Qq Rr Ss Tt Uu Vv Ww Xx Yy Zz 0123456789 !?&@#$%:;"*

The quick brown fox jumps over the lazy dog.

D

Mockingbird Regular
Graphic Script | Erratic Weight | Erratic Baseline |

Garage Fonts Type Foundry
www.garagefonts.com
info@garagefonts.com
800.681.9375

Aa Bb Cc Dd Ee Ff Gg Hh Ii Jj Kk Ll
Mm Nn Oo Pp Qq Rr Ss Tt Uu Vv Ww
Xx Yy Zz 0123456789 !?&@ #$%*

The quick brown fox jumps over the lazy dog.

D *t*

Vestige Oblique
Stylized Sans Serif | Moderate Contrast | Moderate Posture |

Garage Fonts Type Foundry
www.garagefonts.com
info@garagefonts.com
800.681.9375

Aa Bb Cc Dd Ee Ff Gg Hh Ii Jj Kk Ll Mm Nn Oo Pp Qq Rr Ss Tt Uu Vv Ww Xx Yy Zz 0123456789 !?&@#$%:;"*

The quick brown fox jumps over the lazy dog.

D

Ingredients: Aspartame
Graphic | Erratic Posture | Lighter Medium Weight |

T.26 Digital Type Foundry
www.t26.com
info@t26.com
888.T26.FONT

**Aa Bb Cc Dd Ee Ff Gg Hh Ii Jj Kk Ll Mm Nn
Oo Pp Qq Rr Ss Tt Uu Vv Ww Xx Yy Zz 0123
456789 !?@#$%&*(){}:;""**

The quick brown fox jumps over the lazy dog.

D *t*

Ad Hoc™ Roman
Sans Serif | Bold Weight | Brush Details | Erratic Terminal Heights | Slightly Condensed |

Linotype Library GmbH
www.linotype.com
info@linotype.com
+49 (0) 6172 484.418

Aa Bb Cc Dd Ee Ff Gg Hh Ii Jj Kk Ll Mm
Nn Oo Pp Qq Rr Ss Tt Uu Vv Ww Xx Yy Zz
0123456789 !?&@#$%*:;"

The quick brown fox jumps over the lazy dog.

D *t*

Gobbler
Sans Serif | Erratic Width | Medium Weight |

The Chank Company
www.chank.com
friendlyfolks@chank.com
877.GO.CHANK

Aa Bb Cc Dd Ee Ff Gg Hh Ii Jj Kk Ll Mm
Nn Oo Pp Qq Rr Ss Tt Uu Vv Ww Xx Yy Zz
0123456789 !?@#$%&*(){}:;""

The quick brown fox jumps over the lazy dog.

D *t*

ITC Bradley Hand™ Bold
Graphic Sans Serif | Medium Weight | Varied Bowls | Erratic

Linotype Library GmbH
www.linotype.com
info@linotype.com
+49 (0) 6172 484.418

A a B b C c D d E e F f G g H h I i J j K k L l M m N n
O o P p Q q R r S s T t U u V v W w X x Y y Z z 0 1 2 3
4 5 6 7 8 9 ! ? @ # $ % & * ( ) { } : ; " "
The quick brown fox jumps over the lazy dog.

D *t*

Caterina Std Regular
Sans Serif | Medium Weight |
Modulation | Brush Details |

Linotype Library GmbH
www.linotype.com
info@linotype.com
+49 (0) 6172 484.418

A a B b C c D d E e F f G g H h I i J j K k L l M m N n O o
P p Q q R r S s T t U u V v W w X x Y y Z z 0 1 2 3 4 5 6 7
8 9 ! ? $ % & * ( ) : ; " "
The quick brown fox jumps over the lazy dog.

D **T**

Claude™ Sans Regular
Sans Serif | Uniform Light
Weight | Rounded Terminals |

Linotype Library GmbH
www.linotype.com
info@linotype.com
+49 (0) 6172 484.418

A a B b C c D d E e F f G g H h I i J j K k L l M m N n
O o P p Q q R r S s T t U u V v W w X x Y y Z z 0 1 2 3 4
5 6 7 8 9 ! ? & @ $: ; " "
The quick brown fox jumps over the lazy dog.

D

P22 Davinci Forward
Script-Sans Serif Hybrid |
Light Weight | Erratic Width |

P22 Type Foundry
www.p22.com
p22@p22.com
800.P22.5080

A a B b C c D d E e F f G g H h I i J j K k L l M m N n O o
P p Q q R r S s T t U u V v W w X x Y y Z z 0 1 2 3 4 5 6 7
8 9 ! ? $ % & * ( ) : ; " "
The quick brown fox jumps over the lazy dog.

D

Indy™ Italic
Script-Sans Serif Hybrid |
Condensed |
Lighter Medium Weight |

Linotype Library GmbH
www.linotype.com
info@linotype.com
+49 (0) 6172 484.418

A A B B C C D D E E F F G G H H I I J J K K L L M M N N O O
P P Q Q R R S S T T U U V V W W X X Y Y Z Z 0 1 2 3 4 5 6 7
8 9 ! ? @ # $ % & * ( ) ( ) : ; " "
THE QUICK BROWN FOX JUMPS OVER THE LAZY DOG.

D

ITC Matisse™
Graphic | Bolder Medium
Weight | Erratic Width,
Posture, and Height |

Linotype Library GmbH
www.linotype.com
info@linotype.com
+49 (0) 6172 484.418

A a B b C c D d E e F f G g H h I i J j K k L l M m N n O o P p
Q q R r S s T t U u V v W w X x Y y Z z 0 1 2 3 4 5 6 7 8 9 ! ?
$ % & * ( ) { } : ; " "
The quick brown fox jumps over the lazy dog.

D

Mistral™
Script-Sans Serif Hybrid |
Medium Weight | Slight Italic
Posture | Brush Detail |

Linotype Library GmbH
www.linotype.com
info@linotype.com
+49 (0) 6172 484.418

A a B b C c D d E e F f G g H h I i J j K k L l M m N n
O o P p Q q R r S s T t U u V v W w X x Y y Z z 0 1 2 3
4 5 6 7 8 9 ! ? @ # $ % & * ( ) { } : ; " "
The quick brown fox jumps over the lazy dog.

D *t*

Linotype Rana™ Regular
Sans Serif | Medium Weight |
Slight Modulation |

Linotype Library GmbH
www.linotype.com
info@linotype.com
+49 (0) 6172 484.418

A a B b C c D d E e F f G g H h I i J j K k L l M m
N n O o P p Q q R r S s T t U u V v W w X x Y y Z z
0 1 2 3 4 5 6 7 8 9 ! ? @ # $ % & * ( ) { } : ; " "
The quick brown fox jumps over the lazy dog.

D

ReadMyHand™ Regular
Graphic | Erratic Weight |
Brush Detail |

Linotype Library GmbH
www.linotype.com
info@linotype.com
+49 (0) 6172 484.418

A a B b C c D d E e F f G g H h I i J j K k L l M m N n
O o P p Q q R r S s T t U u V v W w X x Y y Z z 0 1 2 3
4 5 6 7 8 9 ! ? ~ Th $ % & * ( ) : ; " "
The quick brown fox jumps over the lazy dog.

D

Riva™
Script | Light Weight |
Erratic Body Heights |

Linotype Library GmbH
www.linotype.com
info@linotype.com
+49 (0) 6172 484.418

A a B b C c D d E e F f G g H h I i J j K k L l M m N n O o
P p Q q R r S s T t U u V v W w X x Y y Z z 0 1 2 3 4 5 6 7
8 9 ! ? $ % & * ( ) : ; " "
The quick brown fox jumps over the lazy dog.

D

Smudger™
Graphic Sans Serif | Bold, Erratic
Weight | Slight Italic Posture |

Linotype Library GmbH
www.linotype.com
info@linotype.com
+49 (0) 6172 484.418

A a B b C c D d E e F f G g H h I i J j K k L l M m N n O o
P p Q q R r S s T t U u V v W w X x Y y Z z 0 1 2 3 4 5
6 7 8 9 ! ? @ # $ % & * ( ) { } : ; " "
The quick brown fox jumps over the lazy dog.

D *t*

Wiesbaden Swing™ Regular
Script-Sans Serif Hybrid |
Light Weight | Erratic Posture |

Linotype Library GmbH
www.linotype.com
info@linotype.com
+49 (0) 6172 484.418

A a B b C c D d E e F f G g H h I i J j K k L l M m N n O o
P p Q q R r S s T t U u V v W w X x Y y Z z 0 1 2 3 4 5
6 7 8 9 ! ? @ # & : ; " "
The quick brown fox jumps over the lazy dog.

D

P22 Freely
Script–Sans Serif Hybrid |
Medium Weight | Moderately
Acute Posture |

P22 Type Foundry
www.p22.com
p22@p22.com
800.P22.5080

ntuitive Color

Saturated, warmer hues of a middle to lighter value bring with them a sense of the intuitive, capitalizing on the metabolic arousal nduced by red, orange, and yellow but tempering their aggressive qualities by lightening them and making them seem a bit more resh. Cooler colors, such as blue and violet, tend to be restful and contemplative, implying thought and consideration, and thus should be avoided in an intuitive palette. As with some other mood categories, the combination of colors is very important in conveying a sense of immediacy. To appear intuitive, colors must seem uncho-sen, or at least chosen with little thought. Combining several ver-sions of a color—or of analogous colors—such as two or three dif-ferent versions of red and orange, suggests a quick sifting of color options after a decision has been made off the cuff. Throwing in an unrelated color as a foil adds to the sense of quick, gut-informed decisions; if the color has some complementary relationship to the base colors—or is slightly off, meaning not an exact complement—this quality may be greatly enhanced.

Sample Color Combinations

0	C
78	M
60	Y
0	K

0	C
39	M
75	Y
0	K

0	C
82	M
34	Y
0	K

0	C
100	M
82	Y
0	K

34	C
0	M
74	Y
0	K

6	C
63	M
42	Y
0	K

0	C
25	M
100	Y
0	K

0	C
11	M
67	Y
0	K

58	C
0	M
20	Y
0	K

12	C
66	M
5	Y
0	K

Austerity and simplicity are the hallmarks of corporate type. These qualities convey notions of authority, credibility, and neutrality that reinforce the image of the corporate environment as a place where business gets done. Corporate typefaces are no-nonsense, strong, and safe, connoting dependability as well as directness. Classical overtones in a corporate typeface lend a sense of precedent and stability.

Corporate

Most typefaces associated with the corporate environment are sans serif, as they are devoid of embellishments and most often exhibit a uniform stroke weight and optically uniform widths. These characteristics result in a formal simplicity and neutrality that helps communicate the corporate sense of professionalism. Because of their uniform stroke weight—and hence, little contrast—sans serifs appear strong, without the potentially brittle quality of the junctures as thin strokes meet thick. Their x-heights tend to be larger, creating a more open, accessible, and legible quality compared to most serif faces. Many sans-serif families are extensive, offering a variety of weights and widths that allow designers to differentiate information and introduce visual contrast without sacrificing overall formal unity. The result is a consistency that speaks to corporate dependability and competence. Serif faces, however, may often be used in corporate communications, as their overtly classical qualities inspire a sense of history—the association being the business "track record." While older serifs tend to feel more organic, transitional and modern serifs, with their sharper serifs, greater stroke contrast and modulation, and upright axes, help convey this conservative quality with a more modern look.

Newsletter Cover
top, and detail, bottom

Gorska Design
Caryl Gorska
San Francisco *USA*

AaBbCcDdEeFfGgHhIiJjKkLlMmNnOoPp
QqRrSsTtUuVvWwXxYyZz0123456789!?
@#$%&*(){}:;""
The quick brown fox jumps over the lazy dog.

D *t*

Rogue Serif Light
Slab Serif | Condensed |
Bold Weight |

Device
www.devicefonts.co.uk
rianhughes@aol.com
44 (0) 7979.602.272

A a B b C c D d E e F f G g H h I i J j K k L l M m
N n O o P p Q q R r S s T t U u V v W w X x Y y
Z z 0 1 2 3 4 5 6 7 8 9 ! ? & @ # $ % * : ; "
The quick brown fox jumps over the lazy dog.

D **T**

Aaux Office Medium
Slab Serif | Condensed |
Medium Weight |

T.26 Digital Type Foundry
www.t26.com
info@t26.com
888.T26.FONT

A a B b C c D d E e F f G g H h I i J j K k L l M m N n O o
P p Q q R r S s T t U u V v W w X x Y y Z z 0 1 2 3 4 5 6 7
8 9 ! ? & @ # $ % * : ; "
The quick brown fox jumps over the lazy dog.

D *t*

Cynapse Bold
Stylized Sans Serif |
Condensed | Medium Weight |

T.26 Digital Type Foundry
www.t26.com
info@t26.com
888.T26.FONT

A a B b C c D d E e F f G g H h I i J j K k L l
M m N n O o P p Q q R r S s T t U u V v W w
X x Y y Z z 0 1 2 3 4 5 6 7 8 9 ! ? & @ # $ % * :
The quick brown fox jumps over the lazy dog.

D **T**

Interviewer Regular
Stylized Serif | Pronounced
Contrast | Medium Weight |

T.26 Digital Type Foundry
www.t26.com
info@t26.com
888.T26.FONT

A a B b C c D d E e F f G g H h I i J j K k L l M m
N n O o P p Q q R r S s T t U u V v W w X x Y y
Z z 0 1 2 3 4 5 6 7 8 9 ! ? & @ # $ % * : ; "
The quick brown fox jumps over the lazy dog.

D **T**

Kaiser Regular
Sans Serif | Slightly
Condensed | Medium Weight |

T.26 Digital Type Foundry
www.t26.com
info@t26.com
888.T26.FONT

A a B b C c D d E e F f G g H h I i J j K k L l M m
N n O o P p Q q R r S s T t U u V v W w X x Y y
Z z 0 1 2 3 4 5 6 7 8 9 ! ? @ # $ % & * ( ) { } : ; " "
The quick brown fox jumps over the lazy dog.

D **T**

Univers™ 55 Roman
Sans Serif | Medium Weight |
Slightly Squared Shoulders |

Linotype Library GmbH
www.linotype.com
info@linotype.com
+49 (0) 6172 484.418

A a B b C c D d E e F f G g H h I i J j K k L l M m
N n O o P p Q q R r S s T t U u V v W w X x Y y
Z z 0 1 2 3 4 5 6 7 8 9 ! ? & @ # $ % * : ; ”

The quick brown fox jumps over the lazy dog.

| D | T |

Pilgrim Regular
Sans Serif | Slightly Condensed | Medium Weight |

T.26 Digital Type Foundry
www.t26.com
info@t26.com
888.T26.FONT

A a B b C c D d E e F f G g H h I i J j K k L l
M m N n O o P p Q q R r S s T t U u V v W w
X x Y y Z z 0 1 2 3 4 5 6 7 8 9 ! ? & @ # $ % * : ; ”

The quick brown fox jumps over the lazy dog.

| D | T |

Alias Union Medium
Serif | Pronounced Contrast | Bolder Medium Weight |

T.26 Digital Type Foundry
www.t26.com
info@t26.com
888.T26.FONT

A a B b C c D d E e F f G g H h I i J j K k L l
M m N n O o P p Q q R r S s T t U u V v W w
X x Y y Z z 0 1 2 3 4 5 6 7 8 9 ! ? & @ # $ % * : ; ”

THE QUICK BROWN FOX JUMPS OVER THE LAZY DOG.

| D |

Alias Union Medium Small Caps
Serif | Pronounced Contrast | Bolder Medium Weight |

T.26 Digital Type Foundry
www.t26.com
info@t26.com
888.T26.FONT

A a B b C c D d E e F f G g H h I i J j K k L l M m
N n O o P p Q q R r S s T t U u V v W w X x Y y Z z
0 1 2 3 4 5 6 7 8 9 ! ? @ # $ % & * ( ) { } : ; “ ”
The quick brown fox jumps over the lazy dog.

| D | T |

Bauer Bodoni™ Roman
Serif | Extreme Contrast | Upright Axis |

Linotype Library GmbH
www.linotype.com
info@linotype.com
+49 (0) 6172 484.418

A a B b C c D d E e F f G g H h I i J j K k L l M m
N n O o P p Q q R r S s T t U u V v W w X x Y y Z z
0 1 2 3 4 5 6 7 8 9 ! ? @ # $ % & * ( ) { } : ; “ ”
The quick brown fox jumps over the lazy dog.

| D | T |

Compatil™ Fact Regular
Sans Serif | Medium Weight | Uniform Strokes |

Linotype Library GmbH
www.linotype.com
info@linotype.com
+49 (0) 6172 484.418

A a B b C c D d E e F f G g H h I i J j K k L l M m N n
O o P p Q q R r S s T t U u V v W w X x Y y Z z 0 1
2 3 4 5 6 7 8 9 ! ? @ # $ % & * ( ) { } : ; “ ”
The quick brown fox jumps over the lazy dog.

| D | T |

Trade Gothic™ Roman
Sans Serif | Medium Weight | Uniform Strokes |

Linotype Library GmbH
www.linotype.com
info@linotype.com
+49 (0) 6172 484.418

A a B b C c D d E e F f G g H h I i J j K k L l M m
N n O o P p Q q R r S s T t U u V v W w X x Y y Z z
0 1 2 3 4 5 6 7 8 9 ! ? @ # $ % & * ( ) { } : ; " "
The quick brown fox jumps over the lazy dog.

D **T**

Compatil™ Letter Regular
Slab Serif | Medium Weight |
Slight Contrast |

Linotype Library GmbH
www.linotype.com
info@linotype.com
+49 (0) 6172 484.418

A a B b C c D d E e F f G g H h I i J j K k L l M m
N n O o P p Q q R r S s T t U u V v W w X x Y y Z z
0 1 2 3 4 5 6 7 8 9 ! ? @ # $ % & * ( ) { } : ; " "
The quick brown fox jumps over the lazy dog.

D **T**

Compatil™ Text Regular
Serif | Medium Weight |
Noticeable Contrast |

Linotype Library GmbH
www.linotype.com
info@linotype.com
+49 (0) 6172 484.418

A a B b C c D d E e F f G g H h I i J j K k L l M m N n
O o P p Q q R r S s T t U u V v W w X x Y y Z z 0 1 2 3
*4 5 6 7 8 9 ! ? @ # $ % & * ( ) { } : ; " "*
The quick brown fox jumps over the lazy dog.

D *t*

Diverda™ Sans Std Italic
Sans Serif | Medium Weight |
Slight Contrast | Occasional
Serif Detail |

Linotype Library GmbH
www.linotype.com
info@linotype.com
+49 (0) 6172 484.418

A a B b C c D d E e F f G g H h I i J j K k L l M m N n
O o P p Q q R r S s T t U u V v W w X x Y y Z z 0 1
2 3 4 5 6 7 8 9 ! ? @ # $ % & * ( ) { } : ; " "
The quick brown fox jumps over the lazy dog.

D **T**

Diverda™ Sans Std Regular
Sans Serif | Medium Weight |
Uniform Strokes |

Linotype Library GmbH
www.linotype.com
info@linotype.com
+49 (0) 6172 484.418

A a B b C c D d E e F f G g H h I i J j K k L l M m N n
O o P p Q q R r S s T t U u V v W w X x Y y Z z 0 1
*2 3 4 5 6 7 8 9 ! ? @ # $ % & * ( ) { } : ; " "*
The quick brown fox jumps over the lazy dog.

D *t*

Diverda™ Serif Std
Regular Italic
Slab Serif | Medium Weight |
Slight Contrast

Linotype Library GmbH
www.linotype.com
info@linotype.com
+49 (0) 6172 484.418

A a B b C c D d E e F f G g H h I i J j K k L l M m N n
O o P p Q q R r S s T t U u V v W w X x Y y Z z 0 1 2 3
4 5 6 7 8 9 ! ? @ # $ % & * ( ) { } : ; " "
The quick brown fox jumps over the lazy dog.

D **T**

Frutiger™ 45 Light
Sans Serif | Uniform Strokes |
Sharp Terminals |

Linotype Library GmbH
www.linotype.com
info@linotype.com
+49 (0) 6172 484.418

A a B b C c D d E e F f G g H h I i J j K k L l M m
N n O o P p Q q R r S s T t U u V v W w X x Y y
Z z 0 1 2 3 4 5 6 7 8 9 ! ? @ # $ % & * ( ) { } : ; " "
The quick brown fox jumps over the lazy dog.

D T

Janson Text™ 55 Roman
Serif | Medium Weight |
Moderate Contrast |

Linotype Library GmbH
www.linotype.com
info@linotype.com
+49 (0) 6172 484.418

A a B b C c D d E e F f G g H h I i J j K k L l M m N n O o
P p Q q R r S s T t U u V v W w X x Y y Z z 0 1 2 3 4 5 6 7
8 9 ! ? @ # $ % & * ( ) { } : ; " "
The quick brown fox jumps over the lazy dog.

D T

ITC Officina® Sans Book
Sans Serif | Lighter Medium
Weight | Slightly Condensed |
Turned Terminals |

Linotype Library GmbH
www.linotype.com
info@linotype.com
+49 (0) 6172 484.418

A a B b C c D d E e F f G g H h I i J j K k L l M m N n O o
P p Q q R r S s T t U u V v W w X x Y y Z z 0 1 2 3 4 5
6 7 8 9 ! ? @ # $ % & * ( ) { } : ; " "
The quick brown fox jumps over the lazy dog.

D T

Rotis® Sans 55 Roman
Sans Serif | Medium Weight |
Slight Contrast |
Slightly Condensed |

Linotype Library GmbH
www.linotype.com
info@linotype.com
+49 (0) 6172 484.418

A a B b C c D d E e F f G g H h I i J j K k L l M m
N n O o P p Q q R r S s T t U u V v W w X x Y y Z z
0 1 2 3 4 5 6 7 8 9 ! ? @ # $ % & * ( ) { } : ; " "
The quick brown fox jumps over the lazy dog.

D T

Linotype Syntax™ Regular
Sans Serif | Medium Weight |
Uniform Strokes |

Linotype Library GmbH
www.linotype.com
info@linotype.com
+49 (0) 6172 484.418

A a B b C c D d E e F f G g H h I i J j K k L l
M m N n O o P p Q q R r S s T t U u V v W w X x
Y y Z z 0 1 2 3 4 5 6 7 8 9 ! ? & @ # $ % * : ; "
The quick brown fox jumps over the lazy dog.

D T

MVB Verdigris OsF
Serif | Medium Weight |
Noticeable Contrast |

MVB Fonts
www.mvbfonts.com
info@mvbfonts.com
510.525.4288

A a B b C c D d E e F f G g H h I i J j K k L l M m
N n O o P p Q q R r S s T t U u V v W w X x Y y Z z
*0 1 2 3 4 5 6 7 8 9 ! ? & @ # $ % * : ; "*
The quick brown fox jumps over the lazy dog.

D T

MVB Verdigris OsF Italic
Serif | Medium Weight |
Noticeable Contrast |

MVB Fonts
www.mvbfonts.com
info@mvbfonts.com
510.525.4288

Corporate Color

Gray and blue are the corporate colors of choice. Their alternate associations of competence, reliability, and calm help assure that a project will communicate these essential business qualities to an audience. Although deeper versions of these colors may be appear powerful at first, they are often perceived as daunting or solemn; medium to lighter tones evoke placid, reasonable, and trustworthy associations. The corporate palette, however, isn't limited to these colors. Red, both vivid and saturated, as well as deeper and cooler, toward burgundy, adds a sense of power that helps invigorate the neutrality and reliability of gray and blue and also implies authority and vitality. Deeper greens and muted, desaturated violets play off the stable quality of blue, injecting a sense of growth and economic status or regal authority, respectively. Mixing gray into a variety of colors—desaturating them and making them more neutral—enhances their sophistication and unifies them. Combining several analogous hues of equal value and low saturation creates an elegant, subdued, and controlled feeling.

Sample Color Combinations

>	0 C	
	0 M	
	0 Y	
	55 K	

>	10 C
	0 M
	0 Y
	35 K

>	65 C
	0 M
	56 Y
	70 K

>	55 C
	0 M
	6 Y
	43 K

>	0 C
	15 M
	15 Y
	60 K

>	80 C
	45 M
	0 Y
	50 K

>	90 C
	40 M
	0 Y
	28 K

>	0 C
	100 M
	100 Y
	25 K

>	12 C
	100 M
	32 Y
	65 K

>	40 C
	65 M
	0 Y
	65 K

Fast and frenetic, electrical and industrial, the techno-influenced designs of the late twentieth and early twenty-first centuries buzz with high-voltage, luminescent combinations of color and typographic design that push conventional boundaries aside. Deriving from the rich palette of the video screen and the drawing capabilities of the computer, colors and type forms in the techno world are radical and dynamic.

im Schtei

Techno

Typefaces reflecting the music scene in the digital age share an extreme quality that communicates not only the technological aspect of the genre but also its high energy. Typefaces used to communicate this genre often push the envelope in terms of legibility, exploring extremes of width, both condensed and extended, as well as the basic structure of the drawings. Simplification and the loss of junctures or strokes is common. Techno typefaces often attempt to reflect the idea of electronic media in their drawing, using bitmaps, pixels, and other modular logic to convey a sense of the digital. Decorative inclusions, such as large dots, graphic shapes, and inlines, are also common among techno typefaces.

Event Poster
top, and detail, bottom

Mixer
Erich Brechbuhl
Lucerne *Switzerland*

AaBbCcDdEeFfGgHhIiJjKkLlMm
NnOoPpQqRrSsTtUuVvWwXxYy
Zz0123456789!?&@#$%*:;"
The quick brown fox jumps over the lazy dog.

D

P22 Basala
Stylized Sans Serif |
Pronounced Contrast |
Extended |

P22 Type Foundry
www.p22.com
p22@p22.com
800.P22.5080

ABCDEFGHIJKLMNOPQRS
TUVWXYZ0123456789!?
N*$%&·()[]!'""
THE QUICK BROWN FOX JUMPS OVER THE LAZY DOG.

D

Monitor
Graphic | All Caps |
Bold Weight | Textural
Counterspaces |

Device
www.devicefonts.co.uk
rianhughes@aol.com
44 (0) 7979.602.272

AaBbCcDdEeFfGgHhIiJjKkLlMm
NnOoPpQqRrSsTtUuVvWwXxYyZz
0123456789!?&@$::"" "

The quick brown fox jumps over the lazy dog.

D

P22 Cusp Square
Graphic | Bold Weight |

P22 Type Foundry
www.p22.com
p22@p22.com
800.P22.5080

AaKbCcDdEeFfGgHhIiJjKk
LlMmNnOoPpQqRrSsTtUuVv
WwXxYyZz0123456789!?&@

The quick brown fox jumps over the lazy dog.

D

Porno Soft
Graphic Serif | Erratic Weight |

Garage Fonts Type Foundry
www.garagefonts.com
info@garagefonts.com
800.681.9375

AaBbCcDdEeFfGgHhIiJjKk
LlMmNnOoPpQqRrSsTtUu
VvWwXxYyZz0123456789!?&

The quick brown fox jumps over the lazy dog.

D

Broken Screen Squares
Graphic | Bold Weight |
Fraktur Structure |

T.26 Digital Type Foundry
www.t26.com
info@t26.com
888.T26.FONT

AaBbCcDdEeFfGgHhIiJjKkL
LMmNnOoPpQqRrSsTtUuVv
WwXxYyZz0123456789!?
@#$%&*()(){}!;""

THE QUICK BROWN FOX JUMPS OVER THE LAZY DOG.

D t

Outlander Nova Medium
Stylized Sans Serif | Extended |

Device
www.devicefonts.co.uk
rianhughes@aol.com
44 (0) 7979.602.272

AaBbCcDdEeFfGgHhIiJjKkLlMm
NnOoPpQqRrSsTtUuVvWwXxYy
ZzO123456789!?&◉⊜⊆$%✳:;"

The quick brown fox jumps over the lazy dog.

D

Pulsar N-Class
Stylized Sans Serif | Extended |

T.26 Digital Type Foundry
www.t26.com
info@t26.com
888.T26.FONT

AaBbCcDdEeFfGgHhIiJjKkLl
MmNnOoPpQqRrSsTtUuVvWw
XxYyZzO123456789!?&◉∫:;""

The quick brown fox jumps over the lazy dog.

D

Urbanite Regular
*Stylized Sans Serif | Medium
Weight | Erratic Baseline |*

T.26 Digital Type Foundry
www.t26.com
info@t26.com
888.T26.FONT

AaBbCcDdEeFfGgHhIiJjKkLlMm
NnOoPpQqRrSsTtUuVvWwXxYyZz
0123456789!?&@$:;""

The quick brown fox jumps over the lazy dog.

D *t*

P22 Cusp Round
Graphic | Bold Weight |

P22 Type Foundry
www.p22.com
p22@p22.com
800.P22.5080

ABCDEFGHIJKLMNOPQRSTUV
WXYZ0123456789!?"$%&!()[]

THE QUICK BROWN FOX JUMPS OVER THE LAZY DOG!

D

Synchro™ Reversed
*Graphic | Medium Weight |
All Capitals | Reverse |*

Linotype Library GmbH
www.linotype.com
info@linotype.com
+49 (0) 6172 484.418

ABCDEFGHIJKLMNOPQRS
TUVWXYZ0123456789!?
#$%&+()!?¡¡""

THE QUICK BROWN FOX JUMPS OVER THE LAZY DOG.

D

Contour Regular
*Graphic | Extended |
Pronounced Contrast |*

Device
www.devicefonts.co.uk
rianhughes@aol.com
44 (0) 7979.602.272

ABCDEFGHIJKLMNOPQRSTU
VWXYZ0123456789
!?#$%&+()!?:""

THE QUICK BROWN FOX JUMPS OVER THE LAZY DOG.

D

Game Over Shaded
Graphic | Inline | Bold Weight |

Device
www.devicefonts.co.uk
rianhughes@aol.com
44 (0) 7979.602.272

AaBbCcDdEeFFGgHhIiJjKKLLMmN
nOoPpQqRrSsTtUuVvWwXxYyZz
0123456789!? ⊡#$%o8P()-[]:;'"

The quick brown Fox Jumps over the lazy dog.

D

Jakita Wide Bold
Stylized Sans Serif | Extended |
Abrupt Joints |

Device
www.devicefonts.co.uk
rianhughes@aol.com
44 (0) 7979.602.272

AaBbCcDdEeFFGgHhIiJjKKLLMmNnOoPpQqRrSsTt
UuVvWwXxYyZz0123456789!?@№$%&*()[]{}¡¿""

The quick brown fox jumps over the lazy dog.

D

Lusta Eighty Sans
Graphic | Inline |
Extra Condensed |

Device
www.devicefonts.co.uk
rianhughes@aol.com
44 (0) 7979.602.272

ABCDEFGHIJKLMNOPQRSTUVWXY
Z0123456789!? #$%&*()!?:;""

THE QUICK BROWN FOX JUMPS OVER THE LAZY DOG.

D

Mastertext Plain
Graphic Sans Serif | Slightly
Condensed | All Caps |

Device
www.devicefonts.co.uk
rianhughes@aol.com
44 (0) 7979.602.272

ABCDEFGHIJKLMNOPQRS
TUVWXYZ0123456789!?@#$
%&*[]{}:;""

THE QUICK BROWN FOX JUMPS OVER THE LAZY DOG.

D

Linotype Franosch™ Medium
Graphic Sans Serif | Medium
Weight | Angular Joints | Abstract
Details | Slightly Extended |

Linotype Library GmbH
www.linotype.com
info@linotype.com
+49 (0) 6172 484.418

aabbccddeeFFgghhiijj
kKLlmmNnOoppqqrrsstt
uuVvWwxxYYzz0123456z
89!!&.();;

the quick brown Fox jumps over the lazy dog.

D

Pargrid™ Std Regular
Graphic | Medium Weight |
Uniform Upper- and Lowercase
Height | Extended

Linotype Library GmbH
www.linotype.com
info@linotype.com
+49 (0) 6172 484.418

ABCDEFGHIJKLMNOPQRSTUVWXYZ0123
456789!?@#$%&*(){}:;""

THE QUICK BROWN FOX JUMPS OVER THE LAZY DOG.

D *t*

Quartz
Graphic | Medium Weight |
Condensed |
Segmented Strokes |

Linotype Library GmbH
www.linotype.com
info@linotype.com
+49 (0) 6172 484.418

*A a B b C c D d E e F f G g H h I i J j K k L l M m N n O o P p Q q R r S s T t U u V v W w X x Y y Z z 0 1 2 3 4 5 6 7 8 9 ! ? @ # $ % & * [ ] { } : ; " "*

The quick brown fox jumps over the lazy dog.

D *t*

Linotype Rezident™ Two
Sans Serif | Medium Weight |
Condensed | Stylized Joints |

Linotype Library GmbH
www.linotype.com
info@linotype.com
+49 (0) 6172 484.418

A a B b C c D d E e F f G g H h I i J j K k L l M m N n O o P p Q q R r S s T t U u V v W w X x Y y Z z 0 1 2 3 4 5 6 7 8 9 ! ? @ $ % & ( ) : ; " "

The quick brown fox jumps over the lazy dog.

D

Linotype Rory™ Oblique
Sans Serif | Pronounced
Contrast | Italic Posture |
Condensed | Angled Joints |

Linotype Library GmbH
www.linotype.com
info@linotype.com
+49 (0) 6172 484.418

A a B b C c D d E e F f G g H h I i J j K k L l M m N n O o P p Q q R r S s T t U u V v W w X x Y y Z z 0 1 2 3 4 5 6 7 8 9 ! ? @ # $ % & * ( ) { } : ; " "

The quick brown fox jumps over the lazy dog.

D *t*

Russell Square™ Roman
Sans Serif | Medium Weight |
Angled Joints | Canted
Terminals | Slightly Extended |

Linotype Library GmbH
www.linotype.com
info@linotype.com
+49 (0) 6172 484.418

A B C D E F G H I J K L M N O P Q R S T U V W X Y Z 0 1 2 3 4 5 6 7 8 9 ! ? $ % & ( ) * : ; "

THE QUICK BROWN FOX JUMPS OVER THE LAZY DOG.

D

Synchro™ Regular
Graphic | Medium Weight |
All Capitals |

Linotype Library GmbH
www.linotype.com
info@linotype.com
+49 (0) 6172 484.418

A a B b C c D d E e F f G g H h I i J j K k L l M m N n O o P p Q q R r S s T t U u V v W w X x Y y Z z 0 1 2 3 4 5 6 7 8 9 ! ? & © # dollar % ´ : ; ˝

the quick brown fox jumps over the lazy dog.

D

Interfacer Regular
Graphic Sans Serif | Bold Weight |

T.26 Digital Type Foundry
www.t26.com
info@t26.com
888.T26.FONT

A a B b C c D d E e F f G g H h I i J j K k L l M m N n O o P p Q q R r S s T t U u V v W w X x Y y Z z 0 1 2 3 4 5 6 7 8 9 ! ? & @ * $ % * : ; "

The quick brown fox jumps over the lazy dog.

D

Hyperion
Graphic | Erratic Weight |
Extreme Contrast |

T.26 Digital Type Foundry
www.t26.com
info@t26.com
888.T26.FONT

Techno Color

Color that expresses the energy of the electronic music scene is vivid and almost garish. Hues all around the color wheel are possible so long as they are highly saturated, to the point where they begin to buzz. Intense orange, pink, blue, green, and yellow are common. Colors that evoke the raw input of the computer monitor—red, blue, and green—are sometimes used in combination. Black is often a major component of techno color schemes, adding depth and contrast to these electric hues. Contrast, in general, is a major hallmark of techno color. Often, combinations of hues that are purposely unrelated—far apart on the color wheel, even complementary—and potentially jarring help reinforce the extreme nature and energy that are symbolic of the techno genre.

Sample Color Combinations

0 C	
29 M	
91 Y	
0 K	

0 C	
100 M	
0 Y	
0 K	

100 C	
60 M	
0 Y	
0 K	

57 C	
0 M	
100 Y	
0 K	

41 C	
0 M	
100 Y	
0 K	

0 C	
95 M	
100 Y	
0 K	

93 C	
0 M	
10 Y	
0 K	

0 C	
67 M	
100 Y	
0 K	

100 C	
85 M	
0 Y	
0 K	

20 C	
20 M	
20 Y	
100 K	

As a category, the idea of "urban" is open to wide interpretation, but it can safely be defined as busy, aggressive, overpopulated, and wild with variety. Every city is different in tone and feeling, but most often the idea of "urban-ness" is associated with large cultural and economic centers. Some are more homogeneous, with residents sharing a common ethnic background, but others are very diverse in their cultural mix. These qualities are reflected in an unusual mix of typefaces, from the strong and cosmopolitan to the funky and stylized.

Urban

Typefaces that read as urban may vary from classical, denoting a cultured, cosmopolitan background, to very stylized, evoking the varied subcultures to be found within the city. As a result, sharp, oldstyle, even archaic serifs; bold, condensed sans serifs; and hip-hop graffiti styles can all equally represent the urban fabric. In more neutral faces, the angularity of curved forms becomes important, creating a kind of formality and tension in normally organic strokes that may convey the density of urban population. The tighter the counterspaces, the more urban the face will feel, beginning to vibrate and create kinetic interplay between dark strokes and slivered counters—those within the letters and those between. Austere, geometric typefaces may also connote "urban;" again, compressed versions help skew the message away from being strictly artificial or industrial. Certain bitmap typefaces based on square grids may begin to resemble urban architecture or display boards, such as are found in stock exchanges or banks.

Event Invitation
top, and detail, bottom

STIM Visual Communication
Timothy Samara
New York City *USA*

ABCDEFGHIJKLMNOPQRST
UVWXYZ0123456789
!?№$%&*[]!?:;""
THE QUICK BROWN FOX JUMPS OVER THE LAZY DOG.

D

Untitled 1
Graphic Sans Serif | Bold Weight | Slightly Extended | Mixed Sharp and Rounded Terminals

Device
www.devicefonts.co.uk
rianhughes@aol.com
44 (0) 7979.602.272

AaBbCcDdEeFfGgHhIiJjKkLlMmNnOoPpQq
RrSsTtUuVvWwXxYyZz0123456789!?@#
$%&*(){}:;""
The quick brown fox jumps over the lazy dog.

D

Anzeigen Grotesk
Sans Serif | Bold Weight | Condensed |

Linotype Library GmbH
www.linotype.com
info@linotype.com
+49 (0) 6172 484.418

AABBCCDDEEFFGGHHIIJJ
KkLLMMNNOOPPQQRRSS
TTUUVVWWXxYYZz012345
6789!?@#$%&*(){}:;""
THE QUICK BROWN FOX JUMPS OVER THE LAZY DOG.

D

ITC Blair™ Medium
Sans Serif | Medium Weight | Slightly Extended | Caps and Small Caps |

Linotype Library GmbH
www.linotype.com
info@linotype.com
+49 (0) 6172 484.418

aaBBCCDDeeFFGGHHIiJjKKLL
MMNNOOPPQQRRSStUUVVWW
XXYYZZ0123456789!?@#$%&*
(){}:;""
THE QUICK BROWN FOX JUMPS OVER THE LAZY DOG.

D *t*

Quartan™ Std Bold
Sans Serif | Unicase | Squared Curves |

Linotype Library GmbH
www.linotype.com
info@linotype.com
+49 (0) 6172 484.418

ABCDEFGHIJKLMNOPQRSTUVW
XYZ0123456789!?$%&[]()*";:
THE QUICK BROWN FOX JUMPS OVER THE LAZY DOG.

D

Buzzer Three™
Sans Serif | Medium Weight | Stylized Joints |

Linotype Library GmbH
www.linotype.com
info@linotype.com
+49 (0) 6172 484.418

AaBbCcDdEeFfGgHhIiJjKkLlMmNn
OoPpQqRrSsTtUuVvWwXxYyZz0123
456789!?@#$%&*(){}:;""
The quick brown fox jumps over the lazy dog.

D **T**

DIN 1451 MittelSchrift
Sans Serif | Medium Weight | Slightly Condensed | Slightly Squared Shoulders |

Linotype Library GmbH
www.linotype.com
info@linotype.com
+49 (0) 6172 484.418

AaBbCcDdEeFfGgHhIiJjKkLl
MmNnOoPpQqRrSsTtUuVvWw
XxYyZz0123456789!?@#$%
&*(){}:;""

The quick brown fox jumps over the lazy dog.

D

F2F El Dee Cons™
Graphic | Erratic Weight and
Body Size | Stroke Distortion |

Linotype Library GmbH
www.linotype.com
info@linotype.com
+49 (0) 6172 484.418

AaBbCcDdEeFfGgHhIiJjKkLlMm
NnOoPpQqRrSsTtUuVvWwXxYy
Zz0123456789!?@#$%&*(){}:;

The quick brown fox jumps over the lazy dog.

D

F2F Lovegrid™
Graphic | Erratic Weight and
Body Size | Stroke Distortion |

Linotype Library GmbH
www.linotype.com
info@linotype.com
+49 (0) 6172 484.418

AaBbCcDdEeFfGgHhIiJjKkLlMM
NNOoPpQqRrSsTtUuVvWwXxYy
Zz0123456789!?@#$%&*(){}:;»«

THE QUICK BROWN FOX JUMPS OVER THE LAZY DOG.

D

F2F TechLand™
Graphic | Erratic Weight and
Body Size | Angled Curves
and Terminals | Positive and
Negative Alternates |

Linotype Library GmbH
www.linotype.com
info@linotype.com
+49 (0) 6172 484.418

AaBbCcDdEeFfGgHhIiJjKkLl
MmNnOoPpQqRrSsTtUuVvWw
XxYyZz0123456789!?&@f:;""

The quick brown fox jumps over the lazy dog.

D t

Urbanite Regular
Stylized Sans Serif | Bold Weight |
Structural Distortion |

T.26 Digital Type Foundry
www.t26.com
info@t26.com
888.T26.FONT

ABCDEFGHIJKLMNOPQRSTUVWXYZ
0123456789!?N$%&*():;""

THE QUICK BROWN FOX JUMPS OVER THE LAZY DOG.

D

Follies™
Sans Serif | Black Weight |
Inline Detail | All Uppercase|

Linotype Library GmbH
www.linotype.com
info@linotype.com
+49 (0) 6172 484.418

AaBbCcDdEeFfGgHhIiJjKkLl
MmNnOoPpQqRrSsTtUuVvWw
XxYyZz0123456789!?@#$%

The quick brown fox jumps over the lazy dog.

D t

Mirogramma Medium
Extended
Sans Serif | Lighter Medium
Weight | Noticeably Squared
Bowls and Shoulders |

Linotype Library GmbH
www.linotype.com
info@linotype.com
+49 (0) 6172 484.418

A a B b C c D d E e F f G g H h I i J j K k L l M m
N n O o P p Q q R r S s T t U u V v W w X x Y y
Z z 0 1 2 3 4 5 6 7 8 9 ! ? @ # $ % & * ( ) { } : ; " "
The quick brown fox jumps over the lazy dog.

D **T**

**Neue Helvetica™ 65
Medium**
*Sans Serif | Bolder Medium
Weight | Uniform Strokes |*

Linotype Library GmbH
www.linotype.com
info@linotype.com
+49 (0) 6172 484.418

A a B b C c D d E e F f G g H h I i J j K k L l M m N n
O o P p Q q R r S s T t U u V v W w X x Y y Z z 0 1 2 3
4 5 6 7 8 9 ! ? $ % & * ( ) : ; " "
The quick brown fox jumps over the lazy dog.

D *t*

Orange™
*Sans Serif | Medium Weight |
Erratic Contrast |*

Linotype Library GmbH
www.linotype.com
info@linotype.com
+49 (0) 6172 484.418

A a B b C c D d E c F f G g H h I i J j K k L l M m N n O o P p
Q q R r S s T t U u V v W w X x Y y Z z 0 1 2 3 4 5 6 7 8 9 ! ?
$ % & * ( ) { } : ; " "
The quick brown fox jumps over the lazy dog.

D

Poplar™
*Sans Serif | Black Weight |
Condensed |*

Linotype Library GmbH
www.linotype.com
info@linotype.com
+49 (0) 6172 484.418

a b c d e f g h i j k l m n o p q r s t u v
w x y z 0 1 2 3 4 5 6 7 8 9 ! ? @ # $ % & * ( ) { }
the quick brown fox jumps over the lazy dog.

D

Linotype Punkt™ Regular
*Graphic Sans Serif | Bold
Weight | Bitmap Texture |*

Linotype Library GmbH
www.linotype.com
info@linotype.com
+49 (0) 6172 484.418

a a B B C C D D e e F F G G H H I i J j K K L L
M M N N O O P P Q Q R r S S T t U U V V W W
X X Y Y Z Z 0 1 2 3 4 5 6 7 8 9 ! ? @ # $ % & * ( )
{ } : ; " "
THE QUICK BROWN FOX JUMPS OVER THE LAZY DOG.

D *t*

Quartan™ Std Book
*Sans Serif | Unicase |
Squared Curves |*

Linotype Library GmbH
www.linotype.com
info@linotype.com
+49 (0) 6172 484.418

A A̤ B B C C D D E̤ E F F G G H H I I̤ J J K K L L M M
N N O̤ O P P Q Q R R S S T T U Ṳ V V W W X X Y Y Z Z
0 1 2 3 4 5 6 7 8 9 ! ? & @ # $ % * : ; "
THE QUICK BROWN FOX JUMPS OVER THE LAZY DOG.

D

Dekapot Deluxxe
*Graphic Sans Serif | Caps and
Alternates | Erratic Baseline |*

The Chank Company
www.chank.com
friendlyfolks@chank.com
877.GO.CHANK

AaBbCcDdEeFfGgHhIiJjKkLlMm
NnOoPpQqRrSsTtUuVvWwXxYyZz
0123456789!?@:;" "
The quick brown fox jumps over the lazy dog.

D

Linotype Red Babe
*Graphic | Bold Weight |
Stroke Distortion |*

Linotype Library GmbH
www.linotype.com
info@linotype.com
+49 (0) 6172 484.418

AaBbCcDdEeFfGgHhIiJjKkLlMmNnOo
PpQqRrSsTtUuVvWwXxYyZz01234567
89!?@#$%&*()<>:;" "
The quick brown fox jumps over the lazy dog.

D *t*

**Linotype Russisch Brot™
Eat Text**
*Graphic Sans Serif | Medium
Weight | Textured Contour |
Slightly Condensed |*

Linotype Library GmbH
www.linotype.com
info@linotype.com
+49 (0) 6172 484.418

AaBbCcDdEeFfGgHhIiJjKkLlMmNnOoPp
QqRrSsTtUuVvWwXxYyZz0123456789
!?@#$%&*(){}:;" "
The quick brown fox jumps over the lazy dog.

D

Linotype Scrap™ Black
*Graphic | Erratic Weight and
Posture | Angular Curves |*

Linotype Library GmbH
www.linotype.com
info@linotype.com
+49 (0) 6172 484.418

AaBbCcDdEeFfGgHhIiJjKkLlMmNnOoPpQq
RrSsTtUuVvWwXxYyZz0123456789!?$%
&*[]:;" "
The quick brown fox jumps over the lazy dog.

D *t*

Scriptek™
*Slab Serif | Medium Weight |
Angled Bowls | Condensed |*

Linotype Library GmbH
www.linotype.com
info@linotype.com
+49 (0) 6172 484.418

AaBbCcDdEeFfGgHhIiJjKkLlMmNn
OoPpQqRrSsTtUuVvWwXxYyZz0123
456789!?@#$%&*(){}:;" "
The quick brown fox jumps over the lazy dog.

D *t*

Linotype Tapeside™ Regular
*Sans Serif | Light Weight | Erratic
Contrast | Structural Distortion |*

Linotype Library GmbH
www.linotype.com
info@linotype.com
+49 (0) 6172 484.418

AaBbCcDdEeFfGgHhIiJjKkLlMmNn
OoPpQqRrSsTtUuVvWwXxYyZz0123
456789!?@#$%&*(){}:;" "
The quick brown fox jumps over the lazy dog.

D **T**

Rotis® Semi Serif 55 Roman
*Serif-Sans Serif Hybrid |
Slight Contrast |
Medium Weight |*

Linotype Library GmbH
www.linotype.com
info@linotype.com
+49 (0) 6172 484.418

Urban Color

If there's any single color associated with the city, it's black. The density and aloof formality of black can connote snobbishness as well as power and superiority; it is the color of choice for musicians, artists, punks, rappers, and the fashionable elite of metropolitan society. Gray comes in a close second, especially darker, charcoal grays, warm or cool. At a value deeper than 50 percent black, gray begins to take on a sense of luxury, the feel of stone and concrete, and the depth of black, without the attitude. Gray is, however, detached—sophisticated yet disconnected despite its density. Other neutrals, especially deep olive, leather brown, and cocoa, enrich and warm the palette, adding a sense of value. The punch of hot, saturated red and orange, along with steely blue-green, reminiscent of glass, act as counterpoints; a pale, creamy yellow, almost white, rounds out the scheme.

Sample Color Combinations

5 C	
5 M	
5 Y	
60 K	

15 C
10 M
0 Y
60 K

20 C
20 M
20 Y
100 K

41 C
0 M
64 Y
75 K

11 C
42 M
62 Y
73 K

0 C
33 M
63 Y
60 K

3 C
3 M
20 Y
3 K

0 C
78 M
100 Y
0 K

35 C
0 M
12 Y
38 K

7 C
0 M
7 Y
28 K

Serenity and a hint of glamour, the contrast of sharp detail and subtle proportion, lightness and curves—a sense of elegance in type can be achieved any number of ways. Above all, it comes down to a sense of restraint enriched by style. Typefaces popular in fashion marketing— as well as sleek corporate styles and classical forms—can be equally effective, given the right space and sensitivity to scale.

Elegant

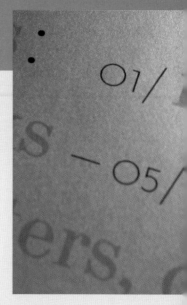

Type styles that are considered elegant fall under many different categories. The very lightweights of corporate sans serifs, for example, are considered elegant, as are script typefaces. Often, a sense of elegance derives from condensed faces with large lower counters or other exaggerated proportions. Contrast in the weight of strokes, in which thicks and thins either come together crisply or round off into each other organically, also creates a sense of elegance. Mixing type styles that are similar in construction but exhibit moderate contrast in their details, weight, or style, imparts a sense of subtle differences that may be perceived as sophisticated.

Call for Entries *details*

**Christine Fent, Manja Uellpap,
Gilmar Wendt**
London *United Kingdom*

Aaβʙ Cc Dᴅ Ee Ff Gɢ Hʜ Iɪ Jⱼ Kᴋ Lʟ
Mм Nɴ Oo Pᴘ Qǫ Rʀ Ss Tᴛ Uu Vv Ww
Xx Yy Zz 0 1 2 3 4 5 6 7 6 9 ! ? ₰ Ⓐ $ :: " "

THE QUICK BROWN FOX JUMPS OVER THE LAZY DOG.

D

Ambient
Stylized Sans Serif |
Light Weight |
Caps and Small Caps |

P22 Type Foundry
www.p22.com
p22@p22.com
800.P22.5080

A a B b C c D d E e F f G g H h I i J j K k L l M m
N n ☉ o P p Q q R s s T t U u V v W w X x Y y Z z
0 1 2 3 4 5 6 7 8 9 ! ? & @ # $ % * : ; "

The quick brown fox jumps over the lazy dog.

D

Zephyr Openface
Stylized Sans Serif |
Inline | Swash Elements |
Light Weight |

P22 Type Foundry
www.p22.com
p22@p22.com
800.P22.5080

AaBbCcDdEeFfGgHhIiJjKkLlMmNnOoPp
QqRrSsTtUuVvWwXxYyZz0123456789
!?@#$%&*(){}:;""
The quick brown fox jumps over the lazy dog.

D T

September Medium
Sans Serif | Slight Contrast |
Bolder Medium Weight |
Slightly Extended |

Device
www.devicefonts.co.uk
rianhughes@aol.com
44 (0) 7979.602.272

A a B b C c D d E e F f G g H h I i J j K k L l M m
N n O o P p Q q R r S s T t U u V v W w X x Y y Z z
0 1 2 3 4 5 6 7 8 9 ! ? & @ # $ % * : ; "

The quick brown fox jumps over the lazy dog.

D T

LTC Californian
Serif | Medium Weight |

P22 Type Foundry
www.p22.com
p22@p22.com
800.P22.5080

A a B b C c D d E e F f G g H h I i J j K k L l M m
N n O o P p Q q R r S s T t U u V v W w X x Y y
Z z 0 1 2 3 4 5 6 7 8 9 ! ? @ # $ % & * ( ) { } : ; " "
The quick brown fox jumps over the lazy dog.

D T

Hiroshige™ Book
Serif | Lighter Medium
Weight | Moderate contrast |
Slight Modulation |

Linotype Library GmbH
www.linotype.com
info@linotype.com
+49 (0) 6172 484.418

A a B b C c D d E e F f G g H h I i J j K k L l M m N n O o
P p Q q R r S s T t U u V v W w X x Y y Z z 0 1 2 3 4 5
6 7 8 9 ! ? @ # $ % & * ( ) { } : ; " "

The quick brown fox jumps over the lazy dog.

D T

Spectrum™ Roman
Serif | Medium Weight |
Pronounced Contrast |
Sharp Serifs |

Linotype Library GmbH
www.linotype.com
info@linotype.com
+49 (0) 6172 484.418

A a B b C c D d E e F f G g H h I i J j K k L l M m
N n O o P p Q q R r S s T t U u V v W w X x Y y Z z
0 1 2 3 4 5 6 7 8 9 ! ? & @ # $ % * : ; ”

The quick brown fox jumps over the lazy dog.

D T

JY Pinnacle Lining
Serif | Lighter Medium Weight |
Fluted Terminals |

JY&A Fonts
www.jyanet.com/fonts

A a B b C c D d E e F f G g H h I i J j K k l l M m N n
O o P p Q q R r S s T t U u V v W w X x Y y Z z 0 1 2
3 4 5 6 7 8 9 ! ? H @ # $ % * : ; ”

The quick brown fox jumps over the lazy dog.

D t

Oplontis Regular
Stylized Sans Serif |
Condensed |

Garage Fonts Type Foundry
www.garagefonts.com
info@garagefonts.com
800.681.9375

A a B b C c D d E e F f G g H h I i J j K k L l M m
N n O o P p Q q R r S s T t U u V v W w X x Y y
Z z 0 1 2 3 4 5 6 7 8 9 ! ? & @ # $ % * : ; ”

The quick brown fox jumps over the lazy dog.

D T

Alias Union Regular
Serif | Medium Weight |

T.26 Digital Type Foundry
www.t26.com
info@t26.com
888.T26.FONT

A a B b C c D d E e F f G g H h I i J j K k L l M m
N n O o P p Q q R r S s T t U u V v W w X x Y y
*Z z 0 1 2 3 4 5 6 7 8 9 ! ? & @ # $ % * : ; ”*

The quick brown fox jumps over the lazy dog.

D T

Alias Union Regular Italic
Serif | Medium Weight |

T.26 Digital Type Foundry
www.t26.com
info@t26.com
888.T26.FONT

A a B b C c D d E e F f G g H h I i J j K k L l M m
N n O o P p Q q R r S s T t U u V v W w X x Y y
Z z 0 1 2 3 4 5 6 7 8 9 ! ? & @ # $ % * : ; ”

The quick brown fox jumps over the lazy dog.

D T

Kurosawa Hand Normal
Serif | Medium Weight |

T.26 Digital Type Foundry
www.t26.com
info@t26.com
888.T26.FONT

A a B b C c D d E e F f G g H h I i J j K k L l M m
N n O o P p Q q R r S s T t U u V v W w X x Y y
Z z 0 1 2 3 4 5 6 7 8 9 ! ? & @ # $ % * : ; ”

The quick brown fox jumps over the lazy dog.

D T

Kurosawa Sans Medium
Sans Serif | Slight Contrast |
Slightly Extended |

T.26 Digital Type Foundry
www.t26.com
info@t26.com
888.T26.FONT

ABCDEFGHIJKLMNOPQR
STUVWXYZO123456789!?&
THE QUICK BROWN FOX JUMPS OVER

D

Oceanus Regular
Sans Serif |
Extra Light Weight |

T.26 Digital Type Foundry
www.t26.com
info@t26.com
888.T26.FONT

A a B b C c D d E e F f G g H h I i J j K k L l M m
N n O o P p Q q R r S s T t U u V v W w X x Y y
Z z 0 1 2 3 4 5 6 7 8 9 ! ? & @ # $ % * : ; "

The quick brown fox jumps over the lazy dog.

D *t*

Slippy Light
Sans Serif | Slight Contrast |

T.26 Digital Type Foundry
www.t26.com
info@t26.com
888.T26.FONT

ABCDEFGHIJKLMNOPORSTU
VWXYZ0123456789!?#$%&*

THE QUICK BROWN FOX JUMPS OVER THE LAZY DOG.

D

Sparrowhawk
Stylized Sans Serif | All Caps |
Slightly Extended |
Bolder Medium Weight |

Device
www.devicefonts.co.uk
rianhughes@aol.com
44 (0) 7979.602.272

A a B b C c D d E e F f G g H h I i J j K k L l
M m N n O o P p Q q R r S s T t U u V v W w
X x Y y Z z 0 1 2 3 4 5 6 7 8 9 ! ? & @ $: ; " "

The quick brown fox jumps over the lazy dog.

D **T**

Venis Italic
Stylized Sans Serif | Medium
Weight | Moderate Posture |

The Chank Company
www.chank.com
friendlyfolks@chank.com
877.GO.CHANK

A a B b C c D d E e F f G g H h I i J j K k L l M m N n O o
P p Q q R r S s T t U u V v W w X x Y y Z z 0 1 2 3 4 5 6 7
8 9 ! ? @ # $ % & * ( ) { } : ; " "

The quick brown fox jumps over the lazy dog.

D *t*

ITC Luna™
Sans Serif | Light Weight |
Slight Contrast |
Exaggerated Proportion |

Linotype Library GmbH
www.linotype.com
info@linotype.com
+49 (0) 6172 484.418

A a B b C c D d E e F f G g H h I i J j K k L l
M m N n O o P p Q q R r S s T t U u V v W w
X x Y y Z z 0 1 2 3 4 5 6 7 8 9 ! ? & @ $: ; " "

The quick brown fox jumps over the lazy dog.

D **T**

Venis
Stylized Sans Serif |
Medium Weight |

The Chank Company
www.chank.com
friendlyfolks@chank.com
877.GO.CHANK

A a B b C c D d E e F f G g H h I i J j K k L l M m
N n O o P p Q q R r S s T t U u V v W w X x Y y Z z
0 1 2 3 4 5 6 7 8 9 ! ? & @ # $ % * : ; "

The quick brown fox jumps over the lazy dog.

D T

RTF Amethyst OsF Light
*Serif | Slight Contrast |
Light Weight |*

P22 Type Foundry
www.p22.com
p22@p22.com
800.P22.5080

A a B b C c D d E e F f G g H h I i J j K k L l M m
N n O o P p Q q R r S s T t U u V v W w X x Y y
Z z 0 1 2 3 4 5 6 7 8 9 ! ? @ # $ % & * ( ) { } : ; " "
The quick brown fox jumps over the lazy dog.

D T

Bembo™ Semi Bold OsF
*Serif | Pronounced Contrast |
Abrupt Ductus |*

Linotype Library GmbH
www.linotype.com
info@linotype.com
+49 (0) 6172 484.418

AaBbCcDdEeFfGgHhIiJjKkLlMmNnOoPpQ
qRrSsTtUuVvWwXxYyZz0123456789
!?@#$%&*()[]:;" "
The quick brown fox jumps over the lazy dog.

D T

Paralucent Condensed
Sans Serif | Light Weight |

Device
www.devicefonts.co.uk
rianhughes@aol.com
44 (0) 7979.602.272

A a B b C c D d E e F f G g H h I i J j K k L l M m
N n O o P p Q q R r S s T t U u V v W w X x Y y Z z
0 1 2 3 4 5 6 7 8 9 ! ? & @ $: ; " "

The quick brown fox jumps over the lazy dog.

D T

P22 Albion Roman
*Serif | Light Weight |
Pronounced Serifs |*

P22 Type Foundry
www.p22.com
p22@p22.com
800.P22.5080

A a B b C c D d E e F f G g H h I i J j K k L l M m
N n O o P p Q q R r S s T t U u V v W w X x Y y Z z
0 1 2 3 4 5 6 7 8 9 ! ? & @ # $ % * : : "

The quick brown fox jumps over the lazy dog.

D

P22 Michelangelo Roman
*Script–Sans Serif Hybrid |
Light Weight | Slight Italic
Posture |*

P22 Type Foundry
www.p22.com
p22@p22.com
800.P22.5080

A B C D E F G H I J K L M N O P Q R S
T U V W X Y Z 0 1 2 3 4 5 6 7 8 9 ! ? & $

THE QUICK BROWN FOX JUMPS OVER THE LAZY DOG.

D

Trajan™ Regular
*Serif | Square Capitals |
Medium Weight |*

Linotype Library GmbH
www.linotype.com
info@linotype.com
+49 (0) 6172 484.418

Elegant Color

Like elegant typography, color becomes elegant when it shows restraint. Colors that are not highly saturated tend to be perceived as elegant; as they approach a more neutral, grayer state, they seem smokier, a little more mysterious and subdued. Pale colors are also considered elegant, but more toward the cooler end of the spectrum: icy blues, violets, and greens. Neutrals such as taupe, gray, and olive also fall into this category. Close-in analogous relationships among colors can provide a sense of elegance, showing restraint in their selection: a warm gray, a cool gray, and an olive green, for example, are close together on the color wheel. Reducing the number of variables that differentiate colors in combination adds sophistication—for example, if the colors being used are all the same value and saturation but change in temperature.

Sample Color Combinations

>	
25	C
25	M
40	Y
45	K

>	
15	C
0	M
10	Y
42	K

>	
0	C
5	M
10	Y
28	K

>	
25	C
3	M
3	Y
14	K

>	
35	C
22	M
8	Y
0	K

>	
22	C
0	M
20	Y
13	K

>	
63	C
37	M
20	Y
34	K

>	
62	C
55	M
28	Y
54	K

>	
25	C
19	M
42	Y
0	K

>	
0	C
33	M
11	Y
45	K

Machines, synthetic materials, gadgets, technology: these are some of the manifestations of "artificial," anything that doesn't occur in nature. Artificial things sometimes lack vitality, appearing dead or static; but overly contrived forms—ones that clearly show evidence of being man-made—also appear fake. Artificial can be fun, but it can run the risk of appearing un-genuine or false.

Artificial

A quality of artificiality can stem from anything at all that refutes a sense of the natural. In typefaces, this can mean proportions between the distribution of stroke weights being reversed; odd proportions between counters or exaggerated changes in body width among letters; dramatically geometric, angular, or abrupt junctures between strokes; or decorative inclusions that allude to mechanical or manmade parts. Because the historical derivation of such proportions creates an expectation of "naturalness," typefaces whose construction is purposely off will feel unnatural or contrived. Extremes of proportion, or stroke structure that pushes the limits of recognizability, may also seem artificial. Some typefaces that exhibit illustrative details, such as highlights or outlines, will seem unnatural or made from a synthetic material, such as plastic. Conversely, very neutral typefaces—lacking in modulation or detail—may seem lifeless and therefore artificial.

Event Collateral
top, and detail, bottom

Crush
Chris Pelling, design and
art direction
Brighton *England*

ABCDEFGHIJKLMNOPQ
RSTUVWXYZ0123456 7
89!?&%*{}{}::˝˝©$¥

THE QUICK BROWN FOX JUMPS OVER THE LAZY DOG.

D

Robot Monster
Graphic Slab Serif |
Extended | Bold Weight |

Nick's Fonts
www.nicksfonts.com

---

abcdefghijklmnopqrstuvwxyz
0123456789!?#$%&+()!?:;˝˝

the quick brown fox jumps over the lazy dog.

D *t*

Drexler Regular
Stylized Sans Serif |
All Lowercase |
Medium Weight |

Device
www.devicefonts.co.uk
rianhughes@aol.com
44 (0) 7979.602.272

AaBb CcDd Ee Ff Gg Hh Ii Jj Kk Ll Mm Nn Oo
Pp Qq Rr Ss Tt Uu Uv Ww Xx Yy Zz 0 1 2 3 4
5 6 7 8 9 !?@#&:;˝˝

The quick brown fox jumps over the lazy dog.

D *t*

P22 Hedonic Medium
Stylized Sans Serif |
Lighter Medium Weight |

P22 Type Foundry
www.p22.com
p22@p22.com
800.P22.5080

AABBCCDDEEFFGGHHIIJJKKLLMM
NNOOPPQQRRSSTTUUVVWWXXYY
ZZ0123456789!?@#$%&+()(}:;""

THE QUICK BROWN FOX JUMPS OVER THE LAZY DOG.

D

Substation
Graphic | Caps and Alternates |
Medium Weight |

Device
www.devicefonts.co.uk
rianhughes@aol.com
44 (0) 7979.602.272

AaBbCcDdEeFfGgHhIiJjKkLlMmNnOo
PpQqRrSsTtUuVvWwXxYyZz012345
6789!?@#$%&*(){}:;""
The quick brown fox jumps over the lazy dog.

D

Linotype Orbit™ Light
Sans Serif | Light Weight |
Dot Details |

Linotype Library GmbH
www.linotype.com
info@linotype.com
+49 (0) 6172 484.418

AaBbCcDdEeFfGgHhIiJjKkLlMm
NnOoPpQqRrSsTtUuVvWwXxYy
Zz0123456789!?&@#$%*:;"

The quick brown fox jumps over the lazy dog.

D

Gimp Round Black
Serif–Sans Serif Hybrid |
Erratic Weight |

Garage Fonts Type Foundry
www.garagefonts.com
info@garagefonts.com
800.681.9375

A a B b C c D d E e F f G g H h l i j j K k L l M m N n O o P p Q q R r S s T t U u V v W w X x Y y Z z 0 1 2 3 4 5 6 7 8 9 ! ? G @ # 2 % * : ; "

The quick brown fox jumps over the lazy dog.

Droplet Closed
Stylized Sans Serif |
Pronounced Contrast |
Bold Weight |

T.26 Digital Type Foundry
www.t26.com
info@t26.com
888.T26.FONT

ABCDEFGHIJKLMNOPQR
STUVWXYZ0123456789
!?✱$%&✱()!?;`"
THE QUICK BROWN FOX JUMPS OVER THE LAZY DOG.

Klaxon Two
Graphic Sans Serif |
Medium Weight | Modular
Stroke and Joint Structure |

Device
www.devicefonts.co.uk
rianhughes@aol.com
44 (0) 7979.602.272

A a B b C c D d E e F f G g H h l i j j K k L l M m N n O o P p Q q R r S s T t U u V v W w X x Y y Z z 0 1 2 3 4 5 6 7 8 9 ! ? & @ # $ % * : ; "

The quick brown fox jumps over the lazy dog.

Tonic Ingear
Graphic | Light Weight |

T.26 Digital Type Foundry
www.t26.com
info@t26.com
888.T26.FONT

A a B b C c D d E e F f G g H h I i J j K k L l M m N n O o P p Q q R r S S T t U u V v W w X x Y y Z z 0 1 2 3 4 5 6 7 8 9 ! ? & @ # $ % * : ; "

The quick brown fox jumps over the lazy dog.

Orbital
Graphic | Medium Weight |

The Chank Company
www.chank.com
friendlyfolks@chank.com
877.GO.CHANK

A a B b C c D d E e F f G g H h I i J j K k L l M m N n O o P p Q q R r S s T t U u V v W w X x Y y Z z 0 1 2 3 4 5 6 7 8 9 ! ? & @ # $ % * : ; "

The quick brown fox jumps over the lazy dog.

UNDA Triangle
Graphic | Uniform Cap and
Lowercase Heights |

T.26 Digital Type Foundry
www.t26.com
info@t26.com
888.T26.FONT

A a B b C c D d E e F f G g H h I i J j K k L l M m N n O o P p Q q R r S s T t U u V v W w X x Y y Z z 0 1 2 3 4 5 6 7 8 9 ! ? & @ # $ % * : ; "

The quick brown fox jumps over the lazy dog.

Ecliptica Round
Stylized Sans Serif | Extra
Condensed | Bold Weight |

Garage Fonts Type Foundry
www.garagefonts.com
info@garagefonts.com
800.681.9375

ABCDEFGHIJKLMNOPQRSTUVWX
YZ0123456789!?№$%&*()!?:;""

THE QUICK BROWN FOX JUMPS OVER THE LAZY DOG.

D

Amorphous
Stylized Sans Serif | All Caps |
Bold Weight |

Device
www.devicefonts.co.uk
rianhughes@aol.com
44 (0) 7979.602.272

ABCDEFGHIJKLMNOPQRSTUV
WXYZ0123456789!?&@#$%*:

The QUICK BROWN FOX JUMPS OVER THE LAZY DOG.

D

Entropy Regular
Graphic | Medium Weight |

T.26 Digital Type Foundry
www.t26.com
info@t26.com
888.T26.FONT

AaBbCcDdEeFFGgHhIiJjKkLl
MmNnOoPpQqRrSsTtUuVvWwXx
YyZz0123456789!?&@#$%*:;"

The quick brown fox jumps over the lazy dog.

D

Tiraso Allegre
Graphic | Medium Weight |

T.26 Digital Type Foundry
www.t26.com
info@t26.com
888.T26.FONT

ABCDEFGHIJKLMNOPQRS
TUVWXYZ0123456789!!
&*#$*:;"

THE QUICK BROWN FOX JUMPS OVER THE LAZY DOG.

D

Shipflat Regular
Graphic | Black Weight |
Inline Texture Detail |

T.26 Digital Type Foundry
www.t26.com
info@t26.com
888.T26.FONT

AaBbCcDdEeFfGgHhIiJjKkLlMmN
nOoPpQqRrSsTtUuVvWwXxYyZz
0123456789!?@#$%&*(){}:;""

The quick brown fox jumps over the lazy dog.

D t

Popgod Regular
Stylized Sans Serif | Bold
Weight | Slightly Extended |

Device
www.devicefonts.co.uk
rianhughes@aol.com
44 (0) 7979.602.272

AaBbCcDdEeFfGgHhIiJjKkLlMmNnOo
PpQqRrSsTtUuVvWwXxYyZz012345
6789!?@#$%&*(){}:;""

The quick brown fox jumps over the lazy dog.

D t

Linotype Cineplex™ Regular
Sans Serif | Uniform Light
Weight | Rounded Terminals |

Linotype Library GmbH
www.linotype.com
info@linotype.com
+49 (0) 6172 484.418

A a B b C c D d E e F f G g H h I i J j K k L l M m N n O o
P p Q q R r S s T t U u V v W w X x Y y Z z 0 1 2 3 4 5 6 7
8 9 ! ? @ # $ % & * ( ) { } : ; " "
The quick brown fox jumps over the lazy dog.

D *t*

Isonorm™ Regular
*Sans Serif | Uniform Medium
Weight | Rounded Terminals |
Slightly Condensed |*

Linotype Library GmbH
www.linotype.com
info@linotype.com
+49 (0) 6172 484.418

A a B b C c D d E e F f G g H h J i J j K k L l M m
N n O o P p Q q R r S s T t U u V v W w X x Y y
Z z 0 1 2 3 4 5 6 7 8 9 ! ? @ # $ % & * ( ) { } : ; " "
The quick brown fox jumps over the lazy dog.

D

Linotype Konflikt™
*Graphic | Structural
Combination | Bold Weight |
Erratic Posture |*

Linotype Library GmbH
www.linotype.com
info@linotype.com
+49 (0) 6172 484.418

A a B b C c D d E e F f G g H h I i J J K K
L l M m N n O o P p Q q R S s T t U U V V
W W X x Y y z 0 1 2 3 4 5 6 7 8 9 ! ? @ #
$ % & * ( ) : ;
The quick brown fox jumps over the lazy dog.

D

Ned™ Std
*Sans Serif | Light Weight |
Hexagonal Curves |*

Linotype Library GmbH
www.linotype.com
info@linotype.com
+49 (0) 6172 484.418

A a B b C c D d E e F f G g H h I i J j K k L l M m
N n O o P p Q q R r S s T t U u V v W w X x Y y Z z
0 1 2 3 4 5 6 7 8 9 ! ? @ # $ % * : ; "
The quick brown fox jumps over the lazy dog.

D *t*

Ultranova Regular
*Stylized Sans Serif |
Condensed | Medium Weight |*

T.26 Digital Type Foundry
www.t26.com
info@t26.com
888.T26.FONT

A a B b C c D d E e F f G g H h I i J j K k L l M m
N n O o P p Q q R r S s T t U u V v W w X x Y y
Z z 0 1 2 3 4 5 6 7 8 9 ! ? & @ # $ % * : ; "
The quick brown fox jumps over the lazy dog.

D

JY Circles
Graphic | Condensed |

JY&A Fonts
www.jyanet.com/fonts

A a B b C c D d E e F f G g H h I i J j K k L l M m N n
O o P p Q q R r S s T t U u V v W w X x Y y Z z 0 1 2
3 4 5 6 7 8 9 ! ? & @ # $ % ° : ; "
The quick brown fox jumps over the lazy dog.

D **T**

Qwerty One
*Graphic | Bitmap Structure |
Shaded Inline |*

T.26 Digital Type Foundry
www.t26.com
info@t26.com
888.T26.FONT

Artificial Color

Colors that occur rarely in nature are often perceived as artificial: extremely bright blues, fluorescent oranges and yellows, and acidic greens. Purposeful combination of colors such as these, in which their presence next to one another creates jarring or unexpected relationships, contributes to a sense of them occurring by artifice and design rather than through natural processes. Mixing colors with extreme variation in temperature but similar value—especially complements—causes severe optical buzzing that may appear electric and unnatural. Colors that exhibit very little chroma, especially gray and black and other hues with very low saturation, may feel lifeless and therefore artificial as well.

Sample Color Combinations

100 C	
0 M	
0 Y	
0 K	

0 C	
73 M	
100 Y	
0 K	

0 C	
15 M	
100 Y	
0 K	

17 C	
0 M	
100 Y	
0 K	

20 C	
20 M	
20 Y	
100 K	

5 C	
0 M	
0 Y	
30 K	

11 C	
100 M	
0 Y	
0 K	

100 C	
0 M	
30 Y	
0 K	

0 C	
100 M	
60 Y	
0 K	

0 C	
0 M	
0 Y	
25 K	

As the diametric opposite of "artificial," design, type, and color that are organic capture everything that is natural and alive. This sense of the natural encompasses everything from forms that are outright biological or vegetal in reference to more subtle formal relationships that evoke movement, rhythm, and growth.

Organic

Typefaces that can be considered organic span a number of classifications, although oldstyle serifs are often seen as the most organic overall. Their rhythmic alternation between thin and thick, the curving flow of their junctures, their oblique axes, and the plantlike extensions of their lowercase branches, ascenders, and descenders make them feel inherently natural. Some sans serifs, especially more recently developed, humanistic faces, show modulation in their stroke weights and references to such oldstyle forms, imparting a healthy vigor to a class that is often thought of as mechanical. Toward the more decorative extreme, typefaces with illustrative references to plants, cellular forms, amoebas, or exaggerated, sloping curves on wide bodies, offer a more pictorial representation of organic form. Script forms, though often delicate and somewhat romantic, may sometimes convey a sense of the natural, evoking plant tendrils or curling vines.

Spa Collateral
top, and detail, bottom

STIM Visual Communication
Timothy Samara
New York City *USA*

AaBbCcDdEeFfGgHhIiJjKƙLIMm
NnOoPpQqRrSsTtUuVvWwXxYy
ZzO123456789!?@#$%&*(){}:;
" "

The quick brown fox jumps over the lazy dog.

Linotype BioPlasm™
*Sans serif | Pronounced
Contrast | Stroke Distortion |
Rounded Terminals |*

Linotype Library GmbH
www.linotype.com
info@linotype.com
+49 (0) 6172 484.418

AaBbCcDdEeFfGgHhIiJjKkLLMm
NnOoPpQqRrSsTtUuVvWwXxYy
Zz0123456789!?:;

The quick brown fox jumps over the lazy dog.

P22 Infestia Regular
*Graphic | Erratic Width |
Erratic Cap- and Baselines |
Medium Weight |*

P22 Type Foundry
www.p22.com
p22@p22.com
800.P22.5080

AaBbCcDdEeFfGgHhIiJjKkLlMmNn
OoPpQqRrSsTtUuVvWwXxYyZzO123
456789!?@#$%&*(){}:;" "

The quick brown fox jumps over the lazy dog.

Caterina Std Regular
*Serif | Medium Weight |
Moderate Contrast |
Modulation | Brush Detail |*

Linotype Library GmbH
www.linotype.com
info@linotype.com
+49 (0) 6172 484.418

Linotype Grassy™
*Graphic | Light Weight |
Linear Inclusions |*

Linotype Library GmbH
www.linotype.com
info@linotype.com
+49 (0) 6172 484.418

AaBbCcDdEeFfGgHhIiJjKkLlMm
NnOoPpQqRrSsTtUuVvWwXxYyZz
0123456789!?&@#$%*:;"

The quick brown fox jumps over the lazy dog.

MVB Café Mimi Regular
*Modified Script |
Medium Weight |*

MVB Fonts
www.mvbfonts.com
info@mvbfonts.com
510.525.4288

AaBbCcDdEeFfGgHhIiJjKkLlMm
NnOoPpQqRrSsTtUuVvWwXxYyZz
0123456789!?&@#$%*:;"

The quick brown fox jumps over the lazy dog.

MVB Café Mimi Bold
*Modified Script | Noticeable
Contrast | Erratic Posture |*

MVB Fonts
www.mvbfonts.com
info@mvbfonts.com
510.525.4288

A a B b C c D d E e F f G g H h I i J j K k L l M m N n O o P p Q q R r S s T t U u V v W w X x Y y Z z 0 1 2 3 4 5 6 7 8 9 ! ? & @ # $ % * : :

The quick brown fox jumps over the lazy dog

Garden Weasel
Script | Light Weight |

Garage Fonts Type Foundry
www.garagefonts.com
info@garagefonts.com
800.681.9375

A a B b C c D d E e F f G g H h I i J j K k L l M m N n O o P p Q q R r S s T t U u V v W w X x Y y Z z 0 1 2 3 4 5 6 7 8 9 ! ? & @ $ % * : ; "

The quick brown fox jumps over the lazy dog.

Karazan
Graphic | Medium Weight |
Textured Contour |

Garage Fonts Type Foundry
www.garagefonts.com
info@garagefonts.com
800.681.9375

A a B b C c D d E e F f G g H h I i J j K k L l M m N n O o P p Q q R r S s T t U u V v W w X x Y y Z z 0 1 2 3 4 5 6 7 8 9 ! ? & ☺ №° $ % * : ; "

The quick brown fox jumps over the lazy dog.

Mistic Art
Stylized Sans Serif |
Condensed | Light Weight |

Garage Fonts Type Foundry
www.garagefonts.com
info@garagefonts.com
800.681.9375

a b c d e f g h i j k l m n o p q r s t u v w x y z 0 1 2 3 4 5 6 7 8 9 ! ? ( ) [ ] . . "

t he quick br⌐wn f⌐x jumps ⌐ver the lazy d⌐g.

Aurelius Regular
Stylized Serif |
Extra Condensed |
Light Weight |

T.26 Digital Type Foundry
www.t26.com
info@t26.com
888.T26.FONT

A a B b C c D d E e F f G g H h I i J j K k L l M m N n O o P p Q q R r S s T t U u V v W w X x Y y Z z 0 1 2 3 4 5 6 7 8 9 ! ? & @ # $ % * . ; "

The quick brown fox jumps over the lazy dog.

Wet
Stylized Sans Serif |
Erratic Weight |

Garage Fonts Type Foundry
www.garagefonts.com
info@garagefonts.com
800.681.9375

A a B b C c D d E e F f G g H h I i J j K k L l M m N n O o P p Q q R r S s T t U u V v W w X x Y y Z z 0 1 2 3 4 5 6 7 8 9 ! ? & @ # $ % * : ; "

The quick brown fox jumps over the lazy dog.

Waterproof
Graphic | Erratic Weight |
Erratic Baseline |

Garage Fonts Type Foundry
www.garagefonts.com
info@garagefonts.com
800.681.9375

A a B b C c D d E e F f G g H h I i J j K k L l M m
N n O o P p Q q R r S s T t U u V v W w X x Y y Z z
0 1 2 3 4 5 6 7 8 9 ! ? & @ # $ % * : ; "

The quick brown fox jumps over the lazy dog.

D *t*

Two Four Two
Stylized Sans Serif |
Light Weight |

Garage Fonts Type Foundry
www.garagefonts.com
info@garagefonts.com
800.681.9375

A a B b C c D d E e F f G g H h I i J j K k L l M m
N n O O P p Q q R r S s T t U u V v W w X x Y y
Z z 0 1 2 3 4 5 6 7 8 9 ! ? & # $ % : ; "

The quick brown fox jumps over the lazy dog.

D

Fur Regular
Stylized Sans Serif |
Erratic Weight |
Rounded Contours |

T.26 Digital Type Foundry
www.t26.com
info@t26.com
888.T26.FONT

A a B b C c D d E e F f G g H h I i J j K k L l
M m N n O o P p Q q R r S s T t U u V v W w
X x Y y Z z 0 1 2 3 4 5 6 7 8 9 ! ? & @ # $ %

The quick brown fox jumps over the lazy dog.

D

Frazzle Regular
Graphic | Erratic Weight |
Outline Detail |

T.26 Digital Type Foundry
www.t26.com
info@t26.com
888.T26.FONT

A a B b C c D d E e F f G g H h I i J j K k L l M m
N n O o P p Q q R r S s T t U u V v W w X x Y y
Z z 0 1 2 3 4 5 6 7 8 9 ! ? @ # $ % & * ( ) { } : ;
" "

The quick brown fox jumps over the lazy dog.

D *t*

Byngve™ Std Bold
Serif | Bold Weight |
Modulation | Brush Detail |

Linotype Library GmbH
www.linotype.com
info@linotype.com
+49 (0) 6172 484.418

A a B b C c D d E e F f G g H h I i J j K k L l M m
N n O o P p Q q R r S s T t U u V v W w X x Y y
Z z 0 1 2 3 4 5 6 7 8 9 ! ? & @ # $ % * : ; "

The quick brown fox jumps over the lazy dog.

D

Septa Regular
Stylized Sans Serif |
Erratic Weight |
Stroke Distortion |

T.26 Digital Type Foundry
www.t26.com
info@t26.com
888.T26.FONT

A a B b C c D d E e F f G g H h I i J j K k L l
M m N n O o P p Q q R r S s T t U u V v W w X x
Y y Z z 0 1 2 3 4 5 6 7 8 9 ! ? & @ # $ % * : ; "

The quick brown fox jumps over the lazy dog.

D

Feltrinelli
Script | Medium Weight |

T.26 Digital Type Foundry
www.t26.com
info@t26.com
888.T26.FONT

A a B b C c D d E e F f G g H h I i J j K k L l M m
N n O o P p Q q R r S s T t U u V v W w X x Y y
Z z 0 1 2 3 4 5 6 7 8 9 ! ! ? & @ № S % * : ; ”

The quick brown fox jumps over the lazy dog.

D

Task Hairy
Graphic Sans Serif |
Erratic Weight |

T.26 Digital Type Foundry
www.t26.com
info@t26.com
888.T26.FONT

A a B b C c D ə E e F f G g H h I i J j K k L l M m N n
O o P p Q q R r S s T t U u V v W w X x Y y Z z 0 1 2 3 4
5 6 7 8 9 ! ? & @ # $ % * : ; ”

The quick brown fox jumps over the lazy dog.

D *t*

Fatso Regular
Stylized Sans Serif |
Condensed | Bold Weight |

T.26 Digital Type Foundry
www.t26.com
info@t26.com
888.T26.FONT

A A B B C C D D E E F F G G H H I I J J K K L L
M M N N O O P P Q Q R R S S T T U U V V W W
X X Y Y Z Z 0 1 2 3 4 5 6 7 8 9 ! ? ET @ $: ; “ ”

THE QUICK BROWN FOX JUMPS OVER THE LAZY DOG.

D

P22 Woodcut Sans
Graphic | Bold Weight |
Caps and Alternates |

P22 Type Foundry
www.p22.com
p22@p22.com
800.P22.5080

A a B b C c D d E e F f G g H h I i J j K k L l M m N n O o P p
Q q R r S s T t U u V v W w X x Y y Z z 0 1 2 3 4 5 6 7 8 9 ! ? &
@ $: ; ” ”

The quick brown fox jumps over the lazy dog.

D **T**

P22 Plymouth
Serif | Condensed |
Pronounced Contrast |
Slight Italic Posture |

P22 Type Foundry
www.p22.com
p22@p22.com
800.P22.5080

A a B b C c D d E e F f G g H h I i J j K k L l M m
N n O o P p Q q R r S s T t U u V v W w X x Y y
Z z 0 1 2 3 4 5 6 7 8 9 ! ? @ # $ % & * ( ) { } : ; “ ”
The quick brown fox jumps over the lazy dog.

D

F2F Whale Tree™
Graphic | Erratic Weight |
Pronounced Contrast |

Linotype Library GmbH
www.linotype.com
info@linotype.com
+49 (0) 6172 484.418

A a B b C c D d E e F f G g H h I i J j K k L l M m N n
O o P p Q q R r S s T t U u V v W w X x Y y Z z 0 1 2 3 4 5
6 7 8 9 ! ? & @ $: ; “ ”

The quick brown fox jumps over the lazy dog.

D

P22 Aglio
Graphic | Light Weight |
Erratic Posture |

P22 Type Foundry
www.p22.com
p22@p22.com
800.P22.5080

Organic Color

Wood, vegetation, earth—deep, saturated neutrals and a variety of green hues, from bright and leafy to dark, grassy, and olive—all convey a sense of natural, growing things. Browns, whether muted and cooler or rich and warm, connote natural materials and ground viewers emotionally. They also provide a backdrop for more vibrant colors, especially green. In combination with jewel tones (saturated violets and fuchsia, deep reds, and amber), brown and green evoke the garden, the landscape, and vegetables. Intense colors hint at vitality, health, and energy. Combining rich colors, including saturated neutrals, creates a sense of sensuous growth and abundance. Mixing analogous colors in ranges of neutral greens, golds, and browns adds subtlety, sophistication, and a sense of ecological thoughtfulness.

Sample Color Combinations

> 5 C
> 63 M
> 74 Y
> 50 K

> 15 C
> 75 M
> 100 Y
> 71 K

> 83 C
> 0 M
> 100 Y
> 0 K

> 100 C
> 0 M
> 100 Y
> 25 K

> 48 C
> 0 M
> 100 Y
> 60 K

> 50 C
> 28 M
> 100 Y
> 58 K

> 15 C
> 45 M
> 100 Y
> 24 K

> 0 C
> 100 M
> 64 Y
> 36 K

> 72 C
> 100 M
> 0 Y
> 20 K

> 0 C
> 100 M
> 14 Y
> 25 K

The grinding gears of machinery, clouds of smoke and steam, concrete, steel, iron, and oil—the colors of industry, as well as appropriate type-faces that feel industrial, bring to mind the grand strength and grime of the factory.

Industrial

It will come as no surprise that type and color associated with industrial processes or environments will seem mechanical—either in the geometric quality of the typefaces' structure or decorative details or in the colors' associations with raw materials. Similar to some "artificial" typefaces, overtly industrial typefaces exhibit extremely geometric construction and near–mathematically uniform proportions. Typefaces whose structure is based on a square, in which curves are replaced by horizontal and vertical strokes, are an exceptionally austere example of this kind of structure. Some bitmap typefaces, whose compositional elements fall on a grid and are more square themselves, feel industrial. Although bold and heavy sans serifs most often communicate the heavy, machine-weight quality of industry, some serifs—especially slab serifs and hybrid serif gothics such as Copperplate or Bank Gothic—have industrial qualities because their serifs are small and their curved forms are squared out. Condensed, heavyweight faces in which the shoulders and branches are forced to turn abruptly are also strongly indus-trial in quality. Typefaces that include the evidence of industrial processes, such as etching, bleaching, scoring, routing, or patterning, or abstract graphic references to gears, nuts and bolts, and so on, impart a decidedly industrial message.

Catalog Cover
top, and detail, bottom

Untitled
Zoe Scutts
Kent *United Kingdom*

ÅAＣ₹(CＤＤＥＥＰＦＦＧＧＨＨ|]]ＪＸＬＬ
ＭＭＮＮＯＯＰＰＰＱＱＲＲＳＳＴＴＵＵＶＶＷＷ
ＸＸＹЧＺＺＯＩ２３４{５６７８9Ｉ？₹ᶜ#₹½%

The quick brown fox jumps over the lazy dog.

D

Five Link Chain
Graphic | Medium Weight |
Mixed Case with Alternates |

Garage Fonts Type Foundry
www.garagefonts.com
info@garagefonts.com
800.681.9375

aBCDEFGHIJKLMNOPQRSTUVWX
YZ0123456789!?⁰₤%6&*()!?:;""

THE QUICK BROWN FOX JUMPS OVER THE LAZY DOG.

D

Scrotnig Heavy
Stylized Sans Serif | Unicase |
Bold Weight

Device
www.devicefonts.co.uk
rianhughes@aol.com
44 (0) 7979.602.272

A a B b C c D d E e F f G g H h I i J j K k L l M m
N n O o P p Q q R r S s T t U u V v W w X x Y y Z z 01
2 3 4 5 6 7 8 9 ! ? & @ $: ; ""

The quick brown fox jumps over the lazy dog.

D T

P22 Typewriter
Graphic Serif | Lighter
Medium Weight |

P22 Type Foundry
www.p22.com
p22@p22.com
800.P22.5080

A B C D E F G H I J K L M N O P Q R S T U V W
X Y Z 0 1 2 3 4 5 6 7 8 9 ! ? & ( ) { } :; " "

THE QUICK BROWN FOX JUMPS OVER THE LAZY DOG.

D

Linotype Alphabat™
Graphic | Medium Weight |
Reversed Thicks and Thins |

Linotype Library GmbH
www.linotype.com
info@linotype.com
+49 (0) 6172 484.418

A a B b C c D d E e F f G g H h I i J j K k L l M m
N n O o P p Q q R r S s T t U u V v W w X x Y y Z z
0 1 2 3 4 5 6 7 8 9 ! ? & @ + $ % * : ; "

The quick brown fox jumps over the lazy dog.

D

Player Piano
Graphic | Medium Weight |

The Chank Company
www.chank.com
friendlyfolks@chank.com
877.GO.CHANK

A a B b C c D d E e F f G g H h I i J j K k L l
M m N n O o P p Q q R r S s T t U u V v W w
X x Y y Z z 0 1 2 3 4 5 6 7 8 9 ! ? & @ # $ % * : ; "

The quick brown fox jumps over the lazy dog.

D t

Klif Slim
Stylized Sans Serif |
Light Weight |

Garage Fonts Type Foundry
www.garagefonts.com
info@garagefonts.com
800.681.9375

ABCDEFGHIJKLMNOPQRSTUVW
XYZ0123456789!?&@#$%":;"

THE QUICK BROWN FOX JUMPS OVER THE LAZY DOG.

D

LTC Octic Gothic
Sans Serif | Bold Weight |
All Caps |

P22 Type Foundry
www.p22.com
p22@p22.com
800.P22.5080

AaBbCcDdEeFfGgHhIiJjKkLl
MmNnOoPpQqRrSsTtUuVvWwXx
YyZz0123456789!?&@#$%*

The quick brown fox jumps over the lazy dog.

D

Charter D Normal
Graphic | Erratic Weight |
Moderate Italic Posture |

Garage Fonts Type Foundry
www.garagefonts.com
info@garagefonts.com
800.681.9375

ABCDEFGHIJKLMNOPQRSTUVWXYZ
0123456789!?#$%&*[]!?;""

THE QUICK BROWN FOX JUMPS OVER THE LAZY DOG.

D

Hounslow Solid
Graphic | Condensed | Inline
Detail | Black Weight |

Device
www.devicefonts.co.uk
rianhughes@aol.com
44 (0) 7979.602.272

AaBbCcDdEeFfGgHhIiJjKkLlMmN
nOoPpQqRrSsTtUuVvWwXxYyZz
0123456789!?@#$%&*(){}:;""

The quick brown fox jumps over the lazy dog.

D *t*

Paralucent Stencil Heavy
Sans Serif | Bold Weight |

Device
www.devicefonts.co.uk
rianhughes@aol.com
44 (0) 7979.602.272

AaBbCcDdEeFfGgHhIiJjKkLlMm
NnOoPpQqRrSsTtUuVvWwXxYy
Zz0123456789!?@#$%&*(){}:;""

The quick brown fox jumps over the lazy dog.

D **T**

Glypha™ 65 Bold
Slab Serif | Bold Weight |
Slight Contrast |

Linotype Library GmbH
www.linotype.com
info@linotype.com
+49 (0) 6172 484.418

aabbccddeeffgghhiijjkkllmm
nnooppqqrrssttuuvvwwxxyyzz
0123456789!?&@#$%*:;"

the quick brown fox jumps over the lazy dog.

D

Gideon
Stylized Sans Serif |
All Lowercase with Alternate
Widths | Bold Weight |

The Chank Company
www.chank.com
friendlyfolks@chank.com
877.GO.CHANK

A a B b C c D d E e F f G g H h I i J j K k L l M m n N n O o P p Q q
R r S s T t U u U u W w X x Y y Z z 0 1 2 3 4 5 6 7 8 9 ! ? & @ # $
? * [ ] [ ] : ; "

The quick brown fox jumps over the lazy dog.

D *t*

Tube
*Stylized Sans Serif |
Extra Condensed |
Medium Weight |*

T.26 Digital Type Foundry
www.t26.com
info@t26.com
888.T26.FONT

A a B b C c D d E e F f G g H h I i J j K K
L l M m N n O o P p Q q R r S s T t U u V v
W w X x Y y Z z 0 1 2 3 4 5 6 7 8 9 ! ? $ %
& ( ) { } : ; " "

The quick brown fox jumps over the lazy dog.

D

Linotype Element™
*Graphic | Bold Weight | Inline |
Rounded Terminals |*

Linotype Library GmbH
www.linotype.com
info@linotype.com
+49 (0) 6172 484.418

A a B b C c D d E e F f G g H h I i J j K k L l M m N n
O o P p Q q R r S s T t U u V v W w X x Y y Z z 0 1 2 3 4
5 6 7 8 9 ! ? & @ * $ 2 * :; "

The quick brown fox jumps over the lazy dog.

D *t*

Board Original
*Stylized Sans Serif |
Condensed |
Medium Weight |*

T.26 Digital Type Foundry
www.t26.com
info@t26.com
888.T26.FONT

A a B b C c D d E e F f G g H h I i J j K k L l M m
N n O o P p Q q R r S s T t U u V v W w X x Y y Z z
0 1 2 3 4 5 6 7 8 9 ! ? & @ # $ % * : ; "

The quick brown fox jumps over the lazy dog.

D

Sabeh Light
Graphic | Light Weight |

Garage Fonts Type Foundry
www.garagefonts.com
info@garagefonts.com
800.681.9375

A a B b C c D d E e F f G g H h I i J j K k L l M m
N n O o P p Q q R r S s T t U u V v W w X x Y y Z z
0 1 2 3 4 5 6 7 8 9 ! ? & @ # $ % * : ; "

The quick brown fox jumps over the lazy dog.

D *t*

Sauerkrauto
*Stylized Sans Serif | Medium
Weight | Condensed |*

The Chank Company
www.chank.com
friendlyfolks@chank.com
877.GO.CHANK

A A B B C C D D E E F F G G H H I I J J K K L L M M N
N O O P P Q Q R R S S T T U U V V W W X X Y Y Z Z
0 1 2 3 4 5 6 7 8 9 ! ? @ № $ % & + ( ) ; " "

THE QUICK BROWN FOX JUMPS OVER THE LAZY DOG.

D

Payload Spraycan
Graphic | Bold Weight |

Device
www.devicefonts.co.uk
rianhughes@aol.com
44 (0) 7979.602.272

AaBbCcDdEeFfGgHhIiJjKkLlMmNnOoPpQqRrSsTt
UuVvWwXxYyZz0123456789!?@#$%&*()[]{}:;""

The quick brown fox jumps over the lazy dog.

D

Flak Nailed
*Stylized Sans Serif |
Condensed | Bold Weight |*

Device
www.devicefonts.co.uk
rianhughes@aol.com
44 (0) 7979.602.272

A a B b C c D d E e F f G g H h I i J j K k L l M m
N n O o P p Q q R r S s T t U u V v W w X x Y y Z z
0 1 2 3 4 5 6 7 8 9 ! ? & @ # $ % * : ; "

The quick brown fox jumps over the lazy dog.

D *t*

CA Aires Pro
*Sans Serif | Condensed |
Bold Weight |*

The Chank Company
www.chank.com
friendlyfolks@chank.com
877.GO.CHANK

A a B b C c D d E e F f G g H h I i J j K k L l M m N n O o P p Q q
R r S s T t U u V v W w X x Y y Z z 0 1 2 3 4 5 6 7 8 9 ! ? @ # $ %
& * [ ] { } : ; " "

The quick brown fox jumps over the lazy dog.

D *t*

**Linotype Case Study No.1™
Regular**
*Sans Serif | Light Weight |
Condensed |
Squared Shoulders |*

Linotype Library GmbH
www.linotype.com
info@linotype.com
+49 (0) 6172 484.418

ABCDEFGHIJKLMNOPQRSTUVWXYZ
0123456789!?@#$%&*()[]?;;""

THE QUICK BROWN FOX JUMPS OVER THE LAZY DOG.

D

Telecast Regular
*Graphic | Bold Weight |
Textural Detail |*

Device
www.devicefonts.co.uk
rianhughes@aol.com
44 (0) 7979.602.272

A a B b C c D d E e F f G g H h I i J j K k L l M m
N n O o P p Q q R r S s T t U u V v W w X x Y y Z z
0 1 2 3 4 5 6 7 8 9 ! ? & @ # $ % * : ; "

The quick brown fox jumps over the lazy dog.

D *t*

Hamilton Offset
Graphic | Erratic Weight |

The Chank Company
www.chank.com
friendlyfolks@chank.com
877.GO.CHANK

A a B b C c D d E e F f G g H h I i J j K k L l M m N n O o
P p Q q R r S s T t U u V v W w X x Y y Z z 0 1 2 3 4 5 6 7
8 9 ! ? @ # $ % & * ( ) { } : ; " "

The quick brown fox jumps over the lazy dog.

D

Linotype Zensur™
*Graphic | Medium Weight |
Broken Strokes |*

Linotype Library GmbH
www.linotype.com
info@linotype.com
+49 (0) 6172 484.418

Industrial Color

The factory and chemical processes are the inspiration for the industrial color palette. Black, deep grays, and warm neutrals with almost no color form a background for steel blue, copper, and aluminum gray. Bright yellow (think caution markers on machinery) adds contrast, as do bright orange (think hard-hats) and very saturated red. Acid green, sometimes with a slightly blue cast, brings to mind chemical cleaners, mixing agents, and solvents. In combination, small doses of saturated hues enliven the mass and darkness of the industrial color base of neutrals.

Sample Color Combinations

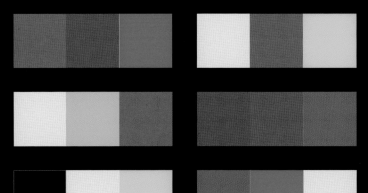

›	5 C
	0 M
	0 Y
	65 K

›	20 C
	0 M
	0 Y
	70 K

›	0 C
	0 M
	10 Y
	70 K

›	51 C
	12 M
	0 Y
	53 K

›	20 C
	20 M
	20 Y
	100 K

›	0 C
	64 M
	64 Y
	46 K

›	5 C
	0 M
	5 Y
	10 K

›	0 C
	0 M
	100 Y
	0 K

›	0 C
	100 M
	100 Y
	0 K

›	25 C
	0 M
	100 Y
	0 K

All things magical, mystical, occult, and fictional combine in the fantastic—elves and monsters, magicians and seers, pixies, aliens, and robots. Typefaces and color that embody fantasy borrow from all these genres in literature, film, and art.

Fantasy

Type of a fantastic nature brings a number of characteristics, taken from history and culture, together in exaggerated forms. First, type styles that derive from archaic and medieval forms convey the historical sense of ritual that is often a context for fantasy-based imagery or stories—for example, styles associated with stone-cut capitals, or blackletter or textura forms used in manuscript illumination and scrolls. Added to these forms, exaggerated details, such as cross-strokes that extend past stems, oversized serifs, extended legs or tails, or runic or glyphic ornamentation, augment the fantastic qualities of such faces and help them transcend mere historical reference. Hybrid faces that mix script and sans-serif details may appear runic or symbolic, alluding to scrolls for incantation or lost languages. Illustrative inclusions, such as star- or diamondlike shapes, added to characters or replacing cross-strokes or marks such as tittles, bring a similarly runic, fantastic quality. Furthermore, some organic serifs or script forms feature highly modulated strokes and unusual junctures that lend a sense of fairytale woodland magic. Bizarre structures in seemingly classical type styles, or highly stylized construction overall, convey the sense of things that are not of this world.

Logotype
top, and detail, bottom

Brand Engine
Eric Read, art director
Deborah Smith Read, designer
Sausalito [CA] *USA*

A a B b C c Ö D E e F f G g H h l i J j K k L L ɯ N n
O o P p Q q R r S s T t U u V v W ɯ X x Y y Z z 0 1
2 3 4 5 6 7 8 9 ! ? @ # $ % & * ( ) { } : ; " "
The quick brown fox jumps over the lazy dog.

ITC Korigan™ Light
Sans Serif | Moderate Contrast | Medium Weight | Uncial Structure |

Linotype Library GmbH
www.linotype.com
info@linotype.com
+49 (0) 6172 484.418

A a B b C c D d E e F f G g H h I i J j K k L J
M m N n O o P p Q q R r S s T t U u V v W w
X x Y y Z z 0 1 2 3 4 5 6 7 8 9 ! ? & @ # $ % * : ; "
The quick brown fox jumps over the lazy dog.

Darwin Normal
Serif | Medium Weight |

Garage Fonts Type Foundry
www.garagefonts.com
info@garagefonts.com
800.681.9375

A a B b C c D d E e F f G g H h l i J j K k L L M m N n O o P p
Q q R r S s T t U u V u W w X x Y y Z z 0 1 2 3 4 5 6 7 8 9 ! ?
@ # $ % et * [ ] { } : ; " "
The quick brown fox jumps over the lazy dog.

Linotype Gotharda™
Sans Serif | Bold Weight | Condensed | Blackletter Details |

Linotype Library GmbH
www.linotype.com
info@linotype.com
+49 (0) 6172 484.418

A a B b C r D d E e F F G g H h l i J j K k L l M m
N n O o P p Q q R r S s T t U u V u W w X x Y y Z z
0 1 2 3 4 5 6 7 8 9 ! ? G @ # $ % * : ; "
The quick brown fox jumps over the lazy dog.

Interrobang Serif
Serif–Sans Serif Hybrid | Pronounced Contrast | Condensed | Medium Weight |

Garage Fonts Type Foundry
www.garagefonts.com
info@garagefonts.com
800.681.9375

O a B b C c D d E e F F G g O h l i J J K k L L
M m N n O o P p Q q R r S s T t U u O o W w
X x Y y Z z 0 1 2 3 4 5 6 7 8 9 ! ? & @ # $ % * : ;
The quick brown fox jumps over the lazy dog.

Quiver
Graphic Sans Serif | Extended | Bold Weight |

Garage Fonts Type Foundry
www.garagefonts.com
info@garagefonts.com
800.681.9375

A a B b C c D D E e F F G g H H I I J J K K L L M m
N N O O P P Q Q R R S S T T U U V V W W X x Y Y
Z Z 0 1 2 3 4 5 6 7 8 9 ! ? ( ) : ;
THE QUICK BROWN FOX JUMPS OVER THE LAZY DOG.

Merlin™
Graphic | Erratic Weight and Contrast | Glyphic Detail |

Linotype Library GmbH
www.linotype.com
info@linotype.com
+49 (0) 6172 484.418

AaBbCcDdEeFfGgHhIiJjKkLlMmNnOoPpQqRrSsTtU
uVvWwXxYyZz0123456789!?@№§%&*[][]:;""

The quick brown fox jumps over the lazy dog.

D *t*

Gargoyle Black
Textura–Sans Serif Hybrid |
Bold Weight | Condensed |

Device
www.devicefonts.co.uk
rianhughes@aol.com
44 (0) 7979.602.272

AaBbCcDdEeFfGgHhIiJjKK
LlMmNnOoPpQqRrSsTtUuVV
WwXxYyZz0123456789!?@J
$%&*[]{}:;""

the quick brown fox jumps over the lazy dog.

D *t*

Beluga™ LT Regular
Serif | Gothic Details |
Heavier Medium Weight |

Linotype Library GmbH
www.linotype.com
info@linotype.com
+49 (0) 6172 484.418

AaBbCcDdEeFfGgHhIiJjKkLlMm
NnOoPpQqRrSsTtUuVvWwXxYyZz
0123456789!?&@$:;""

The quick brown fox jumps over the lazy dog.

D

Calligraphica Regular
Archaic–Serif Hybrid | Inline |
Pronounced Contrast |

P22 Type Foundry
www.p22.com
p22@p22.com
800.P22.5080

AaBbCcDdEeFfGgHhIiJjKkLlMmNnOoPp
QqRrSsTtUuVvWwXxYyZz0123456789!?
@#$%&*(){}:;""

The quick brown fox jumps over the lazy dog.

D

Tarragon™
Serif | Medium Weight |
Brush Detail | Condensed |

Linotype Library GmbH
www.linotype.com
info@linotype.com
+49 (0) 6172 484.418

AaBbCcDdEeFfGgHhIiJjKkLlMmNnOoPpQqRrSsTtUuVvWwXxYyZz0123456789!?@#$%&*()(){}:;""

The quick brown fox jumps over the lazy dog.

D

Linotype Besque™
Graphic | Stroke Distortion |
Pronounced Contrast |

Linotype Library GmbH
www.linotype.com
info@linotype.com
+49 (0) 6172 484.418

AaBbCcDdEeFfGgHhIiJjKkLlMm
NnOoPpQqRrSsTtUuVvWwXxYy
Zz0123456789!?@#$%&*(){}:;""

The quick brown fox jumps over the lazy dog.

D *t*

Blue Island™
Serif | Lighter Medium
Weight | Moderate Contrast |
Stylized Joints |

Linotype Library GmbH
www.linotype.com
info@linotype.com
+49 (0) 6172 484.418

a b c d e f g h i j k L m n o p q r s t u v w x y z ⊙ 1 2 3 4 5 6 7 8 9 ! ? ✳ $ % & ( ) * : ; £ 🦜

the quick brown fox jumps over the Lazy dog.

D

Frances Uncial
Serif | Medium Weight | Unicase | Erratic Modulation |

Linotype Library GmbH
www.linotype.com
info@linotype.com
+49 (0) 6172 484.418

A Q B D C C D O E C F F G Q H H I I J J K K L L M M N J O O P Q Q R P S S T T U V V V W W X X Y Y Z Z O 1 2 3 4 5 6 7 8 9 ! ? & @ # $ % * : ; "

The qvick brown fox jvmps over the Lazy dog.

D

Eremaeus
Serif | Light Weight | Moderate Contrast | Uncial and Glyphic Details |

T.26 Digital Type Foundry
www.t26.com
info@t26.com
888.T26.FONT

A a B b C c D d E e F f G g H h I i J j K k L L M m M n O o P p Q q R e S s T t U u V v W w X x Y y Z z 0 1 2 3 4 5 6 7 8 9 ! ? @ # $ % & * ( ) { } : ; " "

The quick brown fox jumps over the lazy dog.

D

Grace™
Serif | Light Weight | Noticeably Condensed | Script and Blackletter Details |

Linotype Library GmbH
www.linotype.com
info@linotype.com
+49 (0) 6172 484.418

A a B b C c D d E e F f G g H h I i J j k L L M m N n O o P p Q q R r S s T t U u V v W w X x Y y Z z 0 1 2 3 4 5 6 7 8 9 ! ? @ # $ % & ( ) [ ] : ;

The quick brown fox jumps over the lazy dog.

D

Moonstone
Stylized Serif | Condensed | Medium Weight | Pinched Bowls and Flared Shoulders |

Device
www.devicefonts.co.uk
rianhughes@aol.com
44 (0) 7979.602.272

A a B b C c D d E e F f G g H h I i J j K k L l M m N n O o P p Q q R r S s T t U u V v W w X x Y y Z z 0 1 2 3 4 5 6 7 8 9 ! ? & @ * $ % * : ; "

the quick brown fox jumps over the lazy dog.

D

El Diablo Regular
Stylized Sans Serif | Lighter Medium Weight | Glyphic Details |

Garage Fonts Type Foundry
www.garagefonts.com
info@garagefonts.com
800.681.9375

A a B b C c D d E e F f G g H h I i J j K k L l M m N n O o P p Q q R r S s T t U u V v W w X x Y y Z z 0 1 2 3 4 5 6 7 8 9 ! ? @ # $ % & * ( ) { } : ; " "

The quick brown fox jumps over the lazy dog.

D *t*

Romic™ Medium
Serif | Bold Weight | Noticeable Modulation |

Linotype Library GmbH
www.linotype.com
info@linotype.com
+49 (0) 6172 484.418

ABCDEFGHIJKLMNOP
QRSTUVWXYZ0123456789
!?[]3&3()::""

The quick brown fox jumps over the lazy dog.

D

Linotype Sangue™
*Gothic Script | Pronounced
Contrast | Upright Posture |
Ultra Condensed Lowercase |*

Linotype Library GmbH
www.linotype.com
info@linotype.com
+49 (0) 6172 484.418

AaBbCcDdEeFfGgHhIiJjKkLlMmNnOoPpQqRrSs
TtUuVvWwXxYyZz0123456789!?@N°$%&*(){}.;""

The quick brown fox jumps over the lazy dog.

D **t**

Yolanda Princess
*Graphic Sans Serif |
Medium Weight | Decorative
Inclusions |*

Device
www.devicefonts.co.uk
rianhughes@aol.com
44 (0) 7979.602.272

AaBbCcDdEeFfGgHhIiJjKkLlMmNnOo
PpQqRrSsTtUuVvWwXxYyZz012345
6789!?@#$%&*(){}:;""
The quick brown fox jumps over the lazy dog.

D

Visigoth™
*Serif | Black Weight |
Pronounced Contrast | Brush
Detail | Slight Italic Posture |*

Linotype Library GmbH
www.linotype.com
info@linotype.com
+49 (0) 6172 484.418

AaBbCcDdEeFfGgHhIiJjKkLlMmNn
OoPpQqRrSsTtUuVvWwXxYyZz01
23456789!?@#$%&*(){}:;""
The quick brown fox jumps over the lazy dog.

D **T**

Semper™ Roman
*Serif | Medium Weight |
Moderate Contrast | Sharp
Terminals |*

Linotype Library GmbH
www.linotype.com
info@linotype.com
+49 (0) 6172 484.418

AaBbCcDdEeFfGgHhIiJjKkLlMmNnOo
PpQqRrSsTtUuVvWwXxYyZz01234567
89!?@#$%&*(){}:;""
The quick brown fox jumps over the lazy dog.

D **T**

ITC Woodland™ Medium
*Sans Serif | Medium Weight |
Cursive Influence | Modulation |*

Linotype Library GmbH
www.linotype.com
info@linotype.com
+49 (0) 6172 484.418

AABBCCDDEEFFGGHHIIJJKKLLMM
NNØØPPQQRRSSTTUUVVΨΨXXYYZZ
Ø1234567891?&@#$&°:;"
THE QUICK BROWN FOX JUMPS OVER THE LAZY DOG.

D

Bad Angel Sinner
Graphic | Medium Weight |

T.26 Digital Type Foundry
www.t26.com
info@t26.com
888.T26.FONT

Fantasy Color

The fantastic in color is embodied by hues that are deep, rich, cool, and jewel-like to the point of being unnatural. Supersaturated blues, burgundies, deep pinks, and violets—ultramarine blue, in particular—that occur rarely in nature, form a base palette for warmer colors such as blood red and deep, warm gold. Alternately, yellowish and brownish greens evoke the scales and hides of monsters and creatures from lagoons or outer space. Black and cold charcoal gray add depth and, when used to surround or contrast the vivid tones of the palette, help enhance their unreal saturation. The hint of mineral colors, such as copper, bronze, deep umber, and silver gray evoke rocks and metal, minerals used for incantation, or alien spacecraft.

Sample Color Combinations

100	C
100	M
0	Y
60	K

77	C
100	M
65	Y
0	K

40	C
100	M
0	Y
24	K

100	C
66	M
0	Y
46	K

100	C
100	M
0	Y
0	K

0	C
100	M
100	Y
42	K

0	C
38	M
100	Y
25	K

70	C
57	M
100	Y
0	K

0	C
72	M
100	Y
72	K

12	C
0	M
0	Y
30	K

In the design world, work that challenges expectation and points to new ways of thinking about visual communication is abundant. Sometimes the challenge comes as a test of legibility, sometimes as an unexpected juxtaposition of content or color. Typography that attempts to see the future through undiscovered technology or inventive use of form asks what can be rather than showing us what already is.

Progressive

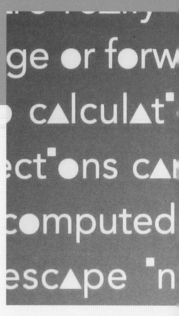

... are really only two escape routes from wr't'ng: back to the 'mage or forward to the codes. Back to the 'mag'nat'on or forward 'nto calculat'on. These reflect'ons put forward that these two d'rect'ons can merge surpr's'ngly 'nto one another. F'gures can be computed to 'mages. From textual wr't'ng/th'nk'ng we can try to escape 'nto 'mag'ned calculat'ons. 'f we succeeded, the calculat'ng and 'mag'nat've th'nk'ng would be sublated 'nto textual th'nk'ng. Wr'ters then would have swallowed and d'gested mathemat'c'ans and 'mage-makers and thus l'fted themselves

onto ▲ new level of th'nk'ng

With so much recent exploration in typographic form, a great many type-faces in use today can be considered progressive. Often, however, the results of this experimentation invite the mind to make concrete associations that aren't strictly evolutionary. Typefaces that feel inherently progressive fall into two major categories: those with conventional structure but whose details clearly explore fundamental mutation in the form, and those whose structure differs dramatically from convention. In the first category, serif/sans-serif hybrids with unusually shaped counters, terminals, and junctures feel innovative because they use the conventional form as a basis and actively seek to alter it. In doing so, they exude a sense of purposeful investigation away from the historical form while simultaneously paying homage to it. The second category includes typefaces whose characters push the limits of legibility, approaching a level of abstraction or symbolic representation, suggesting a new way of representing language altogether. Typefaces whose strokes or counters are replaced by abstract graphic elements, whose overall shapes deviate from the letter archetypes, or whose characters are simplified to the extreme—even missing information important for recognizability—all are attempts to evolve typographic form beyond existing notions.

Conceptual Type Revision
top, and detail, bottom

LSD
Sonia Díaz, Gabriel Martínez
*Based on Avenir Roman,
designed by Adrian Frutiger*
Madrid *Spain*

ʌʌ b̲b c̲c d̲d ԑԑ f̲f ɡ̲ɡ h̲h i̲i j̲j k̲k l̲l m̲m
n̲n o̲o p̲p Q̲Q ʀ̲ʀ s̲s t̲t u̲u v̲v w̲w xx Y̲Y
z̲z 0 1 2 3 4 5 6 7 8 9 ! ? & @ :; " " `

t̲he quick bʀown fox jumps oveʀ the lʌzy doɡ.

D

P22 Bayer Fonetik
Stylized Sans Serif |
Medium Weight |
Unicase with Alternates |

P22 Type Foundry
www.p22.com
p22@p22.com
800.P22.5080

A a B b C c O d E e F F G ɡ H h I i ꓴ j K K
L I M m N n O o P p Q q R r S s T t U u V v
W w X x Y y Z Z 0 1 2 3 4 5 6 7 8 9 ! ? & *

The quick brown fox jumps over the lazy dog.

D

Ambex Thin
Sans Serif | Extended |
Light Weight |

T.26 Digital Type Foundry
www.t26.com
info@t26.com
888.T26.FONT

A a B b C c D d E e F f G g H h I i J j K K L I M m
N n O o P p Q q R r S s T t U u V v W w X x Y y
Z Z 0 1 2 3 4 5 6 7 8 9 ! ? & @ # $ % * :: "

The quick brown fox jumps over the lazy dog.

D *t*

Distilla Regular
Stylized Sans Serif |
Medium Weight |

T.26 Digital Type Foundry
www.t26.com
info@t26.com
888.T26.FONT

ʌ a ʒ b C c D d ԑ e f̄ ſ G ʒ ꜧ ꜧ I i J ʝ ⟨ ʌ L l M m
N n C o ? p Q ɢ ꞃ r S s T t L ɩ v v W w X x ꓩ ʝ Z z
0 1 ꝫ 4 ſ 6 7 8 ꝫ ! ! ? ʓ @ # ¶ % * : ; "

The quicʌ brown fox jumps over the lazy doʒ.

D *t*

Edit Roman
Graphic | Lighter
Medium Weight |

T.26 Digital Type Foundry
www.t26.com
info@t26.com
888.T26.FONT

AaBbCcDdEeFfGgHhIiJjKkLlMmN
nOoPpQqRrSsTtUuVvWwXxYyZz
0123456789!?@#$%&*(){}:;""

The quick brown fox jumps over the lazy dog.

D *t*

Quagmire Bold Extended
Sans Serif | Extended |
Bold Weight |

Device
www.devicefonts.co.uk
rianhughes@aol.com
44 (0) 7979.602.272

A a B b C c D d E e F f G g H h I i J j K k L l M m N n
O o P p Q q R r S s T t U u V v W w X x Y y Z z 0 1 2 3
4 5 6 7 8 9 ! ? @ # $ % & * ( ) { } : ; " "

The quick brown fox jumps over the lazy dog.

D *t*

ITC Binary™
Serif | Moderate Contrast |
Stylized Joints |
Slightly Condensed |

Linotype Library GmbH
www.linotype.com
info@linotype.com
+49 (0) 6172 484.418

AaBbCcDdEeFfGgHhIiJjKkLIMmNn
OoPpQqRrSsTtUuVvWwXxYyZzOI
23456789!?@#$%&*(){}:;" "
The quick brown fox jumps over the lazy dog.

D *t*

Seebad™ Std Bold
Sans Serif | Bold Weight |
Rounded Joints | Condensed |

Linotype Library GmbH
www.linotype.com
info@linotype.com
+49 (0) 6172 484.418

AaBbCcDdEeFfGgHhIiJjKkLlMm
NnOoPpQqRrSsTtUuVvWwXxYyZz
0123456789!?@#$%&*(){}:;" "
The quick brown fox jumps over the lazy dog.

D

Linotype Arab Stroke™
Regular
Sans Serif | Lighter Medium
Weight | Brush Influence |
Irregular Terminals |

Linotype Library GmbH
www.linotype.com
info@linotype.com
+49 (0) 6172 484.418

AaBbCcDdEeFfGgHhIiJjKkLlMmNnOoPp
QqRrSsTtUuVvWwXxYyZz0123456789
!?@#$%&*(){};; " "
The quick brown fox jumps over the lazy dog.

D *t*

Egret Light
Stylized Sans Serif |
Condensed |
Medium Weight |

Device
www.devicefonts.co.uk
rianhughes@aol.com
44 (0) 7979.602.272

ʌaß6(⊏⊃dɛeɸfGg开flij⅃kKLl™mʍn
o°PeQgR®SsttuⵙvvWwxxYyz≠0!
z34sb789!?@#$%&*[|[]:; " "
The quick brown fox jumps over the lazy dog.

D

F2F Metamorfosi™
Graphic | Medium Weight |
Substituted Characters |
Erratic Orientation |

Linotype Library GmbH
www.linotype.com
info@linotype.com
+49 (0) 6172 484.418

AaBbCcDdEeFfGgHhIiJjKkLlMmNnOoPp
QqRrSsTtUuVvWwXxYyZz0123456789!?
@#$%&*(){}:;" "
the quick brown fox jumps over the lazy dog.

D *t*

Linotype Scott™ Venus
Sans serif | Medium Weight |
Uniform Case Body Heights |

Linotype Library GmbH
www.linotype.com
info@linotype.com
+49 (0) 6172 484.418

AaBbCcDdEeFfGgHhIiJjKkLlMmNnOoPpQqRrSs
TtUuVvWwXxYyZz0123456789!?@#$%&*()

The quick brown fox jumps over the lazy dog.

D *t*

Gravel Medium
Stylized Sans Serif | Condensed |
Medium Weight |

Device
www.devicefonts.co.uk
rianhughes@aol.com
44 (0) 7979.602.272

Progressive Color

Like progressive typefaces, progressive color is primarily a matter of finding previously unimagined combinations—a difficult task. Beginning with medium-value hues that are far apart on the color wheel, or that appear to have no harmonic relationships, is a start: violet and green, blue-violet and brown, olive and neutral gray. Keeping the colors desaturated, as well as closer in value to each other, forces their hues and temperatures to interact more intensely and implies a studiousness that conveys purposeful exploration. Color combinations that have historically been labeled a color faux pas, such as red and pink, also transmit the idea of looking past convention to find something new. Extremely bright colors that refer to technology as part of the combination base, especially when they interact with muted hues that are nearly complementary or different in value, create a jarring effect that may seem futuristic in outlook.

Sample Color Combinations

>	60 C / 63 M / 0 Y / 0 K
>	65 C / 0 M / 67 Y / 0 K
>	76 C / 55 M / 0 Y / 0 K
>	55 C / 66 M / 80 Y / 0 K
>	0 C / 0 M / 100 Y / 56 K
>	0 C / 8 M / 0 Y / 50 K
>	100 C / 15 M / 15 Y / 18 K
>	0 C / 84 M / 40 Y / 0 K
>	0 C / 100 M / 100 Y / 0 K
>	53 C / 0 M / 100 Y / 0 K

Extremeness in design involves severity or opposition—harsh combinations of form or aggressive figure-ground relationships— as well
as a sense of the exotic, alien, or extravagant. Stark, minimal layouts,
for example, may pit extravagant white space against exceptionally
bold forms, while maximalist work can be extreme in its over-the-top
complexity and unusual detail. Weirdness—idiosyncratic or foreign
elements—contributes to the exotic quality of extreme design.

Extreme

Along with proportional manipulation that may push the envelope on legibility—typefaces that are so condensed or bold that their counters become
line or dot elements, or so extended that they begin to fall apart—severe
bolding, posture, and disjointed stroke configuration all characterize the
extreme in typefaces. Separation between strokes, replacement of strokes
with forms that visually disconnect from letters, and manipulated stroke
proportions within individual characters further enhance the alien quality
of these typefaces. Forms that are exceptionally decorative or mannered,
even older forms such as highly detailed gothic blackletters, may feel
extreme because of their excessive complexity. Additionally, the introduction of characteristics that contradict the overall proportion or rhythm of
the typeface, such as abstract graphic shapes, sharp angles juxtaposed with
curves, and so on, create an intense, dynamic severity.

T-Shirt Design *details*

Q
Marcel Kummerer
Wiesbaden *Germany*

The quick brown fox jumps over the lazy dog.

D

Linotype Submerge™ Two Regular
Sans Serif | Slight Contrast | Elliptical Structure | Unicase with Selected Alternates |

Linotype Library GmbH
www.linotype.com
info@linotype.com
+49 (0) 6172 484.418

THE QUICK BROWN FOX JUMPS OVER THE LAZY DOG.

D

Gusto Solid
Graphic | Black Weight |

Device
www.devicefonts.co.uk
rianhughes@aol.com
44 (0) 7979.602.272

The quick brown fox jumps over the lazy dog.

D

Special K
Graphic | Condensed | Light Weight |

Garage Fonts Type Foundry
www.garagefonts.com
info@garagefonts.com
800.681.9375

THE QUICK BROWN FOX JUMPS OVER THE LAZY dOG.

D

Linotype Killer™
Sans Serif | Black Weight | Geometric | Pronounced Contrast | Extended |

Linotype Library GmbH
www.linotype.com
info@linotype.com
+49 (0) 6172 484.418

The quick brown fox jumps over the lazy dog.

D

Terminal Regular
Stylized Sans Serif | Extended | Bold Weight |

T.26 Digital Type Foundry
www.t26.com
info@t26.com
888.T26.FONT

The quick brown fox jumps over the lazy dog.

D

Droplet Extra
Stylized Sans Serif | Erratic Weight |

T.26 Digital Type Foundry
www.t26.com
info@t26.com
888.T26.FONT

AaBbCoDEeFGoHHnIiJkKLlMnn
OpPQQArsTtUvVwWxYu220123
456789!?6回#5%*:;"

The quick brown fox jumps over the lazy dog.

D

Kunstware Alphabet
*Stylized Sans Serif | Extended |
Caps with Selected Alternates |*

T.26 Digital Type Foundry
www.t26.com
info@t26.com
888.T26.FONT

AABBCDEEFFGGHHIJ
KKLMNOPPPQRRSTUVW
XYZ0123456789!?6@#$

THE QUICK BROWN FOX JUMPS OVER THE

D

Mata
*Stylized Sans Serif | Extended |
Caps with Selected Alternates |*

T.26 Digital Type Foundry
www.t26.com
info@t26.com
888.T26.FONT

RaBbcˌɕdᴈ3ƺƼ5ᵧggᵪɕɛɛᵧ᷄ʄXʋᴜᵯ
ɴɴooPpQQᵲ,SᵧᵗᵗᵾᴜᵥᵣWᵯxXYᵧ
ʋʋ₀₍ᵌᵧᵧᵌᵧ6ᵧ89!?ᵧᵾᵿ₀ʂ0%ᵟᵌᵧ;"

ᵲɦᵧ quᵢᵪX bᵣoᵥᵥᵥ ᶠoX ᵧᵾᵯᵨᵧ oᵥᵧᵣ ᵲɦᵧ ᵥᵤᵢᵧ ᵈoᵧ.

D

Oeiller Simple
Graphic | Medium Weight |

T.26 Digital Type Foundry
www.t26.com
info@t26.com
888.T26.FONT

AABBCCDDEEFFGGHHiIjJkKLLMMNNOOPPQQRRSSTTUUU
WWxXYY2201234561891?@#$%&*[]{}:;"'

The quick brown fox jumps over the lazy dog.

D

Quasaria™ Regular
*Sans Serif | Lighter Medium
Weight | Extremely Condensed*

Linotype Library GmbH
www.linotype.com
info@linotype.com
+49 (0) 6172 484.418

AaebcIod3ÆFIGᵹHhIiJKKLIMm
nIoᴀPPaQRᴀSᴀTYⅥUUUWWXIY
ᵶᵪ0123456789!?&@f5$%°×:;"

The quick brown fox jumps over the lazy dog.

D

Process Regular
*Graphic | Erratic Weight |
Pronounced Contrast |*

T.26 Digital Type Foundry
www.t26.com
info@t26.com
888.T26.FONT

AABCDEFGHHIJKLMNOPᴙRSTU
UVWWXYZ0123456789!?6⬦H
5%*:;"

THE QUICK BROWN FOX JUMPS OVER THE LAZY DOG.

D

Wackelkontakt
*Stylized Sans Serif |
All Caps with Alternates |
Medium Weight |*

Garage Fonts Type Foundry
www.garagefonts.com
info@garagefonts.com
800.681.9375

The quick brown fox jumps over the lazy dog.

D

Silesia Light
Graphic | Light Weight |
Modular Structure |

Device
www.devicefonts.co.uk
rianhughes@aol.com
44 (0) 7979.602.272

the quick brown fox jumps over the lazy dog.

D

Acid Queen
Graphic | Pronounced Contrast |
Unicase with Alternates |

Garage Fonts Type Foundry
www.garagefonts.com
info@garagefonts.com
800.681.9375

A a B b C c D d E e F f G g H h I i J j K k L l M m N n O o P p Q q R r S s T t U u V v W w X x Y y Z z 0 1 2 3 4 5 6 7 8 9 ! ? @ # $ % & * ( ) { } : ; " "

The quick brown fox jumps over the lazy dog.

D

Linotype Bariton™
Sans Serif | Black Weight |
Contoured Terminals |

Linotype Library GmbH
www.linotype.com
info@linotype.com
+49 (0) 6172 484.418

THE QUICK BROWN FOX JUMPS OVER THE LAZY DOG.

D

Bubba Enbloque Normal
Graphic | Black Weight |

Garage Fonts Type Foundry
www.garagefonts.com
info@garagefonts.com
800.681.9375

the quick brown fox jumps over the lazy dog.

D

Panic Plain
Graphic | Extended |
Bold Weight |

T.26 Digital Type Foundry
www.t26.com
info@t26.com
888.T26.FONT

The quick brown fox jumps over the lazy dog.

D

Rayzor Sharp
Graphic | Bold Weight |

T.26 Digital Type Foundry
www.t26.com
info@t26.com
888.T26.FONT

A a B b C c D d E e F f G g H h I i J j K k L l M m N n O o P p Q q R r S s T t U u V v W w X x Y y Z z 0 1 2 3 4 5 6 7 8 9 ! ? $ % & * ( ) : ; " "

The quick brown fox jumps over the lazy dog.

D

Bigband™
Sans Serif | Black Weight |
Slightly Extended |

Linotype Library GmbH
www.linotype.com
info@linotype.com
+49 (0) 6172 484.418

A a B b C c D d E e F f G g H h I i J j K k L l M m N n O o P p Q q R r S s T t U u V v W w X x Y y Z z 0 1 2 3 4 5 6 7 8 9 ! ? @ # $ % & * ( ) { } : ; " "

The quick brown fox jumps over the lazy dog.

D

Univers™ 39 Thin
Ultra Condensed
Sans Serif | Ultra Light Weight |
Extremely Condensed |

Linotype Library GmbH
www.linotype.com
info@linotype.com
+49 (0) 6172 484.418

A B C D E F G H I J K L M N O P Q R S T U V W X Y Z 0 1 2 3 4 5 6 7 8 9 ! ? J Ł % &

THE QUICK BROWN FOX JUMPS OVER THE LAZY DOG.

D

Vienna™ Extended
Sans Serif | Light Weight |
Very Extended | Exaggerated
Proportion |

Linotype Library GmbH
www.linotype.com
info@linotype.com
+49 (0) 6172 484.418

D

Digital Waste Regular
Graphic | Bold Weight |
Abstract Inclusions |

T.26 Digital Type Foundry
www.t26.com
info@t26.com
888.T26.FONT

A B C D E F G H I J K L M N O P Q R S T U V W X Y Z 0 1 2 3 4 5 6 7 8 9 ! ? £ # $ %
※ : ; "

THE QUICK BROWN FOX JUMPS OVER THE LAZY DOG.

D

Gemini X Regular
Graphic | Extremely Extended |
Inline Detail |

T.26 Digital Type Foundry
www.t26.com
info@t26.com
888.T26.FONT

A a B b C D E F F G g H h I i J i K K L l M n O P q R r S T t U u V w X Y y Z 0 1 2 3 4 5 6 7 8 9 ! ? £ & # $ % X : ; "

The quick brown fox jumps over the lazy dog.

D

Makro Regular
Stylized Sans Serif | Extreme
Contrast | Geometric Structure |

T.26 Digital Type Foundry
www.t26.com
info@t26.com
888.T26.FONT

Extreme Color

Extreme color stems from opposition—first off, complementaries such as blue and orange, violet and yellow, red and green. This clash can be enhanced by value relationships that create a jarring effect, especially in cases where intrinsic value assumptions are reversed (for example, a pale violet and a deep yellow) or pushed as far apart as possible (a blue so dark it is almost black against an orange that is so intense and bright it is electric). Black against white is the ultimate contrast in this regard, although black against a vibrant orange-yellow may appear to have even more contrast. A hot red and a very cool red in close proximity to intense yellow-orange, although analogous, play off the temperature difference between themselves and the warmer, more intense identity of the latter.

Sample Color Combinations

100 C	
35 M	
0 Y	
0 K	

0 C	
68 M	
100 Y	
0 K	

75 C	
100 M	
0 Y	
0 K	

0 C	
5 M	
100 Y	
0 K	

100 C	
43 M	
0 Y	
75 K	

0 C	
22 M	
100 Y	
0 K	

0 C	
79 M	
100 Y	
0 K	

0 C	
100 M	
51 Y	
0 K	

0 C	
100 M	
100 Y	
0 K	

93 C	
0 M	
100 Y	
0 K	

From the regal authority of aristocracy to the credible public presence of police, power is linked to money and force. It follows that powerful type and color exude qualities of strength, untouchable refinement and taste, and rugged durability—boldness and aggression tempered by wealth and stability.

Powerful

In terms of typefaces, power can be signified by a number of characteristics, some purely visual and others through association. Extremely heavy sans serifs, for example, are visually dominant in composition to lighter faces, and their compressed counters create a dynamic energy among their massive strokes. Squared-off curves and junctures in such faces add an aggressive quality. Archaic Roman capitals, on the other hand, connote power through their formality and imperial association. Typefaces that include only capitals enforce a sense of power through their generally angular and consistently rectangular forms; spacing a line of capitals creates a wall of type. Medium-weight to semibold sans serifs, especially those with angular junctures or a substitution of angles for curves, have a rugged presence that is pronounced in the rhythmic regularity of a medium width. At the more decorative end of the scale, typefaces that allude to wealth, elegance, or classicism present a message more associated with power in heavier weights.

Beverage Bottle
top, and detail, bottom

Creuna Design
Brita Bergsnov-Hansen
Oslo *Norway*

A a B b C c D d E e F f G g H h I i J j K k L l
M m N n O o P p Q q R r S s T t U u V v W w
X x Y y Z z 0 1 2 3 4 5 6 7 8 9 ! ? & @ № $ %

The QUICK BROWN FOX JUMPS OVER the LAZY DOG.

D

Fono Expanded Unicase
Stylized Sans Serif |
Bold Weight |
Caps and Small Caps |

Garage Fonts Type Foundry
www.garagefonts.com
info@garagefonts.com
800.681.9375

A a B b C c D d E e F f G g H h I i J j K k L l M m
N n O o P p Q q R r S s T t U u V v W w X x Y y
Z z 0 1 2 3 4 5 6 7 8 9 ! ? $ % & * ( ) { } : ; " "

The quick brown fox jumps over the lazy dog.

D *t*

Aachen™ Bold
Slab Serif | Heavier Bold Weight |
Slightly Condensed |

Linotype Library GmbH
www.linotype.com
info@linotype.com
+49 (0) 6172 484.418

A a B b C c D d E e F f G g H h I i J j K k L l M m
N n O o P p Q q R r S s T t U u V v W w X x Y y
Z z 0 1 2 3 4 5 6 7 8 9 ! ? & @ # $ % * : ; "

The quick brown fox jumps over the lazy dog.

D *t*

Modus Extra Bold
Sans Serif | Bold Weight |

Garage Fonts Type Foundry
www.garagefonts.com
info@garagefonts.com
800.681.9375

A a B b C c D d E e F F G g H h I i J j K k
L l M m N n O o P p Q e R r S s T t U u V v
W w X x Y y Z z 0 1 2 3 4 5 6 7 8 9 ! ? & @ #

The quick brown Fox jumps over the lazy dog.

D *t*

Rubber Large
Stylized Sans Serif |
Heavier Bold Weight |

Garage Fonts Type Foundry
www.garagefonts.com
info@garagefonts.com
800.681.9375

A a B b C c D d E e F f G g H h I i J j K k L l
M m N n O o P p Q q R r S s T t U u V v W w X x
Y y Z z 0 1 2 3 4 5 6 7 8 9 ! ? & @ # $ % * : ;

The quick brown fox jumps over the lazy dog.

D

Sanos Black
Sans Serif | Black Weight |
Slight Contrast | Stylized
Terminals | Extended |

T.26 Digital Type Foundry
www.t26.com
info@t26.com
888.T26.FONT

A a B b C c D d E e F f G g H h I i J j K k L l M m
N n O o P p Q q R r S s T t U u V v W w X x Y y
1 2 0 1 2 3 4 5 6 7 8 9 ! ? & @ # $ % * : ; "

The quick brown fox jumps over the lazy dog.

D

Dimentia Medium
Stylized Sans Serif |
Pronounced Contrast |

T.26 Digital Type Foundry
www.t26.com
info@t26.com
888.T26.FONT

ABCDEFGHIJKLMNOPQRSTUVW
XYZ0123456789!?¶$%*:;"

THE QUICK BROWN FOX JUMPS OVER THE LAZY DOG.

D

Mammoth Regular
*Graphic | Extra Black Weight |
All Caps |*

T.26 Digital Type Foundry
www.t26.com
info@t26.com
888.T26.FONT

ABCDEFGHIJKLMNOPQRSTUVWXYZ
0123456789!?Nº$%º6*[]!?:;""

THE QUICK BROWN FOX JUMPS OVER THE LAZY DOG.

D

Judgement A Medium
*Stylized Sans Serif |
Bold Weight | All Caps |*

Device
www.devicefonts.co.uk
rianhughes@aol.com
44 (0) 7979.602.272

AaBbCcDdEeFfGgHhIi
JjKkLlMmNnOoPpQqRr
SsTtUuVvWwXxYyZzO1
23456789!?%®#$%•:;"

The quick brown fox jumps over the

D

Kamaro Big
*Stylized Sans Serif | Extremely
Extended | Medium Weight |*

Garage Fonts Type Foundry
www.garagefonts.com
800.681.9375
301.260.2285
info@garagefonts.com

A B C D E F G H I J K L M N O P Q R S T U V
W X Y Z 0 1 2 3 4 5 6 7 8 9 ! ? @ # $ % & * ( )

THE QUICK BROWN FOX JUMPS OVER THE LAZY DOG.

D

ITC Machine® Medium
*Sans Serif | Bold Weight |
Angled Shoulders | Condensed |*

Linotype Library GmbH
www.linotype.com
info@linotype.com
+49 (0) 6172 484.418

A a B b C c D d E e F f G g H h I i J j K k L l M m
N n O o P p Q q R r S s T t U u V v W w X x Y y Z z
0 1 2 3 4 5 6 7 8 9 ! ? @ # $ % & * ( ) { } : ; " "

The quick brown fox jumps over the lazy dog.

D T

Meridien™ Roman
*Serif | Moderate Contrast |
Sharp Serifs |*

Linotype Library GmbH
www.linotype.com
info@linotype.com
+49 (0) 6172 484.418

A a B b C c D d E e F f G g H h I i J j K k L l M m N n
O o P p Q q R r S s T t U u V v W w X x Y y Z z 0 1 2 3
4 5 6 7 8 9 ! ? & @ # $ % * : ; "

The quick brown fox jumps over the lazy dog.

D t

Compressor Slab Serif
*Slab Serif | Bold Weight |
Condensed |*

T.26 Digital Type Foundry
www.t26.com
info@t26.com
888.T26.FONT

Powerful Color

Color that feels reliable, has visual depth or complexity, and creates an emotional response of arousal communicates a sense of power. Deep, navy blue has a massive quality tempered by its calming effect; violet, historically expensive to produce, carries associations with royalty. Deep burgundy, a variation on the passionate message conveyed by red, has a violet character that alludes to fine wine. Hunter green connotes wealth and stability, while dark grays, particularly cooler varieties, create a sense of sophistication while referring to the more identifiable hues in the palette. Black is a powerful addition to the palette and, coupled with these other colors, reinforces their intensity.

Sample Color Combinations

100 C	
55 M	
0 Y	
60 K	

| 100 C |
| 77 M |
| 38 Y |
| 0 K |

| 81 C |
| 100 M |
| 0 Y |
| 20 K |

| 0 C |
| 100 M |
| 0 Y |
| 74 K |

| 100 C |
| 62 M |
| 100 Y |
| 0 K |

| 25 C |
| 12 M |
| 0 Y |
| 65 K |

| 30 C |
| 20 M |
| 5 Y |
| 70 K |

| 20 C |
| 20 M |
| 20 Y |
| 100 K |

| 15 C |
| 100 M |
| 36 Y |
| 71 K |

| 0 C |
| 100 M |
| 100 Y |
| 32 K |

Bringing together the world's varied visual languages, multicultural design depends largely on context. In one sense, it may be approached as universal—and therefore neutral—in presentation, but it may also be more consciously considered a grab bag of styles and color that references disparate cultural qualities to create an eclectic visual hybrid of form.

Multicultural

The idea of multiculturalism in type can be conveyed in two diametrically opposed ways: as absolutely neutral and therefore universal, or as a mixture of formal qualities that evoke varied writing systems. In the first camp, sans serifs with little or no variation in body width among characters, large x-heights, regularized curves in shoulders and bowls, and perpendicular terminals—essentially those without any character whatsoever—have been conventionally thought of as international, eschewing any trace of regional or historical origin. However, the alternative—type styles that clearly reference culturally distinct writing systems—may more readily convey the sense of disparate cultures and people coming together. Roman forms, for example, with linear junctures along the cap- or baseline, may carry structural associations with Hindi or Arabic, while some geometrically simplified, angular characters may refer to ideographic or glyphic forms, such as in Asian or Hebraic writing, respectively. Typefaces with swash or curlicue details, or abstract inclusions, may similarly feel as though they are "foreign" as compared to more neutral faces, whether serif or sans serif.

Identity Applications
top, and details, bottom

Lure Design, Inc.
Jeff Matz
Orlando [FL] *USA*

A a B b C c D d E e F f G g H h I i J j K k L l
M m N n O o P p Q q R r S s T t U u V v W w
X x Y y Z z 0 1 2 3 4 5 6 7 8 9 ! ? & @ : ; " "

The quick brown fox jumps over the lazy dog.

D

P22 Daddy-O Junkie
*Graphic Wedge Serif |
Erratic Baseline |
Conflicting Posture |*

P22 Type Foundry
www.p22.com
p22@p22.com
800.P22.5080

A a B b C c D d E e F f G g H h I i J j K k L l
M m N n O o P p Q q R r S s T t U u V v W w
X x Y y Z z 0 1 2 3 4 5 6 7 8 9 ! ? @ # $ %
& * ( ) { } : ; " "

THE QUICK BROWN FOX JUMPS OVER THE LAZY DOG.

D

ITC Juanita™ Xilo
*Sans Serif | Black Weight |
Graphic Detail |
Noticeable Contrast |*

Linotype Library GmbH
www.linotype.com
info@linotype.com
+49 (0) 6172 484.418

A a B b C c D d E e F f G g H h I i J j K k L l
M m N n O o P p Q q R r S s T t U u V v W w
X x Y y Z z 0 1 2 3 4 5 6 7 8 9 ! ? & @ # $ % * : ;

the quick brown fox jumps over the lazy dog.

D

Devine Town Regular
*Sans Serif–Sanskrit Hybrid |
Medium Weight | Sanskrit
Influence | Capline Joints |*

T.26 Digital Type Foundry
www.t26.com
info@t26.com
888.T26.FONT

a a b c d e F g h i j K L M n o o P Q R s t u u v w
x y z 0 1 2 3 4 5 6 7 8 9 ! ? & @ # $ % * : ; "

the quick brown fox jumps over the lazy dog.

D *t*

Expresso
*Graphic | Medium Weight |
Double Lowercase |*

Garage Fonts Type Foundry
www.garagefonts.com
info@garagefonts.com
800.681.9375

A a B b C c D d E e F f G g H h I i J j K k L l M m N n
O o P p Q q R r S s T t U u V v W w X x Y y Z z 0 1 2 3
4 5 6 7 8 9 ! ? ⊙ # $ % & * ( ) { } : ; " "

The quick brown fox jumps over the lazy dog.

D

F2F MadZine™ Wip
*Graphic | Medium Weight |
Condensed | Modulation |
Abstract Inclusions |*

Linotype Library GmbH
www.linotype.com
info@linotype.com
+49 (0) 6172 484.418

A a B b C c D d E e F f G g H h I i J j K k L l M m N n
O o P p Q q R r S s T t U u V v W w X x Y y Z z 0 1
2 3 4 5 6 7 8 9 ! ? ⊛ # $ % * : ; "

THE QUICK BROWN FOX JUMPS OVER THE LAZY DOG.

D

Modern Blues Regular
*Graphic | Glyph Details |
Light Weight | Caps and
Small Caps |*

T.26 Digital Type Foundry
www.t26.com
info@t26.com
888.T26.FONT

A a B b C c D d E e F f G g H h I i J j K k L l M m N n
O o P p Q q R r S s T t U u V v W w X x Y y Z z 0 1 2 3
4 5 6 7 8 9 ! ? @ # $ % & * ( ) { } : ; " "

The quick brown fox jumps over the lazy dog.

D t

Sho™
*Graphic Sans Serif |
Bold Weight | Modulation |
Brush Influence |*

Linotype Library GmbH
www.linotype.com
info@linotype.com
+49 (0) 6172 484.418

a a B b c c D d e e F f G g H h i i J j K k
U l m m n n O o P p Q q R r S s T t U u
V v W w X x Y y Z z 0 1 2 3 4 5 6 7 8 9 ! ?
@ # $ % & * ( ) { } : ; " "

The quick brown fox jumps over the lazy dog.

D

Linotype SinahSans™
*Graphic Sans Serif |
Bold Weight | Noticeable
Contrast | Looping Detail |*

Linotype Library GmbH
www.linotype.com
info@linotype.com
+49 (0) 6172 484.418

A a B b C c D d E e F f G g H h I i J j K k
L l M m N n O o P p Q q R r S s T t U u V v
W w X x Y y Z z 0 1 2 3 4 5 6 7 8 9 ! ? @ #

The quick brown fox jumps over the lazy dog.

D t

Linotype Dharma™
*Serif-Sans Serif Hybrid |
Black Weight |
Pronounced Contrast |*

Linotype Library GmbH
www.linotype.com
info@linotype.com
+49 (0) 6172 484.418

A a B b C c D d E e F f G g H h I i J j K k L l M m N n O o
P p Q q R r S s T t U u V v W w X x Y y Z z 0 1 2 3 4 5 6 7
8 9 ! ? & @ # $ % * : ; :

The quick brown fox jumps over the lazy dog.

D

El Chamuco Condensed
*Stylized Sans Serif | Pronounced
Contrast | Medium Weight |*

T.26 Digital Type Foundry
www.t26.com
info@t26.com
888.T26.FONT

A a B b C c D d E e F f G g H h I i J j K k L l M m N n O o P p
Q q R r S s T t U u V v W w X x Y y Z z 0 1 2 3 4 5 6 7 8 9 ! ?
$ % & * ( ) : ; " "

The quick brown fox jumps over the lazy dog.

D t

ITC Honda®
*Sans Serif | Black Weight |
Condensed |*

Linotype Library GmbH
www.linotype.com
info@linotype.com
+49 (0) 6172 484.418

A a B b C c D d E e F f g g H h I i J j K k L l M m N n O o
P p Q q R r S s T t U u V v W w X x Y y Z z 0 1 2 3 4 5 6 7 8 9
! ? @ # $ % & * ( ) { } : ; " "

The quick brown fox jumps over the lazy dog.

D

ITC Jambalaya™ Regular
*Graphic | Varied Weight and
Contrast | Illustrative Detail |*

Linotype Library GmbH
www.linotype.com
info@linotype.com
+49 (0) 6172 484.418

A a B b C C D d E e F f G g H h I i J J K k L l M m
N n O O P P Q q R r S S T t U U V V W W X X Y Y
Z Z @ 1 2 3 4 5 6 7 8 9 ! ? & @ # $ % * : ; "

The quick brown fox jumps over the lazy dog.

D

Mantra
Graphic | Glyphic Details | Pronounced Contrast | Light Weight | Mixed Heights |

T.26 Digital Type Foundry
www.t26.com
info@t26.com
888.T26.FONT

A a B b C c D d E e F f G g H h I i J j K k L l M m N n O o
P p Q q R r S s T t U u V v W w X x Y y Z z 0 1 2 3 4 5
6 7 8 9 ! ? @ # $ % & * ( ) { } : ; " "

The quick brown fox jumps over the lazy dog.

D

Kigali™ Roman
Graphic Serif | Black Weight | Pronounced Contrast | Brush Influence |

Linotype Library GmbH
www.linotype.com
info@linotype.com
+49 (0) 6172 484.418

A a B b C c D d E e F f G g H h I i J j K k L l M m
N n O o P p Q q R r S s T t U u V v W w X x Y y Z z
0 1 2 3 4 5 6 7 8 9 ! ? $ % & * ( ) : ; " "

The quick brown fox jumps over the lazy dog.

D

Kismet™
Serif | Light Weight | Graphic Inclusions |

Linotype Library GmbH
www.linotype.com
info@linotype.com
+49 (0) 6172 484.418

A a B b C c D d E e F f G g H h I i J j K k L l M m N n O o
P p Q q R r S s T t U u V v W w X x Y y Z z 0 1 2 3 4 5
6 7 8 9 ! ? @ @ $ % & * ( ) : ; " "

The quick brown fox jumps over the lazy dog.

D

Lambada™
Serif | Bolder Medium Weight | Slight Contrast | Looped Serifs and Joint Structure |

Linotype Library GmbH
www.linotype.com
info@linotype.com
+49 (0) 6172 484.418

A a B b C c D d E e F f G g H h I i J j K k L l M m N n
O o P p Q q R r S s T t U u V v W w X x Y y Z z 0 1
2 3 4 5 6 7 8 9 ! ? @ # $ % & * ( ) { } : ; " "

The quick brown fox jumps over the lazy dog.

D t

Matura™
Sans Serif | Black Weight | Moderate Contrast | Brush Influence |

Linotype Library GmbH
www.linotype.com
info@linotype.com
+49 (0) 6172 484.418

A α β δ C c d δ E ε f f G g H h l i J j K k L l M m
N η O σ P ρ φ q R r S s T τ U u V v Ω ω X χ Y y Z z
0 1 2 3 4 5 6 7 8 9 ! ? @ % & ( ) : ;

The quick brown fox jumps over the lazy dog.

D

Morocco™ Std
Graphic | Medium Weight | Greek-Roman Hybrid |

Linotype Library GmbH
www.linotype.com
info@linotype.com
+49 (0) 6172 484.418

ℶℶℷℷℸℸℸℷℸℸ etc.
The quick brown fox jumps over the lazy dog.

D

Talmud Regular
Graphic | Bold Weight |
Short Overall Body |
Hebrew-Roman Hybrid |

T.26 Digital Type Foundry
www.t26.com
info@t26.com
888.T26.FONT

AaBbCcDdEeFfGgHhIiJjKkLlMmNn
OoPpQqRrSsTtUuVvWwXxYyZz 0 1 2 3 4 5
6 7 8 9 ! ? @ N $ % & + ( ) { } : ; " "
The quick brown fox jumps over the lazy dog.

D

Linotype Pide Nashi™ Two
Sans Serif | Bold Weight |
Pronounced Descenders |
Arabic Influence |

Linotype Library GmbH
www.linotype.com
info@linotype.com
+49 (0) 6172 484.418

AaBbCcDdEeFfGgHhIiJjKkLl
MmNnOoPpQqRrSsTtUuVvWw
XxYyZz0123456789!?&@#$%
The quick brown fox jumps over the lazy dog.

D **£**

Rappongi Normal
Stylized Sans Serif | Extended |
Medium Weight |

T.26 Digital Type Foundry
www.t26.com
info@t26.com
888.T26.FONT

ā a b b c̄ c δ δ Ē e f f ḡ g h h ī i j j k k l l m̄ m n̄ n
σ̄ σ p̄ p q̄ q r̄ r s̄ s t̄ t ū u v̄ v w̄ w x̄ x ȳ y z̄ z 0 1
2 3 4 5 6 7 8 9 ! ? @ # $ % & * ( ) { } : ; " "
The quick brown fox jumps over the lazy dog.

D

ITC Simran™
Sans Serif | Heavier Medium
Weight | Noticeable Contrast |
Unicase with Alternates |

Linotype Library GmbH
www.linotype.com
info@linotype.com
+49 (0) 6172 484.418

AABBCCDDEEFFGGHHIIJJKKLLMMNN
OOPPQQRRSSTTUUVVWWXXYYZZ0123
456789!?&@$:;""
THE QUICK BROWN FOX JUMPS OVER THE LAZY DOG.

D

P22 Shibumi
Stylized Sans Serif | Medium
Weight | Pronounced
Contrast | Brush Forms |

P22 Type Foundry
www.p22.com
p22@p22.com
800.P22.5080

AaBbCcDdEeFfGgHhIiJjKkLlMm
NnOoPpQqRrSsTtUuVvWwXxYy
ZzZz0123456789!?@#$%&*(){} :;""
The quick brown fox jumps over the lazy dog.

D

Slogan™ Regular
Script | Medium Weight |
Pronounced Contrast |
Semi-Swash Capitals |

Linotype Library GmbH
www.linotype.com
info@linotype.com
+49 (0) 6172 484.418

Multicultural Color

As with typefaces, color schemes that attempt to convey a multicultural idea may be either severely limited or quite open in terms of the number and kinds of colors that are used. A limited palette of gray, black, white, red, and golden yellow—the extremes of value and a concentration on two hues with universal associations of energy—is a popular color approach for design that is intended to be as international as possible. On the other hand, a wide range of colors mixed together in very basic presentation also conveys the sense of many kinds of visual traditions being brought together. Middle values of blue, green, red, orange, gold, ochre, brown, and fuchsia together—controlled so that their values are as similar as possible—reference the environment seen in all parts of the world: grass, earth, sky, water, sun, animals, and so on. In combining colors of similar value, the interaction of hues becomes more pronounced and speaks more clearly of their multicultural mixing.

Sample Color Combinations

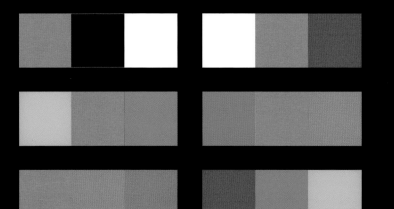

>	
20 C	
20 M	
20 Y	
100 K	

>	
0 C	
0 M	
0 Y	
0 K	

>	
0 C	
100 M	
100 Y	
10 K	

>	
5 C	
5 M	
5 Y	
45 K	

>	
0 C	
25 M	
100 Y	
0 K	

>	
80 C	
25 M	
0 Y	
0 K	

>	
80 C	
0 M	
60 Y	
10 K	

>	
0 C	
45 M	
75 Y	
20 K	

>	
27 C	
38 M	
47 Y	
20 K	

>	
0 C	
63 M	
0 Y	
23 K	

From the haze of prehistory to the cultures of early human civilization—the Sumerians, Phoenicians, Egyptians, ancient Greeks, and imperial Romans—the archaic in type and color embodies the ancient.

Archaic

Type that is classified as archaic in the Western tradition harks back to the simple, lapidary (stone-carved) forms derived initially from Sumerian cuneiform—sharp, angular, and chiseled strokes—and later refined by the Greeks and Romans. All-capital faces dominate this category, as these forms were the first to be developed. Simple construction, geometrically circular curves, abrupt junctures, and quadrant-based proportions in width—in which the O, A, H, and N define a square, supported by letters with half-square widths, such as E, F, L, S, B, and R—join with brush or pen-inspired strokes. Faces that reference older forms tend to be uniform in overall weight, while those that evoke the refined culture of Rome show contrast among the strokes. Archaic typefaces may have serifs—evidence of the chisel and the brush as drawing method—or may not. Single-weight script forms—sometimes clearly hand drawn—allude to casual writing from the era. Geometric glyphlike alphabets round out the category. Modern interpretations of archaic forms sometimes include lowercase forms, integrating the past with present needs for text.

Catalog Cover *top, and detail*

STIM Visual Communication
Timothy Samara
New York City *USA*

A B C D E F G H I J K L M N O P Q R S
T U V W X Y Z O 1 2 3 4 5 6 7 8 9 ! ? $ % &
( ) { } * : ; " "
THE QUICK BROWN FOX JUMPS OVER THE LAZY DOG.

Lithos™ Light
Sans Serif | Uniform Weight | Square Capital Proportion | Modulation |

Linotype Library GmbH
www.linotype.com
info@linotype.com
+49 (0) 6172 484.418

A A B B C C D D E E F F G G H H I I J J K K L L M M
N N O O P P Q Q R R S S T T U U V V W W X X Y Y
Z Z 0 1 2 3 4 5 6 7 8 9 ! ? @ # $ % & * ( ) { } : ; " "
THE QUICK BROWN FOX JUMPS OVER THE LAZY DOG.

Herculanum™ Roman
Sans Serif | Medium Weight | Caps with Selected Alternates | Brush Influence |

Linotype Library GmbH
www.linotype.com
info@linotype.com
+49 (0) 6172 484.418

A B C D E F G H I J K L M N O P Q R S T U V
W X Y Z 0 1 2 3 4 5 6 7 8 9 ! ? & @ # $ % * : ; "

THE QUICK BROWN FOX JUMPS OVER THE LAZY DOG.

Minerva Display Caelatura
Archaic Serif | All Caps | Lighter Medium Weight |

T.26 Digital Type Foundry
www.t26.com
info@t26.com
888.T26.FONT

A B C D E F G H I J K K L M N O P Q R S T
U V W X Y Z 0 1 2 3 4 5 6 7 8 9 ! ? & $ % : ; "

THE QUICK BROWN FOX JUMPS OVER THE LAZY DOG.

RTF Cadmus
Archaic Sans Serif | Uniform Lighter Medium Weight |

P22 Type Foundry
www.p22.com
p22@p22.com
800.P22.5080

A B C D E F G H I J K L M N O P Q R S T
U V W X Y Z 0 1 2 3 4 5 6 7 8 9 ! ? @ # $ % &
* ( ) { } : ; " "
THE QUICK BROWN FOX JUMPS OVER THE LAZY DOG.

Pompeijana™
Serif | Medium Weight | Pronounced Contrast | Rustic Influence | Brush Detail |

Linotype Library GmbH
www.linotype.com
info@linotype.com
+49 (0) 6172 484.418

A a B b C c D d E e F f G g H h I i J j K k L l M m N n
O o P p Q q R r S s T t U u V v W w X x Y y Z z 0 1
2 3 4 5 6 7 8 9 ! ? @ # $ % & * ( ) { } : ; " "
The quick brown fox jumps over the lazy dog.

Albertus™ Roman
Serif-Sans Serif Hybrid | Medium Weight | Varied Contrast | Modulation |

Linotype Library GmbH
www.linotype.com
info@linotype.com
+49 (0) 6172 484.418

ABCDEFGHIJKLMNOPQRSTUVWX
YZ0123456789!9 ◂ $%&* ():; " "

THE QUICK BROWN FOX JUMPS OVER THE LAZY DOG.

D

Augustea Open™
Serif | Square Capitals |
Light Weight | Inline Detail |

Linotype Library GmbH
www.linotype.com
info@linotype.com
+49 (0) 6172 484.418

AaBbCcDdEefGgHhIiJjKkLlMm
NnOoPpQqRrSsTtUuVvWwXxYy
Zz0123456789!?@#$%℮*(){}:; ""
The quick brown fox jumps over the lazy dog.

D *t*

ITC Braganza™
Graphic Script | Medium
Weight | Pronounced Contrast |
Cursive Influence |

Linotype Library GmbH
www.linotype.com
info@linotype.com
+49 (0) 6172 484.418

A B C D E F G H I J K L M N O P
Q R S T U V W X Y Z 0 1 2 3 4 5 6 7 8
9 ! ? $ % & * ( ) { } : ; " "

THE QUICK BROWN FOX JUMPS OVER THE LAZY DOG.

D

Castellar™ Roman
Serif | Medium Weight |
Pronounced Contrast | Inline
Detail | Sharp Serifs |

Linotype Library GmbH
www.linotype.com
info@linotype.com
+49 (0) 6172 484.418

A B C D E F G H I J K L M N O P Q
R S T U V W X Y Z 0 1 2 3 4 5 6 7 8 9 ! ?
$ % & * ( ) { } : ; " "

THE QUICK BROWN FOX JUMPS OVER THE LAZY DOG.

D

Charlemagne™
Serif | Medium Weight |
Moderate Contrast |
Sharp Serifs |

Linotype Library GmbH
www.linotype.com
info@linotype.com
+49 (0) 6172 484.418

AaBbCcDdEeFfGgHhIiJjKkLlMm
NnOoPpQqRrSsTtUuVvWwXxYy
Zz0123456789!?@#$%&*(){}:; " "
The quick brown fox jumps over the lazy dog.

D *t*

Codex™
Serif-Sans Serif Hybrid |
Medium Weight | Noticeable
Contrast | Cursive Influence |

Linotype Library GmbH
www.linotype.com
info@linotype.com
+49 (0) 6172 484.418

AaBbCcDdEeFfGgHhIiJjKkLlMmNnOoPpQqRrSsTt
UuVvWwXxYyZz0123456789!?H($%&*( ) MV:; " "

The quick brown fox jumps over the lazy dog.

D

Etruscan™
Sans Serif | Light Weight |
Condensed | Lapidary
Influence | Glyphic Detail |

Linotype Library GmbH
www.linotype.com
info@linotype.com
+49 (0) 6172 484.418

ABCDEFGHIJKLMNOPQRSTUVWXYZ
0123456789!?@#$%&*(){}:;" "

THE QUICK BROWN FOX JUMPS OVER THE LAZY DOG.

D

Persephone NF
Archaic Sans Serif |
Uniform Medium Weight |
Slight Modulation |

Nick's Fonts
www.nicksfonts.com

A a B b C c D d E e F f G g H h I i J j K k L l M m N n O o
P p Q q R r S s T t U u V v W w X x Y y Z z 0 1 2 3 4 5 6 7
8 9 ! ? @ # $ % & * ( ) { } : ; " "
The quick brown fox jumps over the lazy dog.

D   t

Koch™ Antiqua
Serif | Light Weight | Notable
Contrast | Small x-Height |
Upper Stroke Emphasis |

Linotype Library GmbH
www.linotype.com
info@linotype.com
+49 (0) 6172 484.418

ABCDEFGHIJKLMNOPQRSTU
VWXYZ0123456789!?$%&*(){}
:;" "

THE QUICK BROWN FOX JUMPS OVER THE LAZY DOG.

D

Lithos™ Bold
Sans Serif | Uniform Weight |
Square Capital Proportion |
Modulation |

Linotype Library GmbH
www.linotype.com
info@linotype.com
+49 (0) 6172 484.418

ABCDEFGHIJKLMNOPQRSTUV
WXYZ0123456789!?&#$%:;"

THE QUICK BROWN FOX JUMPS OVER THE LAZY DOG.

D

RTF Lancelot Title
Archaic Serif | All Caps |
Moderate Contrast |

P22 Type Foundry
www.p22.com
p22@p22.com
800.P22.5080

A A B C D E E F G G H I J J K K L M N O P P
Q R R S T U U V W X Y Z 0 1 2 3 4 5 6 7 8 9 ! ?
@ # $ % & * ( ) { } : ; " "
THE QUICK BROWN FOX JUMPS OVER THE LAZY DOG.

D

Moonglow™ Std Regular
Sans Serif | Medium Weight |
Modulation | Inline Stroke |

Linotype Library GmbH
www.linotype.com
info@linotype.com
+49 (0) 6172 484.418

A a B b C c D d E e F f G g H h I i J j K k L l M m N n
O o P p Q q R r S s T t U u V v W w X x Y y Z z 0 1
2 3 4 5 6 7 8 9 ! ? @ # $ % & * ( ) { } : ; " "
The quick brown fox jumps over the lazy dog.

D   t

ITC Motter Sparta™
Sans Serif | Bold Weight |
Graphic Brush Detail

Linotype Library GmbH
www.linotype.com
info@linotype.com
+49 (0) 6172 484.418

A a B b C c D d E e F f G g H h I i J j K k L l M m N n O o P p Q q R r
S s T t U u V v W w X x Y y Z z 0 1 2 3 4 5 6 7 8 9 ! ? @ # $ % & *
( ) { } : ; " "

The quick brown fox jumps over the lazy dog.

ITC Noovo™ Light
Sans Serif | Light Weight |
Condensed |
Textured Contour |

Linotype Library GmbH
www.linotype.com
info@linotype.com
+49 (0) 6172 484.418

a b c d e f g h i j k l m n o p q r s t u
v w x y z 0 1 2 3 4 5 6 7 8 9 ! ? $ % & * ( ) { } : ; "

the quick brown fox jumps over the lazy dog.

Omnia™
Serif | Bold Weight | Unicase |
Uncial Influence |
Noticeable Contrast |

Linotype Library GmbH
www.linotype.com
info@linotype.com
+49 (0) 6172 484.418

A A B B C C D D E E F F G G H H I I J J K K L L
M M N N O O P P Q Q R R S S T T U U V V W W
X X Y Y Z Z O 1 2 3 4 5 6 7 8 9 ! ? & # $ % *

THE QUICK BROWN FOX JUMPS OVER THE LAZY DOG.

The Boustrophedon Plain
Archaic Sans Serif |
Greek Lapidary Detail |
Caps with Alternates |

Garage Fonts Type Foundry
www.garagefonts.com
info@garagefonts.com
800.681.9375

A B C D E F G H I J K L M N O P Q R S T
U V W X Y Z 0 1 2 3 4 5 6 7 8 9 ! ? $ % & ( )
{ } : ; " "   *

THE QUICK BROWN FOX JUMPS OVER THE LAZY DOG.

Rusticana™
Sans Serif | Medium Weight |
Square Capital Proportion |
Modulation |

Linotype Library GmbH
www.linotype.com
info@linotype.com
+49 (0) 6172 484.418

A a B b C c D d E e F f G g H h I i J j K k L l M m N n O o
P p Q q R r S s T t U u V v W w X x Y y Z z 0 1 2 3 4 5
6 7 8 9 ! ? @ # $ % & * ( ) { } : ; " "

The quick brown fox jumps over the lazy dog.

Silentium® Pro Roman 1
Serif | Bold Weight |
Pronounced Contrast |
Brush Detail |
Slight Italic Posture |

Linotype Library GmbH
www.linotype.com
info@linotype.com
+49 (0) 6172 484.418

Λ Λ B b C c D d E ε F ϝ G ç H h I i J j K k L l M m
N и O o P p Q q R r S s T t U u V v W w X x Y y
Z z 0 1 2 3 4 5 6 7 8 9 ! ? @ # $ % & * ( ) { } : ; " "

The quick brown fox jumps over the lazy dog.

Linotype Syntax™ Lapidar
Serif Text
Serif | Medium Weight | Varied
Posture | Caps with Alternates |

Linotype Library GmbH
www.linotype.com
info@linotype.com
+49 (0) 6172 484.418

Archaic Color

Given the simple technology and craft of the ancient world, archaic color reflects the use of natural materials in building, imagery, and the making of objects. Colors evocative of stone, clay, animal skins, and furs—warm neutrals, chalky grays and ivories, terra-cotta, umber, ochre, and black—are supported by colors from early metalwork in iron, copper, bronze, and gold. Additionally, however, rich hues of blue, green, deep red, and violet are important components of an archaic palette, referring to pigments developed from minerals and plants. With natural, earthy tones as a base, these more saturated colors add vitality and contrast.

Sample Color Combinations

0 C	
5 M	
10 Y	
22 K	

0 C	
0 M	
0 Y	
35 K	

36 C	
35 M	
55 Y	
0 K	

15 C	
57 M	
84 Y	
61 K	

5 C	
5 M	
12 Y	
0 K	

2 C	
2 M	
10 Y	
13 K	

0 C	
50 M	
100 Y	
41 K	

100 C	
66 M	
0 Y	
42 K	

0 C	
100 M	
100 Y	
56 K	

81 C	
0 M	
100 Y	
73 K	

European feudal society—following the fall of Rome and continuing up through the late Gothic period, prior to the Renaissance—provides the context for medieval type and color. The decorative manuscript work of scribes, heraldic symbols, pageantry, and ritual inform the visual style of this category.

Medieval

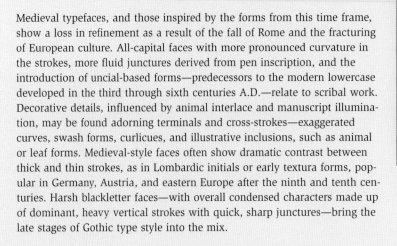

Medieval typefaces, and those inspired by the forms from this time frame, show a loss in refinement as a result of the fall of Rome and the fracturing of European culture. All-capital faces with more pronounced curvature in the strokes, more fluid junctures derived from pen inscription, and the introduction of uncial-based forms—predecessors to the modern lowercase developed in the third through sixth centuries A.D.—relate to scribal work. Decorative details, influenced by animal interlace and manuscript illumination, may be found adorning terminals and cross-strokes—exaggerated curves, swash forms, curlicues, and illustrative inclusions, such as animal or leaf forms. Medieval-style faces often show dramatic contrast between thick and thin strokes, as in Lombardic initials or early textura forms, popular in Germany, Austria, and eastern Europe after the ninth and tenth centuries. Harsh blackletter faces—with overall condensed characters made up of dominant, heavy vertical strokes with quick, sharp junctures—bring the late stages of Gothic type style into the mix.

Packaging *top, and detail*

Love Communications
Preston Wood, Amy Veach,
Scott Greer
Salt Lake City [UT] *USA*

ABCDEFGHIJKLMNOPQ
RSTUVWXYZ&

THE QUICK BROWN FOX JUMPS OVER THE LAZY

D

LTC Jacobean Initials B
Lombardic Initials | Caps |
Lacking Numerals |

P22 Type Foundry
www.p22.com
p22@p22.com
800.P22.5080

A a B b C c D ∂ E e F f G g H h I i J j K k L l
M m N n O o P p Q q R r S s T t U u V v W w
X x Y y Z z 0 1 2 3 4 5 6 7 8 9 ! ? @ # $ %
& * ( ) { } : ; " "

The quick brown fox jumps over the lazy dog.

D *t*

Neue Hammer Unziale™ 1
Regular
Sans Serif | Moderate Contrast |
Medium Weight | Sharp
Terminals | Uncial Influence |

Linotype Library GmbH
www.linotype.com
info@linotype.com
+49 (0) 6172 484.418

A a B b C c D ∂ E e F f G g H h I i J j K k L M m
N n O o P p Q q R r S s T t U u V v W w X x Y y
Z z 0 1 2 3 4 5 6 7 8 9 ! ? @ # & : ; " "

The quick brown fox jumps over the lazy dog.

D

P22 Elven
Half Uncial–Sans Serif Hybrid |
Lighter Medium Weight |

P22 Type Foundry
www.p22.com
p22@p22.com
800.P22.5080

a a b b c c d d e e f f g g h h i i j j k k l l m m n n o o
p p q q R R s s T T u u v v w w x x g y z z 0 1 2 3 4 5 6
7 8 9 ! ? : ; " "

the quick brown fox jumps over the lazy dog.

D

P22 Kells Round
Half Uncial–Sans Serif Hybrid |
Lighter Medium Weight |

P22 Type Foundry
www.p22.com
p22@p22.com
800.P22.5080

D

P22 Amelia
Cloister Initials |
Floral Frame Detail |
Lacking Numerals |

P22 Type Foundry
www.p22.com
p22@p22.com
800.P22.5080

A a B b C c D d E e f f G g H h I i J j K k L l M m N n O o
P p Q q R r S s T t U u V v W w X x Y y Z z 0 1 2 3 4 5 6 7
8 9 ! ? & @ $: ; " "

The quick brown fox jumps over the lazy dog.

D *t*

P22 Morris Troy
Lombardic–Uncial Hybrid |
Medium Weight |
Pronounced Contrast |

P22 Type Foundry
www.p22.com
p22@p22.com

P22 Morris Ornaments
Lombardic–Cloister Initial Hybrid | Caps with Alternates |

P22 Type Foundry
www.p22.com
p22@p22.com
800.P22.5080

The quick brown fox jumps over the lazy dog.

Schwarzkopf Oldstyle
Fraktur | Medium Weight | Pronounced Contrast |

P22 Type Foundry
www.p22.com
p22@p22.com
800.P22.5080

LTC Jacobean Initials A
Cloister Initials | Caps | Floral Frame Detail |

P22 Type Foundry
www.p22.com
p22@p22.com
800.P22.5080

The quick brown fox jumps over the lazy dog.

P22 Dwiggins Uncial
Uncial-Serif Hybrid | Pronounced Contrast | Medium Weight |

P22 Type Foundry
www.p22.com
p22@p22.com
800.P22.5080

LTC Jacobean Initials C
Lombardic Initials | Caps in Reverse | Floral Frame Detail |

P22 Type Foundry
www.p22.com
p22@p22.com
800.P22.5080

The quick brown fox jumps over the lazy dog.

Almonda
Stylized Sans Serif | Fraktur Details | Bolder Medium Weight |

T.26 Digital Type Foundry
www.t26.com
info@t26.com
888.T26.FONT

𝔄𝔞𝔅𝔟ℭ𝔠𝔇𝔡𝔈𝔢𝔉𝔣𝔊𝔤ℌ𝔥𝔍𝔦𝔍𝔧𝔎𝔨𝔏𝔩𝔐𝔪
𝔑𝔫𝔒𝔬𝔓𝔭𝔔𝔮ℜ𝔯𝔖𝔰𝔗𝔱𝔘𝔲𝔙𝔳𝔚𝔴𝔛𝔵𝔜𝔶
𝔷ʒ0123456789!?@#$%&*(){}:;""
The quick brown fox jumps over the lazy dog.

D

Fette Fraktur™
Graphic | Black Weight | Pronounced Contrast | Blackletter Gothic | Curved Shoulders |

Linotype Library GmbH
www.linotype.com
info@linotype.com
+49 (0) 6172 484.418

AaßbCcDdEeFfGgHkIiJjKkLlmΛnOo
PpQqRrSsTtUuVvWwXxYyZʒ0123456
789!?8@*$%*::"

The quick brown fox jumps over the lazy dog.

D *t*

Text Regular
Stylized Sans Serif | Fraktur Brush Details | Condensed | Medium Weight |

T.26 Digital Type Foundry
www.t26.com
info@t26.com
888.T26.FONT

AaBbCcDdEeFfGgHhIiJjKkLlMmNn
OoPpQqRrSsTtUuVvWwXxYyZz01
23456789!?& #$%*:;"

The quick brown fox jumps over the lazy dog.

D *t*

RTF Alexander Quill
Stylized Sans Serif | Moderate Contrast | Medium Weight |

P22 Type Foundry
www.p22.com
p22@p22.com
800.P22.5080

𝔄𝔞𝔅𝔟ℭ𝔠𝔇𝔡𝔈𝔢𝔉𝔣𝔊𝔤ℌ𝔥𝔍𝔦𝔍𝔧𝔎𝔨𝔏𝔩𝔐𝔪
𝔘𝔫𝔒𝔬𝔓𝔭𝔔𝔮ℜ𝔯𝔖𝔰𝔗𝔱𝔘𝔲𝔙𝔳𝔚𝔴𝔛𝔵𝔜𝔶
𝔷ʒ0123456789!?@ß§%&*(){}:;""
The quick brown fox jumps over the lazy dog.

D

Fette Gotisch
Graphic | Black Weight | Pronounced Contrast | Blackletter Gothic | Angled Shoulders |

Linotype Library GmbH
www.linotype.com
info@linotype.com
+49 (0) 6172 484.418

AaßbCcDdEeFfGgHhIiJjKkLlMmNn
OoPpQqRrSsTtUuVvWwXxYyZz01
23456789!?&@#$%*:;"

The quick brown fox jumps over the lazy dog.

D *t*

RTF Fellowship Normal
Stylized Sans Serif | Moderate Contrast | Slight Italic Posture |

P22 Type Foundry
www.p22.com
p22@p22.com
800.P22.5080

ĀĀBbCDDEFGĦIIJKLMNNOQPQ9RRSST
UVVWXYZ0123456789!?K⊠⚥:;""

D

P22 Kells Square
Stylized Wedge Serif | Glyphic Detail | All Caps with Selected Alternates |

P22 Type Foundry
www.p22.com
p22@p22.com
800.P22.5080

THE QUICK BROWN FOX JUMPS OVER THE LAZY DOG.

A a B b e c D d E e F f G g h I i J j K k L l M m
N n O o P p Q q R r S s T t U u V v W w X x Y y Z z
0 1 2 3 4 5 6 7 8 9 ! ? @ # $ % & * ( ) { } : ; " "
The quick brown fox jumps over the lazy dog.

D

Beneta™ Regular
*Graphic Sans Serif | Bold
Weight | Pronounced Contrast |
Brush Influence |*

Linotype Library GmbH
www.linotype.com
info@linotype.com
+49 (0) 6172 484.418

A A A B B C D E F G G H H H I J K L L
M M N N O P Q Q R R R S S T U U V W U
X Y Z 0 1 2 3 4 5 6 7 8 9 ! ? $ % & [ ] ( ) * : ;

THE QUICK BROWN FOX JUMPS OVER THE LAZY DOG.

D

Aquitaine™ Initials
*Serif | Bold Weight |
Pronounced Contrast |
Inline Detail |*

Linotype Library GmbH
www.linotype.com
info@linotype.com
+49 (0) 6172 484.418

A a B b C c D d E e F f G g H h I i J j K k L l M m
N n O o P p Q q R r S s T t U u V v W w X x Y y
Z z 0 1 2 3 4 5 6 7 8 9 ! ? & @ # $ % * : ; "

THE QUICK BROWN FOX JUMPS OVER THE LAZY DOG.

D

Archangel
*Stylized Sans Serif |
Pronounced Contrast |
Caps and Small Caps |*

T.26 Digital Type Foundry
www.t26.com
info@t26.com
888.T26.FONT

A a b b c c d d E e F f G g b h I i j j k k L l m m
n n o o p p q q R r s s t t u u v v w w x x y
z z 0 1 2 3 4 5 6 7 8 9 ! ? & @ # $ % * : ; "

THE QUICK BROWN fox jumps over THE lazy DOG.

D *t*

Idiosynoptium Bold
*Stylized Sans Serif | Moderate
Contrast | Uniform Cap and
Lowercase Height |*

T.26 Digital Type Foundry
www.t26.com
info@t26.com
888.T26.FONT

A a B b C c D e E f F g G h H i I j J k K l L m m n n o o
p p Q q R r S s T t u u V v W w X x Y z Z 0 1 2 3 4 5
6 7 8 9 ! ? @ s _ % c r a ( ) { } : ; " ß
The quick brown fox jumps over the lazy dog.

D

**Linotype Textur™
Lombardisch DFR**
*Graphic | Bold Weight |
Inline and Linear Detail |
Lombardic Influence |*

Linotype Library GmbH
www.linotype.com
info@linotype.com
+49 (0) 6172 484.418

A a B b C c D d E e F f G g H h I i J j K k L l M m n N
O o P p Q q R r S s T t U u V v W w X x Y y Z z 0 1
2 3 4 5 6 7 8 9 ! ? @ # $ % & * ( ) { } : ; " "
The quick brown fox jumps over the lazy dog.

D *t*

Carolina™
*Serif | Lighter Medium Weight |
Slight Italic Posture |*

Linotype Library GmbH
www.linotype.com
info@linotype.com
+49 (0) 6172 484.418

Medieval Color

Most of feudal society during the Middle Ages was governed by the interaction of competing lords and kings and by the influence of the Catholic Church. The symbolic coloring that these groups used for identification in battle and ritual contributes to the medieval palette: red, golden yellow, royal blue, forest and emerald greens, black, and white. The nobility of the period is reflected in the color violet, a rare and expensive pigment to procure at the time. The Church, similarly, is evoked through violet, red and, especially, gold and white, the colors of the popes. Rich reds and burgundies, mid-value browns, ochre, and desaturated green derive from textiles and tapestries, adding depth to the striking heraldic palette of the aristocracy.

Sample Color Combinations

0	C	
100	M	
100	Y	
10	K	

0	C
20	M
100	Y
0	K

100	C
45	M
0	Y
0	K

100	C
68	M
100	Y
0	K

100	C
27	M
100	Y
0	K

78	C
100	M
0	Y
20	K

0	C
32	M
100	Y
35	K

24	C
100	M
0	Y
65	K

0	C
58	M
78	Y
52	K

14	C
0	M
0	Y
26	K

In Europe, the late thirteenth through early sixteenth centuries were marked by a tremendous expansion in scholarly activity. Following the rediscovery of ancient learning lost in the Middle Ages, this burst of creativity affected literature, science, and the arts—among them, type design. A shift from an agrarian, feudal society toward a culture of commerce, exploration, and humanism is reflected in type and color of increased richness, subtlety, and refinement.

Renaissance

Renaissance type styles include Gothic styles still in use after the Medieval period—frakturs, textura, and blackletter forms—as well as humanistic styles incorporating Carolingian forms into the new modern alphabet of fifty-two characters: the upper- and lowercase serifs. These new faces, which would eventually be known as oldstyle, refer to archaic capital structure in their proportions, with some characters markedly wider than others, but integrate the soft, rounded pen strokes of uncials and minuscules. Renaissance oldstyle faces are remarkably organic, with fluid shading and minimal contrast between thick and thin strokes, a small x-height in the lowercase, teardrop, brush-formed serifs, and soft, rounded terminals. Their curved characters, in both upper- and lowercase, show a pronounced oblique axis, further evidence of their derivation from the brush. Overall, Renaissance faces tend to be more extended than those considered conventionally regular in width. Italics, which first made their appearance in the fourteenth century, are also generally useful for imparting a Renaissance quality to typography, especially if they exhibit scriptlike junctures.

Magazine Page Spread
top, and detail, bottom

Flat
Petter Ringbom, Tsia Carson
New York City *USA*

A a B b C c D d E e F f G g H h I i J j K k L l M m
N n O o P p Q q R r S s T t U u V v W w X x Y y Z z
0 1 2 3 4 5 6 7 8 9 ! ? @ # $ % & * ( ) { } : ; " "
The quick brown fox jumps over the lazy dog.

Alcuin™ Regular
Serif | Medium Weight |
Modulation |
Moderate Contrast |

Linotype Library GmbH
www.linotype.com
info@linotype.com
+49 (0) 6172 484.418

A a B b C c D d E e F f G g H h I i J j K k L l M m N n
O o P p Q q R r S s T t U u V v W w X x Y y Z z 0 1 2 3
4 5 6 7 8 9 ! ? @ # $ % & ★ ( ) { } : ; " "
The quick brown fox jumps over the lazy dog.

Bembo™ Italic OsF
Serif | Medium Weight |
Moderate Contrast |
Slightly Condensed |

Linotype Library GmbH
www.linotype.com
info@linotype.com
+49 (0) 6172 484.418

[Script typeface sample: alphabet A-Z in decorative Fraktur/script style]
The quick brown fox jumps over the lazy dog.

P22 Elizabethan
Graphic Script | Fraktur Detail |
Medium Weight |

P22 Type Foundry
www.p22.com
p22@p22.com
800.P22.5080

A a B b C c D d E e F f G g H h Ii Jj K k L l M m N n O o Þ p
Q q R r S s T t U u V v W w X x Y y Z z 0 1 2 3 4 5 6 7 8 9 ! ? @ #
& : ; " "
The quick brown fox jumps over the lazy dog.

P22 Goudy Aries
Serif | Lombardic Detail |
Moderate Contrast |
Medium Weight |

P22 Type Foundry
www.p22.com
p22@p22.com
800.P22.5080

A a B b C c D d E e F f G g H h I i J j K k L l M m N n O o
P p Q q R r S s T t U u V v W w X x Y y Z z 0 1 2 3 4 5 6 7
8 9 ! ? @ # $ % & * ( ) { } : ; " "
The quick brown fox jumps over the lazy dog.

Linotype Gaius™ Regular
Serif | Light Weight |
Noticeable Contrast | Brush
Detail | Slight Italic Posture |

Linotype Library GmbH
www.linotype.com
info@linotype.com
+49 (0) 6172 484.418

A a B b c c D d E e F f G g H h I i J j K k L l M m N n O o
P p Q q R r S s T t U u V v W w X x Y y Z z 0 1 2 3 4
5 6 7 8 9 ! ? & @ $: ; " "
The quick brown fox jumps over the lazy dog.

P22 Operina Romano
Serif | Italic Lowercase |
Medium Weight |
Slightly Condensed |

P22 Type Foundry
www.p22.com
p22@p22.com
800.P22.5080

A a B b C c D d E e F f G g H h I i J j K k L l M m N n O o
P p Q q R r S s T t U u V v W w X x Y y Z z 0 1 2 3 4
5 6 7 8 9 ! ? & @ $: ; " "

The quick brown fox jumps over the lazy dog.

D

P22 Operina Corsivo
Serif | Slight Italic Overall |
Swash Detail | Medium Weight |
Pronounced Descenders |

P22 Type Foundry
www.p22.com
p22@p22.com
800.P22.5080

A a B b C c D d E e F f G g H h I i J j K k L l M m N n
O o P p Q q R r S s T t U u V v W w X x Y y Z z 0 1 2 3
4 5 6 7 8 9 ! ? & @ $: ; " "

The quick brown fox jumps over the lazy dog.

D **T**

P22 Tynedale
Stylized Serif | Moderate
Contrast | Pronounced Serifs |
Light Weight |

P22 Type Foundry
www.p22.com
p22@p22.com
800.P22.5080

A a B b C c D d E e F f G g H h I i J j K k L l M m
N n O o P p Q q R r S s T t U u V v W w X x Y y Z z
*0 1 2 3 4 5 6 7 8 9 ! ? @ # $ % & * ( ) { } : ; " "*

The quick brown fox jumps over the lazy dog.

D **T**

ITC Galliard® Italic
Serif | Medium Weight |
Moderate Contrast |
Abrupt Joints |

Linotype Library GmbH
www.linotype.com
info@linotype.com
+49 (0) 6172 484.418

A a B b C c D d E e F f G g H h I i J j K k L l M m N n
O o P p Q q R r S s T t U u V v W w X x Y y Z z 0 1 2 3
*4 5 6 7 8 9 ! ? @ # $ % & * ( ) { } : ; " "*

The quick brown fox jumps over the lazy dog.

D **T**

Garamond™ #3 Italic OsF
Serif | Medium Weight |
Soft Terminals | Small x-Height |
Reduced Contrast |

Linotype Library GmbH
www.linotype.com
info@linotype.com
+49 (0) 6172 484.418

A A B B C C D D E E F F G G H H I I J
K K L L M M N N O O P P Q Q R R S S T T
U U V V W W X X Y Y Z Z

THE QUICK BROWN FOX JUMPS OVER THE LAZY DOG

D

P22 Durer Caps
Graphic | Carolingian
Roman Caps |
Sketched Alternates |

P22 Type Foundry
www.p22.com
p22@p22.com
800.P22.5080

A a B b C c D d E e F f G g H h I i J j K k L l M m
N n O o P p Q q R r S s T t U u V v W w X x Y y Z z
0 1 2 3 4 5 6 7 8 9 ! ? & @ # $ % * : ; "

The quick brown fox jumps over the lazy dog.

D *t*

LTC Goudy Thirty
Stylized Serif | Textura Details |
Moderate Contrast |

P22 Type Foundry
www.p22.com
p22@p22.com
800.P22.5080

A a B b C c D d E e F f G g H h I i J j K k L l M m
N n O o P p Q q R r S s T t U u V v W w X x Y y
Z z 0 1 2 3 4 5 6 7 8 9 ! ? & @ # $ % * : ; ”

The quick brown fox jumps over the lazy dog.

D T

Telegdi
*Serif | Moderate Contrast |
Medium Weight |*

P22 Type Foundry
www.p22.com
p22@p22.com
800.P22.5080

A a B b C c D d E e F f G g H h I i F j K k L l M m N n
O o P p Q q R r S s T t U u V v W w X x Y y Z z 0 1 2 3
4 5 6 7 8 9 ! ? & @ # $ % * : ; ”

The quick brown fox jumps over the lazy dog.

D T

Telegdi Italic
*Serif | Moderate Contrast |
Moderate Posture |*

P22 Type Foundry
www.p22.com
p22@p22.com
800.P22.5080

A a B b C c D d E e F f G g H h I i J j K k L l M m N n O o P p
Q q R r S s T t U u V v W w X x Y y Z z 0 1 2 3 4 5 6 7 8 9 ! ?
& @ $: ; " "

The quick brown fox jumps over the lazy dog.

D T

P22 Latimer
*Serif | Lombard and Fraktur
Detail | Condensed | Lighter
Medium Weight |*

P22 Type Foundry
www.p22.com
p22@p22.com
800.P22.5080

A a B b C c D d E e F f G g H h I i J j K k L l
M m N n O o P p Q q R r S s T t U u V v W w
X x Y y Z z 0 1 2 3 4 5 6 7 8 9 ! ? & @ $: ; " "

The quick brown fox jumps over the lazy dog.

D t

P22 Aragon
*Stylized Serif | Swash Details |
Medium Weight |*

P22 Type Foundry
www.p22.com
p22@p22.com
800.P22.5080

A a B b C c D d E e F f G g H h I i J j K k L l M m
N n O o P p Q q R r S s T t U u V v W w X x Y y
Z z 0 1 2 3 4 5 6 7 8 9 ! ? @ # $ % & * ( ) { } : ;

The quick brown fox jumps over the lazy dog.

D T

ITC Cerigo™ Medium
*Serif | Medium Weight |
Brush Influence |
Moderate Contrast |*

Linotype Library GmbH
www.linotype.com
info@linotype.com
+49 (0) 6172 484.418

A a B b C c D d E e F f G g H h I i J j K k L l
M m N n O o P p Q q R r S s T t U u V v W w
X x Y y Z z 0 1 2 3 4 5 6 7 8 9 ! ? & @ $: ; " "

The quick brown fox jumps over the lazy dog.

D t

P22 Avocet
*Serif | Swash Details | Light
Weight | Moderate Italic Posture |*

P22 Type Foundry
www.p22.com
p22@p22.com
800.P22.5080

A a B b C c D d E e F f G g H h I i J j K k L l M m N n
O o P p Q q R r S s T t U u V v W w X x Y y Z z 0 1
2 3 4 5 6 7 8 9 ! ? @ # $ % & * ( ) { } : ; " "
The quick brown fox jumps over the lazy dog.

D **T**

ITC Giovanni® Book
Serif | Medium Weight |
Brush Detail |
Moderate Contrast |

Linotype Library GmbH
www.linotype.com
info@linotype.com
+49 (0) 6172 484.418

A a B b C c D d E e F f G g H h I i J j K k L l M m N n O o
P p Q q R r S s T t U u V v W w X x Y y Z z 0 1 2 3 4 5 6 7 8
*9 ! ? & @ # $ % * : ; "*

The quick brown fox jumps over the lazy dog.

D **t**

P22 Cilati Regular
Serif | Condensed |
Moderate Italic Posture |
Moderate Contrast |

P22 Type Foundry
www.p22.com
p22@p22.com
800.P22.5080

A a B b C c D d E e F f G g H h I i J j K k L l M m
N n O o P p Q q R r S s T t U u V v W w X x Y y Z z
0 1 2 3 4 5 6 7 8 9 ! ? & @ # $ % * : ; "

The Quick Brown Fox Jumps Over the Lazy Dog.

D

P22 Cilati Swash Small Caps
Serif | Condensed |
Moderate Italic Posture |
Script Influence |

P22 Type Foundry
www.p22.com
p22@p22.com
800.P22.5080

A a B b C c D d E e F f G g H h I i J j K k L l M m
N n O o P p Q q R r S s T t U u V v W w X x Y y
Z z 0 1 2 3 4 5 6 7 8 9 ! ? @ # $ % & * ( ) { } : ;
The quick brown fox jumps over the lazy dog.

D **T**

**ITC Mendoza Roman®
Medium**
Serif | Heavier Medium
Weight | Reduced Contrast |
Soft Terminals |

Linotype Library GmbH
www.linotype.com
info@linotype.com
+49 (0) 6172 484.418

A a B b C c D d E e F f G g H h I i J j K k L l M m
N n O o P p Q q R r S s T t U u V v W w X x Y y Z z
0 1 2 3 4 5 6 7 8 9 ! ? @ # $ % & * ( ) { } : ; " "
The quick brown fox jumps over the lazy dog.

D

San Marco™
Sans Serif | Bold Weight |
Gothic Influence |

Linotype Library GmbH
www.linotype.com
info@linotype.com
+49 (0) 6172 484.418

A a B b C c D d E e F f G g H h I i J j K k L l M m N n
O o P p Q q R r S s T t U u V v W w X x Y y Z z 0 1
2 3 4 5 6 7 8 9 ! ? @ # $ % & * ( ) { } : ; " "
The quick brown fox jumps over the lazy dog.

D **T**

Linotype Trajanus™ Roman
Serif | Medium Weight |
Sharp Joints |
Noticeable Contrast |

Linotype Library GmbH
www.linotype.com
info@linotype.com
+49 (0) 6172 484.418

Renaissance Color

Renaissance innovation developed, in part, from an expansion in travel and commerce between Europe and the East brought on by the Crusades; Renaissance color, therefore, includes Eastern and Islamic influence on the core European color scheme of heraldry and ritual. The base color family of red, yellow, blue, green, and violet from the medieval color palette is refined and enriched by desaturating and deepening them, producing an array of burgundies, golden ochres, deeper blues, forest and hunter greens, and burgundy violets of a smokier, more refined value. Exotic rust brown, umber, and olive allude to the spice trade, while parchmentlike neutral, deep burgundy violet, and warm charcoal gray hint at the scholarly aspect of the Renaissance period.

Sample Color Combinations

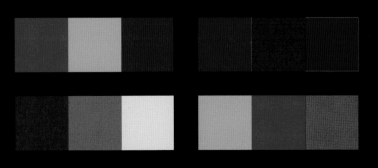

>	
0 C	
100 M	
100 Y	
30 K	

>
0 C
30 M
100 Y
10 K

>
100 C
55 M
0 Y
20 K

>
36 C
66 M
100 Y
68 K

>
100 C
75 M
95 Y
0 K

>
100 C
62 M
0 Y
55 K

>
24 C
100 M
10 Y
77 K

>
37 C
29 M
100 Y
44 K

>
10 C
10 M
25 Y
5 K

>
3 C
5 M
10 Y
70 K

The Baroque era expanded on the cultural rebirth of the Renaissance and its humanistic expression in elaborate detail, emotional and refined decoration, and rich, exaggerated color.

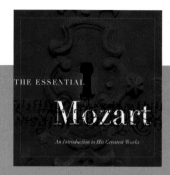

Baroque

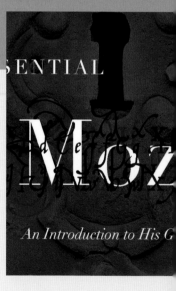

Baroque typography is highly refined and theatrical, evolving the classical forms of Renaissance letters toward a mannered and affected presentation. Textura and script forms with extremes of contrast are common examples of this style, enhanced by highly stylized joints, modulation, and exaggerated ductus in their strokes. Extended serif faces, in which the serifs are larger or more pronounced than in less stylized forms, convey a theatrical quality associated with Baroque architecture: grand, formal, and exuberant. With the Age of Enlightenment following rapidly on the heels of the Baroque era, transitional serif faces—with sharp terminals, pronounced stroke contrast, and a more upright (as opposed to oblique) axis in the curved forms such as O and Q—bring a Baroque quality to the evolution of the serif into its modern form of extreme contrast. Baroque characters tend toward Roman square-capital proportion but are slightly more uniform in overall width relative to each other.

CD Packaging
top, and detail, bottom

STIM Visual Communication
Timothy Samara
New York City *USA*

A B C D E F G H I J K L M N O P Q R S
T U V W X Y Z 0 1 2 3 4 5 6 7 8 9 ! ? $ &
( ) : ; " "

THE QUICK BROWN FOX JUMPS OVER THE LAZY DOG.

D

Smaragd™
Serif | Light Weight | Extreme Contrast | Two-Weight Contour |

Linotype Library GmbH
www.linotype.com
info@linotype.com
+49 (0) 6172 484.418

A a B b C c D d E e F f G g H h I i J j K k L l M m N n O o P p
R r S s T t U u V v W w X x Y y Z z 0 1 2 3 4 5 6 7 8 9 ! ? & @
$: ; " "

The quick brown fox jumps over the lazy dog.

D

P22 Operina Fiore
Serif | More Uniform Weight | Swash Detail | Exaggerated Stems |

P22 Type Foundry
www.p22.com
p22@p22.com
800.P22.5080

A a B b C c D d E e F f G g H h I i J j K k L l M m N n O o
P p Q q R r S s T t U u V v W w X x Y y Z z 0 1 2 3 4 5 6 7
8 9 ! ? @ # $ % & * ( ) { } : ; " "

The quick brown fox jumps over the lazy dog.

D

Linotype Dala™ Text
Serif | Medium Weight | Gothic Influence | Upright Posture | Condensed |

Linotype Library GmbH
www.linotype.com
info@linotype.com
+49 (0) 6172 484.418

A a B b C c D d E e F f G g H h I i J j K k L l M m N n O o P p
Q q R r S s T t U u V v W w X x Y y Z z 0 1 2 3 4 5 6 7 8 9
! ? & @ $: ; " "

The quick brown fox jumps over the lazy dog.

D

La Danse
Script | Swash Caps | Moderate Posture |

P22 Type Foundry
www.p22.com
p22@p22.com
800.P22.5080

A a B b C c D d E e F f G g H h I i J j K k L l M m N n
O o P p Q q R r S s T t U u V v W w X x Y y Z z 0 1 2 3
4 5 6 7 8 9 ! ? $ % & * ( ) : ; " "

The quick brown fox jumps over the lazy dog.

D

Aristocrat™
Script | Light Weight | Double Stroke | Swash Capitals |

Linotype Library GmbH
www.linotype.com
info@linotype.com
+49 (0) 6172 484.418

A a B b C c D d E e F f G g H h I i J j K k L l M m
N n O o P p Q q R r S s T t U u V v W w X x Y y
Z z 0 1 2 3 4 5 6 7 8 9 ! ? @ # $ % & * ( ) { } : ; " "

The quick brown fox jumps over the lazy dog.

D **T**

Linotype Didot™ Roman
Serif | Extreme Contrast | Hairline Serifs |

Linotype Library GmbH
www.linotype.com
info@linotype.com
+49 (0) 6172 484.418

A a B b C c D d E e F f G g H h I i J j K k L l M m
N n O o P p Q q R r S s T t U u V v W w X x Y y Z z
0 1 2 3 4 5 6 7 8 9 ! ? @ # § % & * ( ) p q : : " "

The quick brown fox jumps over the lazy dog.

D

ITC Edwardian Script™ Regular
Script | Medium Weight | Swash Capitals | Noticeable Contrast |

Linotype Library GmbH
www.linotype.com
info@linotype.com
+49 (0) 6172 484.418

A a B b C c D d E e F f G g H h I i J j K k L l M m N n
O o P p Q q R r S s T t U u V v W w X x Y y Z z 0 1 2 3
4 5 6 7 8 9 ! ? w § % § * ( ) ∽ ∽ : ; " "

The quick brown fox jumps over the lazy dog.

D *t*

Greyton™ Script
Script | Bold Weight | Pronounced Contrast | Inline Stroke |

Linotype Library GmbH
www.linotype.com
info@linotype.com
+49 (0) 6172 484.418

A a B b C c D d E e F f G g H h X i J j K k L l
M m N n O o P p Q q R r S s T t U u V v W w
X x Y y Z z 0 1 2 3 4 5 6 7 8 9 ! ? & fi % * [ ] : ;

The quick brown fox jumps over the lazy dog.

D

Boston Blackie
Blackletter | Pronounced Contrast | Heavy Weight | Extended |

Nick's Fonts
www.nicksfonts.com

A a B b C c D d E e F f G g H h I i J j K k L l M m N n O o
P p Q q R r S s T t U u V v W w X x Y y Z z 0 1 2 3 4 5 6 7
8 9 ! ? @ # § % & * ( ) { } : ; " "

The quick brown fox jumps over the lazy dog.

D

Wilhelm Klinspor Gotisch™
Graphic | Bold Weight | Squared Shoulders | Stylized Terminals | Condensed |

Linotype Library GmbH
www.linotype.com
info@linotype.com
+49 (0) 6172 484.418

A a B b C c D d E e F f G g H h I i J j K k L l M m N n
O o P p Q q R r S s T t U u V v W w X x Y y Z z 0 1 2 3 4 5
6 7 8 9 ! ? x w § § § * ( ) a e : : " "

The quick brown fox jumps over the lazy dog.

D

Young Baroque™
Script | Ultra Light Weight | Swash Capitals | Reduced Contrast |

Linotype Library GmbH
www.linotype.com
info@linotype.com
+49 (0) 6172 484.418

A a B b C c D d E e F f G g H h I i J j K k L l M m N n
O o P p Q q R r S s T t U u V v W w X x Y y Z z 0 1 2 3
4 5 6 7 8 9 ! ? @ # § % & * ( ) { } : ; " "

The quick brown fox jumps over the lazy dog.

D

Zapfino™ Three
Script | Light Weight | Moderate Contrast | Small Lowercase | Swash Detail |

Linotype Library GmbH
www.linotype.com
info@linotype.com
+49 (0) 6172 484.418

Baroque Color

Rich jewel tones in the red and violet range—burgundy, deep, bloody red, dark fuchsia, and velvety wine purples—underscore the Baroque palette. Complemented by equally dark yet somewhat desaturated green, bluish green, and ultramarine blues, the palette evokes passion and theatrical ostentation. Deep, saturated golden orange, nearly rustlike in quality, hints at decadence while providing a contrasting warm note to the overall cool backdrop of the Baroque jewel tones.

Sample Color Combinations

>	0 C
	100 M
	62 Y
	72 K

>	36 C
	100 M
	0 Y
	62 K

>	85 C
	100 M
	42 Y
	0 K

>	75 C
	100 M
	52 Y
	38 K

>	70 C
	0 M
	69 Y
	72 K

>	100 C
	32 M
	45 Y
	57 K

>	100 C
	83 M
	35 Y
	0 K

>	0 C
	80 M
	100 Y
	35 K

>	0 C
	100 M
	0 Y
	55 K

>	45 C
	100 M
	95 Y
	17 K

In 1856, English style maven Owen Jones published *The Grammar of Ornament*, an enormous tome of dingbats, borders, swags, and ornamental details culled from around the world—epitomizing the wildly varied and decorative aesthetic of Victorian design.

Victorian

Victorian style is a mixture of styles, competing for attention and highly decorative, yet also refined despite the ornamental incongruities that characterize it. Victorian type styles, whether historical examples or modern interpretations of Victorian spirit, show a kind of restraint in proportion, making them somewhat formal, but an overload of stylistic manipulation—severely modulated strokes, extremes of contrast, exaggerated serif proportions, inconsistencies in weight within thick strokes and within thin strokes. Victorian faces tend to be very active in line setting, with overall condensed widths contributing to the activity of ornament with rapid alternation between counters and strokes. Upright script forms, as opposed to canted, or italic, scripts offer a sense of formality repressing a more expressive urge.

Letterhead *details*

Ph.D
Michael Hodgson and
Clive Piercy, Creative Directors
Tammy Dotson, Design
Santa Monica [CA] *USA*

The quick brown fox jumps over the lazy dog.

D

P22 Broadwindsor
Graphic Script |
Moderate Contrast |

P22 Type Foundry
www.p22.com
p22@p22.com
800.P22.5080

The quick brown fox jumps over the lazy dog.

D

Excelsior Script™
Script | Light Weight | Moderate
Contrast | Stylized Terminals
and Joints | Condensed

Linotype Library GmbH
www.linotype.com
info@linotype.com
+49 (0) 6172 484.418

The quick brown fox jumps over the lazy dog.

D *t*

P22 Folk Art Cross
Graphic | Light Weight |
Textured Detail |

P22 Type Foundry
www.p22.com
p22@p22.com
800.P22.5080

The quick brown fox jumps over the lazy dog.

D *t*

Roman Script™
Script-Serif Hybrid | Bold
Weight | Sans Serif Influence |
Upright Posture |

Linotype Library GmbH
www.linotype.com
info@linotype.com
+49 (0) 6172 484.418

The quick brown fox jumps over the lazy dog.

D **T**

P22 Kane
Serif | Moderate Contrast |
Slightly Extended |

P22 Type Foundry
www.p22.com
p22@p22.com
800.P22.5080

The quick brown fox jumps over the lazy dog.

D

P22 Roanoke Script
Script | Condensed |
Swash Detail | Acute Posture |
Medium Weight |

P22 Type Foundry
www.p22.com
p22@p22.com
800.P22.5080

A a B b C c D d E e F f G g H h I i J j K k L l M m
N n O o P p Q q R r S s T t U u V v W w X x Y y
Z z 0 1 2 3 4 5 6 7 8 9 ! ? & @ $: ; " "

The quick brown fox jumps over the lazy dog.

D T

P22 Sherwood
Serif | Notable Contrast | Medium Weight |

P22 Type Foundry
www.p22.com
p22@p22.com
800.P22.5080

A A B B C C D D E E F F G G H H I I J J K K L L
M M N N O O P P Q Q R R S S T T U U V V W W X X
Y Y Z Z 0 1 2 3 4 5 6 7 8 9 ! ? @ # $ % & * ( ) { }
: ; " "
THE QUICK BROWN FOX JUMPS OVER THE LAZY DOG.

D

Engravers Bold Face #9
Serif | Bold Weight | Extreme Contrast | Bracketed Serifs | Caps and Small Caps |

Linotype Library GmbH
www.linotype.com
info@linotype.com
+49 (0) 6172 484.418

A a B b C c D d E e F f G g H h I i J j K k L l M m
N n O o P p Q q R r S s T t U u V v W w X x Y y
Z z 0 1 2 3 4 5 6 7 8 9 ! ? @ # $ % & * ( ) { } : ; " "

The quick brown fox jumps over the lazy dog.

D

Wexley Oakley Regular
Graphic–Sans Serif Hybrid | Fraktur References | Heavier Medium Weight |

Device
www.devicefonts.co.uk
rianhughes@aol.com
44 (0) 7979.602.272

D

Baroquoco
Graphic Icon Font

Garage Fonts Type Foundry
www.garagefonts.com
info@garagefonts.com
800.681.9375

A a B b C c D d E e F f G g H h I i J j K k L l M m
N n O o P p Q q R r S s T t U u V v W w X x Y y Z z
0 1 2 3 4 5 6 7 8 9 ! ? & @ # $ % * : ; "

The quick brown fox jumps over the lazy dog.

D t

P22 Kilkenny Regular
Serif | Pronounced Contrast | Moderately Condensed |

P22 Type Foundry
www.p22.com
p22@p22.com
800.P22.5080

A a B b C c D d E e F f G g H h I i J j K k L l M m N n O o P p Q q R r S s T t
U u V v W w X x Y y Z z 0 1 2 3 4 5 6 7 8 9 ! ? @ # & : ; " "

The quick brown fox jumps over the lazy dog.

D

P22 Grosvenor
Script | Condensed | Acute Posture | Lighter Medium Weight |

P22 Type Foundry
www.p22.com
p22@p22.com
800.P22.5080

*A a B b C c D d E e F f G g H h I i J j K k L l M m N n O o P p Q g R r S s T t U u V v W w X x Y y Z z 0 1 2 3 4 5 6 7 8 9 ! ? & @ # $ % * : ; "*

The quick brown fox jumps over the lazy dog.

MVB Chanson d'Amour
Script | Lesser Contrast |
Light Weight |

MVB Fonts
www.mvbfonts.com
info@mvbfonts.com
510.525.4288

*A a B b C c D d E e F f G g H h I i J j K k L l M m N n O o P p Q q R r S s T t U u V v W w X x Y y Z z 0 1 2 3 4 5 6 7 8 9 ! ? k b $ % & * ( ) q v : : " "*

The quick brown fox jumps over the lazy dog.

Oberon™
Graphic Script | Bold Weight |
Outline Detail | Swash Detail |

Linotype Library GmbH
www.linotype.com
info@linotype.com
+49 (0) 6172 484.418

AABCDDEEFFGGHIJKKLL MMNOOPQRRSTUUVVWW XYZZ0123456789!?&@#$

THE QUICK BROWN FOX JUMPS OVER THE LAZY DOG.

P22 Victorian Gothic
Stylized Wedge Serif |
Uniform Medium Weight |
Extended | All Caps |

P22 Type Foundry
www.p22.com
p22@p22.com
800.P22.5080

A a B b C c D d E e F f G g H h I i J j K k L l M m N n O o P p Q q R r S s T t U u V v W w X x Y y Z z 0 1 2 3 4 5 6 7 8 9 ! ? & @ # $ % : ; "

The quick brown fox jumps over the lazy dog.

Indelible Victorian
Graphic Script | Light Weight |

T.26 Digital Type Foundry
www.t26.com
info@t26.com
888.T26.FONT

A a B b C c D d E e F f G g H h I i J j K k L l M m N n O o P p Q q R r S s T t U u V v W w X x Y y Z z 0 1 2 3 4 5 6 7 8 9 ! ? @ # & : ; " "

The quick brown fox jumps over the lazy dog.

P22 Escher Hand
Serif | Condensed |
Medium Weight |

P22 Type Foundry
www.p22.com
p22@p22.com
800.P22.5080

A a B b C c D d E e F f G g H h I i J j K k L l M m N n O o P p Q q R r S s T t U u V v W w X x Y y Z z 0 1 2 3 4 5 6 7 8 9 ! ? & @ # $ % * : ; "

The quick brown fox jumps over the lazy dog.

MVB Gryphius
Serif | Moderate Contrast |
Medium Weight |

MVB Fonts
www.mvbfonts.com
info@mvbfonts.com
510.525.4288

A B C D E F G H I J K L M N O P Q R
S T U V W X Y Z

THE QUICK BROWN FOX JUMPS OVER THE LAZY DOG

D

Gill™ Floriated Capitals
*Graphic | Decorative Contour |
Light Weight | Lacking
Numerals and Punctuation|*

Linotype Library GmbH
www.linotype.com
info@linotype.com
+49 (0) 6172 484.418

A B C D E F G H I J K L M
N O P Q R S T U V W X Y Z
0 1 2 3 4 5 6 7 8 9 ! ? & @ $

THE QUICK BROWN FOX JUMPS OVER

D

P22 Toybox Blocks
Graphic | Medium Weight |

P22 Type Foundry
www.p22.com
p22@p22.com
800.P22.5080

A a B b C c D d E e F f G g H h I i J j K k L l M m N n O o
P p Q q R r S ſ T t U u V v W w X x Y y Z z 0 1 2 3 4 5 6 7
8 9 ! ? & s $ % & * ( ) { } : ; " "

The quick brown fox jumps over the lazy dog.

D

Mariage
*Graphic Serif | Medium
Weight | Pronounced Contrast |
Blackletter |*

Linotype Library GmbH
www.linotype.com
info@linotype.com
+49 (0) 6172 484.418

A a B b C c D d E e F f G g H h I i J j K k L l M m N n
O o P p Q q R r S s T t U u V v W w X x Y y Z z 0 1 2 3
4 5 6 7 8 9 ! ? ŋ f $ % & * ( ) : ; " "

The quick brown fox jumps over the lazy dog.

D *t*

Victorian™
*Serif | Bold Weight | Stylized
Serifs and Joints |Pronounced
Contrast | Swash Details*

Linotype Library GmbH
www.linotype.com
info@linotype.com
+49 (0) 6172 484.418

A A B b C c D D E e F f G g H H I i J j K K L l M m
N n O o P p Q q R r S s T t U u V v W w X x Y y
Z z 0 1 2 3 4 5 6 7 8 9 ! ? & @ # $ % * : ; "

The Quick Brown Fox Jumps Over The Lazy Dog.

D

P22 Kilkenny Swash Caps
*Serif | Pronounced Contrast |
Moderately Condensed |*

P22 Type Foundry
www.p22.com
p22@p22.com
800.P22.5080

A a B b C c D d E e F f G g H h I i J j K k L l M m
N n O o P p Q q R r S s T t U u V v W w X x Y y Z z
0 1 2 3 4 5 6 7 8 9 ! ? & @ # $ % * : ; "

The quick brown fox jumps over the lazy dog.

D

P22 Victorian Swash
*Serif | Condensed | Erratic
Height | Lesser Contrast |*

P22 Type Foundry
www.p22.com
p22@p22.com
800.P22.5080

Victorian Color

Deep violet hues are the cornerstone of Victorian color, especially in combination with rich, dark wood tones, such as umber or mahogany. Burgundies that are skewed toward the violet range of the spectrum, almost pink in quality, lend the sense of passion that is curtailed by morality. Blue violet—in both light and deep, smoky values—brings additional depth to the palette. Ivory and a light, coffee-colored neutral brown soften the richness of the base color scheme.

Sample Color Combinations

78 C	
80 M	
0 Y	
20 K	

70 C
75 M
0 Y
36 K

51 C
100 M
100 Y
63 K

0 C
52 M
100 Y
78 K

14 C
100 M
0 Y
71 K

0 C
87 M
0 Y
66 K

23 C
42 M
57 Y
10 K

3 C
3 M
12 Y
0 K

46 C
48 M
19 Y
0 K

94 C
76 M
45 Y
0 K

Gunslingers and ranch-hands, dusty deserts and Navajo rugs—the Wild West presents a wild mix of type and color that is rugged, dynamic, and sultry all at once.

Wild West

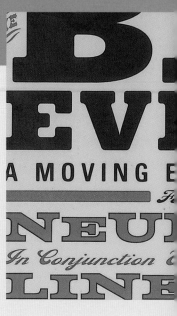

The period between 1800 and 1880 in American history is one of expansion westward into mostly uncharted territory, conflict with indigenous peoples, and a lawlessness made famous in film and literature. The most notable type style of the period is the slab serif, appearing in myriad styles as early advertising spread across the landscape from small cities into smaller cow towns. Slab-serif faces, in all their varieties—often with details or slight degradation that refers to their early production using type cut from wood rather than metal—are instantly evocative of the American West. The slabs may be squared or pointed, crimped or dimpled, but they are consistently pronounced and often dominate the stems of the characters on which they appear. Condensed and extended are equally common; slab serifs of all styles proliferated during this time. Glyphlike variations, more geometric and sans serif in their form, borrow from the language of cattle branding. Additionally, condensed gothic sans-serif faces, such as were used in newspaper and early catalog printing in the latter part of the nineteenth century, are stylistically in tune with the Wild West era.

Print Collateral Poster
top, and detail, bottom

Palazzolo™ Design
Greg Palazzolo
Ada [MI] *USA*

ABCDEFGHIJKLMNOPQRSTUVWXYZ
0123456789!?@#$%&*[]{}:;""

THE QUICK BROWN FOX JUMPS OVER THE LAZY DOG.

D

Falfurrias
Stylized Sans Serif |
Bold Weight | All Caps |

Nick's Fonts
www.nicksfonts.com

AaBbCcDdEeFf GgHhIiJj KkLl MmNn
OoPpQqRr SsTt UuVvWwXxYyZz 01234
56789!?& @ $:;""

THE QUICK BROWN FOX JUMPS OVER THE LAZY DOG.

D

P22 Posada
Stylized Serif | Uniform
Bold Weight | Caps and
Small Caps |

P22 Type Foundry
www.p22.com
p22@p22.com
800.P22.5080

Aa Bb Cc Dd Ee Ff Gg Hh Ii Jj Kk Ll Mm Nn
Oo Pp Qq Rr Ss Tt Uu Vv Ww Xx Yy Zz 0123
456789 !?& fi%*[][]:;""©$¥

The quick brown fox jumps over the lazy dog.

D

Rio Grande
Slab Serif | Extra Bold Weight |

Nick's Fonts
www.nicksfonts.com

Aa Bb Cc Dd Ee Ff Gg Hh Ii Jj Kk Ll Mm Nn Oo
Pp Qq Rr Ss Tt Uu Vv Ww Xx Yy Zz 01234567
89!?&fi%*()[]:;""©$¥

The quick brown fox jumps over the lazy dog.

D t

Mrs. Bathhurst
Serif | Moderate Contrast |

Nick's Fonts
www.nicksfonts.com

AaBbCcDdEeFfGgHhIiJj
KkLLMmNNOoPpQqRRSsTT
UuVvWwXxYyZz01234567
89Y?@#$%&*[]{}:;""

THE QUICK BROWN FOX JUMPS OVER THE LAZY DOG.

D

ITC Buckeroo™
Slab Serif | Black Weight |
Slightly Extended |
Decorative Cut-ins |

Linotype Library GmbH
www.linotype.com
info@linotype.com
+49 (0) 6172 484.418

AaBbCcDdEeFfGgHhIiJjKkLlMmNnOoPpQqRrSsTtUuVvWwXxYy
Zz0123456789!?@#$%&*[]{}:;""

The quick brown fox jumps over the lazy dog.

D

Laguna Madre
Stylized Slab Serif |
Extra Condensed |

Nick's Fonts
www.nicksfonts.com

ABCDEFGHIJKLMNOPQRSTUVWXYZ0123
456789!?@#$%&*( ){ }:;" "

THE QUICK BROWN FOX JUMPS OVER THE LAZY DOG.

D

Pilot Point
*Stylized Slab Serif |
Condensed | Bold Weight |*

Nick's Fonts
www.nicksfonts.com

AABBCCDDEEFFGGHHIIJJKKLLMMNN
OOPPQQRRSSTTUUVVWWXXYYZZ012
3456789!?&@#$%*:;"

THE QUICK BROWN FOX JUMPS OVER THE LAZY DOG.

D

Goshen
*Sans Serif | All Caps with
Alternate Condensed Width |
Moderate Contrast |*

The Chank Company
www.chank.com
friendlyfolks@chank.com
877.GO.CHANK

AaBbCcDdEeFf GgHhIiJjKkLlMm
NnOoPpQqRrSsTt UuVv WwXxYyZz
0123456789!?@#&:;" "

The quick brown fox jumps over the lazy dog.

D *t*

P22 Folk Art Stitch
*Graphic | Condensed |
Medium Weight |*

P22 Type Foundry
www.p22.com
p22@p22.com
800.P22.5080

AaBbCcDdEeFfGgHhIiJjKkLlMm
NnOoPpQqRrSsTtUuVvWwXxYy
ZzO123456789!?&@#$%*:;"

The quick brown fox jumps over the lazy dog.

D

P22 Wayout West
*Stylized Slab Serif | Erratic
Weight | Erratic Posture |*

P22 Type Foundry
www.p22.com
p22@p22.com
800.P22.5080

AaBbCcDdEeFfGgHhIiJjKkLlMmNn
OoPpQqRrSsTtUuVvWwXxYyZz0123
456789!?$%&*( ):;" "

The quick brown fox jumps over the lazy dog.

D

Cabaret™
*Graphic Slab Serif | Bold
Weight | Outline, Shadow, and
Inline Graphic Detail |*

Linotype Library GmbH
www.linotype.com
info@linotype.com
+49 (0) 6172 484.418

AaBbCcDdEeFfGgHhIiJjKkLlMmNnOoPpQqRrSsTt
UuVvWwXxYyZz0123456789!?&@S:;

The quick brown fox jumps over the lazy dog.

D

P22 Woodtype Regular
*Slab Serif | Extra Condensed |
Uniform Medium Weight |*

P22 Type Foundry
www.p22.com
p22@p22.com
800.P22.5080

AaBbCcDdEeFfGgHhIiJjKkLlMmNnOo
PpQqRrSsTtUuVvWwXxYyZz012345678
9!?€@#$%*:;"

The quick brown fox jumps over the lazy dog.

Livery Light
Stylized Slab Serif |
Pronounced Contrast |

Garage Fonts Type Foundry
www.garagefonts.com
info@garagefonts.com
800.681.9375

AaBbCcDDEeFfGgHhIiJjKkLlMm
NnOoPpQqRrSsTtUuVvWwXx
YyZz0123456789!?&AND AT №$%❀:;"

THE QUICK BROWN FOX JUMPS OVER THE LAZY DOG.

Dead Mule Grande
Stylized Slab Serif | Extended |
Heavy Bold Weight |
Caps and Small Caps |

T.26 Digital Type Foundry
www.t26.com
info@t26.com
888.T26.FONT

AaBbCcDdEeFfGHhIiJj
KkLlMmNnOoPpQqRr
SsTtUuVvWwXxYyZz0
123456789!?$%&*(){};;

The quick brown fox jumps over the lazy dog.

Blackoak™
Slab Serif | Black Weight |
Very Extended |

Linotype Library GmbH
www.linotype.com
info@linotype.com
+49 (0) 6172 484.418

AaBbCcDdEeFfGgHhIiJjKkLlMm
NnOoPpQqRrSsTtUuVvWwXxYyZz
0123456789!?&@#$%*:;"

The quick brown fox jumps over the lazy dog.

Prospect Modern
Slab Serif | Condensed |
Bold Weight |

The Chank Company
www.chank.com
friendlyfolks@chank.com
877.GO.CHANK

ABCDEFGHIJKLMNOPQRSTUVW
XYZ0123456789!?$%&(){};;""*

THE QUICK BROWN FOX JUMPS OVER THE LAZY DOG.

Cottonwood™
Graphic Slab Serif | Black
Weight | Extreme Contrast |
Stylized Joints | Horizontal
Emphasis |

Linotype Library GmbH
www.linotype.com
info@linotype.com
+49 (0) 6172 484.418

AaBbCcDdEeFfGgHhIiJjKkLlMm
NnOoPpQqRrSsTtUuVvWwXxYyZz
0123456789!?&@#$%*:;"

The quick brown fox jumps over the lazy dog.

Gomorrah
Slab Serif | Condensed |
Bold Weight |

The Chank Company
www.chank.com
friendlyfolks@chank.com
877.GO.CHANK

A a B b C c D d E e F f G g H h I i J j K k L l M m N n O o
P p Q q R r S s T t U u V v W w X x Y y Z z 0 1 2 3 4 5
6 7 8 9 ! ? @ # $ % & * ( ) { } : ; " "

The quick brown fox jumps over the lazy dog.

D *t*

Giddyup™
Script | Light Weight |
Slight Italic Posture |
Illustrative Inclusions |

Linotype Library GmbH
www.linotype.com
info@linotype.com
+49 (0) 6172 484.418

AaBbCcDdEeFfGgHhIiJj
KkLlMmNnOoPpQqRrSs
TtUuVvWwXxYyZz012345
6789!?$%&*(){}:;" "

The quick brown fox jumps over the lazy dog.

D

Madrone™
Serif | Extra-Black Weight |
Extreme Contrast | Extended |

Linotype Library GmbH
www.linotype.com
info@linotype.com
+49 (0) 6172 484.418

A A B B C C D D E E F F G G H H I I J J K K L L M M N N O O P P Q Q R R S S T T
U U V V W W X X Y Y Z Z 0 1 2 3 4 5 6 7 8 9 ! ? $ % & * ( ) { } : ; " "

THE QUICK BROWN FOX JUMPS OVER THE LAZY DOG.

D

Mesquite™
Graphic Serif | Bold Weight |
Ultra Condensed |

Linotype Library GmbH
www.linotype.com
info@linotype.com
+49 (0) 6172 484.418

ABCDEFGHIJKLM
NOPQRSTUVWXY
Z0123456789!?@#

THE QUICK BROWN FOX JUMPS OVER THE LAZY DOG.

D

Thunderbird Regular
Slab Serif | Medium Weight |
Decorative Contour |

Linotype Library GmbH
www.linotype.com
info@linotype.com
+49 (0) 6172 484.418

A a B b C c D d E e F f G g H h I i J j K k L l M m N n O o P p Q q R
S s T t U u V v W w X x Y y Z z 0 1 2 3 4 5 6 7 8 9 ! ? $ % & * ( ) :
" "

The quick brown fox jumps over the lazy dog.

D

Wanted™
Slab Serif | Black Weight |
Texture Detail | Horizontal
Emphasis |

Linotype Library GmbH
www.linotype.com
info@linotype.com
+49 (0) 6172 484.418

A B C D E F G H I J K L M N O P Q R S
T U V W X Y Z 0 1 2 3 4 5 6 7 8 9 ! ? $ % & *
( ) { } : ; " "

THE QUICK BROWN FOX JUMPS OVER THE LAZY DOG.

D

Zebrawood™ Regular
Graphic | Black Weight |
Illustrative Detail |

Linotype Library GmbH
www.linotype.com
info@linotype.com
+49 (0) 6172 484.418

Wild West Color

Dusty, desaturated neutrals—tan, beige, taupe, and grayish ivory—form a backdrop for the Wild West palette, alluding to the desert and rocky landscape of the western American continent. Deeper browns, brown-oranges, and muted violet also evoke the environment, calling to mind the mountains and mesas of the Southwest. Middle-value and slightly lighter reds, derived from Navajo and Pueblo textiles, add warmth to the palette; black and deep umber round out the color scheme at the darker end of the value scale.

Sample Color Combinations

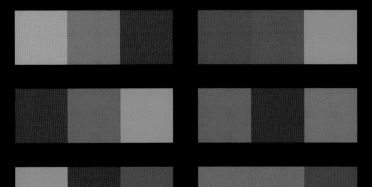

| > |
| 0 C |
| 0 M |
| 6 Y |
| 9 K |

| > |
| 0 C |
| 24 M |
| 45 Y |
| 32 K |

| > |
| 0 C |
| 38 M |
| 54 Y |
| 52 K |

| > |
| 0 C |
| 49 M |
| 83 Y |
| 52 K |

| > |
| 0 C |
| 61 M |
| 100 Y |
| 71 K |

| > |
| 19 C |
| 70 M |
| 100 Y |
| 54 K |

| > |
| 49 C |
| 64 M |
| 35 Y |
| 24 K |

| > |
| 0 C |
| 100 M |
| 100 Y |
| 35 K |

| > |
| 0 C |
| 73 M |
| 77 Y |
| 32 K |

| > |
| 27 C |
| 71 M |
| 57 Y |
| 0 K |

Segueing from the Victorian era's bitty ornamentation into the first phases of modernism, Art Nouveau celebrated the natural and organic while paving the way for the rational aesthetic of the early twentieth century. These two seemingly opposing visual languages inform the Art Nouveau era's typography and color.

Art Nouveau

Art Nouveau, used here as a broad term for the period between 1880 and 1920, encompasses a range of styles that complement each other. In terms of typefaces, Art Nouveau typography is represented primarily by floral, organic forms that are plantlike in shape and detail. Pronounced modulation in strokes, often tapering from capline to baseline, as well as bulbous, stylized serif endings, integrate with sinuous curves and broad, heavier weights to create a sensuous movement among letters. Hybrid serif/sans serif forms allude to the transition between the centuries, referring to early modernist styles such as Arts & Crafts and Jugendstil. Additionally, early grotesk sans serifs that still retain a sense of their origins in brush drawing may be counted among Art Nouveau styles. Unlike later sans serifs of the Machine Age, these typefaces tend to be more condensed overall, with smaller x-heights than their later counterparts, and exhibit a noticeable contrast between thick and thin strokes. Some decorative elements, such as swash forms or exaggerated legs, tails, and bowls—in the R, Q, and lowercase g respectively—contribute to the flowing quality of Art Nouveau type style.

Publication Cover *top, and details, middle and bottom*

The Pushpin Group, Inc.
Seymour Chwast
New York City *USA*

AaBbCcDdEeFfGgHhIiJjKkLlMmNnOoPpQqRrSsTtUu
UυWwXxYy2zO123456789!?@№$%&*()():;""
THE QUICK BROWN FOX JUMPS OVER THE LAZY DOG.

D

Absinthe
Stylized Sans Serif |
Condensed |
Pronounced Contrast |

Device
www.devicefonts.co.uk
rianhughes@aol.com
44 (0) 7979.602.272

AaBbCcDdEeFfGgHhIiJjKkLlMmNn
OoPpQqRrSsTtUuVvWwXxYyZz012
3456789!?&@$:;""

THE QUICK BROWN FOX JUMPS OVER THE LAZY DOG.

D

P22 Dard Arts & Crafts Tall
Stylized Sans Serif | Condensed |
Exaggerated Counters | All Caps
with Selected Alternates |

P22 Type Foundry
www.p22.com
p22@p22.com
800.P22.5080

AaBbCcDdEeFfGgHhIiJjKkLlMmNnOo
PpQqRrSsTtUuVvWwXxYyZz0123456
789!?&@$:;""

The quick brown fox jumps over the lazy dog.

D **T**

P22 Lindum
Semi-Serif | Lesser Contrast |
Light Weight |

P22 Type Foundry
www.p22.com
p22@p22.com
800.P22.5080

AaBbCcDdEeFfGgHhIiJjKkLlMm
NnOoPpQqRrSsTtUuVvWwXxYyZz
0123456789!?&$%&*():;""

THE QUICK BROWN FOX JUMPS OVER THE LAZY DOG.

D

Orlando™
Graphic Serif | Medium Weight |
Outline | Swash Detail |

Linotype Library GmbH
www.linotype.com
info@linotype.com
+49 (0) 6172 484.418

AaBbCcDdEeFfGgHhIiJjKkLlMmNnOo
PpQqRrSsTtUuVvWwXxYyZz01234567
89!?@#$%&*(){}:;""

The quick brown fox jumps over the lazy dog.

D **t**

Rialto™
Serif | Medium Weight |
Reduced Contrast | Stylized
Terminals | Condensed |

Linotype Library GmbH
www.linotype.com
info@linotype.com
+49 (0) 6172 484.418

AaBbCcDdEeFfGgHhIiJjKkLlMmNnOoPp
QqRrSsTtUuVvWwXxYyZz0123456789!
?&@$:;""

The quick brown fox jumps over the lazy dog.

D

P22 Mucha
Stylized Sans Serif |
Erratic Contrast | Runic Detail |
Medium Weight |

P22 Type Foundry
www.p22.com
p22@p22.com
800.P22.5080

A A B B C C D D E E F F G G H H I I J J K H L L M M N N O O P P Q Q R R
S S T T U U V V W W X X Y Y Z Z 0 1 2 3 4 5 6 7 8 9 ! ? & @ $: ; " "

THE QUICK BROWN FOX JUMPS OVER THE LAZY DOG.

D

P22 Parrish Hand
*Stylized Sans Serif | Light
Weight | Extra Condensed |
All Caps with Alternates |*

P22 Type Foundry
www.p22.com
p22@p22.com
800.P22.5080

A a B b C c D d E e F f G g H h I i J j K k L l M m
N n O o P p Q q R r S s T t U u V v W w X x Y y
Z z 0 1 2 3 4 5 6 7 8 9 ! ? @ # $ % & * ( ) { } : ; " "
The quick brown fox jumps over the lazy dog.

D **t**

Arnold Boecklin™ Regular
*Serif | Bold Weight |
Fluid Ductus | Swash Detail |*

Linotype Library GmbH
www.linotype.com
info@linotype.com
+49 (0) 6172 484.418

A a B b C c D d E e F f G g H h I i J j K k L l M m
N n O o P p Q q R r S s T t U u V v W w X x Y y Z z
0 1 2 3 4 5 6 7 8 9 ! ? & @ $: ; " "

The quick brown fox jumps over the lazy dog.

D **T**

P22 St. G Schrift One
Sans Serif | Medium Weight |

P22 Type Foundry
www.p22.com
p22@p22.com
800.P22.5080

A a B b C c D d E e F f G g H h I i J j K k L l M m N n O o
P p Q q R r S s T t U u V v W w X x Y y Z z 0 1 2 3 4 5 6 7
8 9 ! ? $ % & * ( ) : ; " "
The quick brown fox jumps over the lazy dog.

D **t**

Eckmann™
*Graphic Sans Serif | Bold
Weight | Notable Modulation |
Brush Detail | Condensed |*

Linotype Library GmbH
www.linotype.com
info@linotype.com
+49 (0) 6172 484.418

A A B B C C D D E E F F G G H H I I J J K K L L
M M N N O O P P Q Q R R S S T T U U V V W W
X X Y Y Z Z 0 1 2 3 4 5 6 7 8 9 ! ? & @ $: ; " "

THE QUICK BROWN FOX JUMPS OVER THE LAZY DOG.

D

P22 Terracotta Regular
*Semi-Serif | Uniform Light
Weight | Baseline-Shifted Caps
with Lining Small Caps |*

P22 Type Foundry
www.p22.com
p22@p22.com
800.P22.5080

A A B B C C D D E E F F G G H H I I J J K K L L
M M N N O O P P Q Q R R S S T T U U V V
W X X Y Y Z Z 0 1 2 3 4 5 6 7 8 9 ! ? & @ $: ; " "

THE QUICK BROWN FOX JUMPS OVER THE LAZY DOG.

D

P22 Terracotta Alternates
*Semi-Serif | Uniform Light
Weight | Caps with Alternates |*

P22 Type Foundry
www.p22.com
p22@p22.com
800.P22.5080

A a B b C c D d E e F f G g H h I i J j K k L l
M m N n O o P p Q q R r S s T t U u V v W w
X x Y y Z z 0 1 2 3 4 5 6 7 8 9 ! ? & @ $: ;

The quick brown fox jumps over the lazy dog.

D

P22 Dard Hunter
*Serif | Condensed | Medium
Weight | Swash Details |*

P22 Type Foundry
www.p22.com
p22@p22.com
800.P22.5080

A a B b C c D d E e F f G g H h I i J j K K L l M m
N n O o P p Q q R r S s T t U u V v W w X x Y y
Z z 0 1 2 3 4 5 6 7 8 9 ! ? Æ æ Ñ $ % ø : ; "

The quick brown fox jumps over the lazy dog.

D

Widoveil
*Stylized Sans Serif | Bold
Weight | Extended |*

Garage Fonts Type Foundry
www.garagefonts.com
info@garagefonts.com
800.681.9375

A B C D E F G H I J K L M N O P Q R S T U V W X Y Z
0 1 2 3 4 5 6 7 8 9 ! ? & * $ % * : ; "

THE QUICK BROWN FOX JUMPS OVER THE LAZY DOG.

D

Toulouse Lautrec:
Moulin Rouge Outline
*Stylized Sans Serif |
Light Weight | Condensed |*

T.26 Digital Type Foundry
www.t26.com
info@t26.com
888.T26.FONT

A a B b C c D d E e F f G g H h I i J j K k L l M m
N n O o P p Q q R r S s T t U u V v W w X x Y y Z z
0 1 2 3 4 5 6 7 8 9 ! ? & @ # $ % * : ; "

The quick brown fox jumps over the lazy dog.

D *t*

Toulouse Lautrec:
Theatre Antoine
*Stylized Semi-Serif | Uniform
Medium Weight | Condensed |*

T.26 Digital Type Foundry
www.t26.com
info@t26.com
888.T26.FONT

A A B B C C D D E E F F G G H H I I J J K K L L
M M N N O O P P Q Q R R S S T T U U V V W W
X X Y Y Z Z 0 1 2 3 4 5 6 7 8 9 ! ? & @ # $ % * : ; "

THE QUICK BROWN FOX JUMPS OVER THE LAZY DOG.

D

JY Arts & Crafts
*Stylized Sans Serif |
All Caps with Alternates |
Medium Weight |*

JY&A Fonts
www.jyanet.com/fonts

A a B b C c D d E e F f G g H h I i J j K k L l M m
N n O o P p Q q R r S s T t U u V v W w X x Y y
Z z 0 1 2 3 4 5 6 7 8 9 ! ? & @ # $ % : ; "

The quick brown fox jumps over the lazy dog.

D *t*

Toulouse Lautrec:
Le Chat Noir
*Stylized Semi-Serif | Uniform
Medium Weight | Condensed |*

T.26 Digital Type Foundry
www.t26.com
info@t26.com
888.T26.FONT

ABCDEFGHHIIJKLMNOPQRSSTTU
UUUUXXYYZZ0123456789!?&@
#J%*:;"

THE QUICK BROWN FOX JUMPS OVER THE LAZY DOG.

Aa Bb Cc Dd Ee Ff Gg Hh Ii Jj Kk Ll Mm Nn Oo Pp
Qq Rr Ss Tt Uu Vv Ww Xx Yy Zz 0) 23456789
(P & @ $ :: " "

The quick brown fox jumps over the lazy dog.

A a B b C c D d E e F f G g H h I i J j K k L l M m
N n O o P p Q q R r S s T t U u V v W w X x Y y Z z
0 1 2 3 4 5 6 7 8 9 ! ? @ # $ % & * ( ) { } : ; " "

The quick brown fox jumps over the lazy dog.

A A B b C c D D E E F F G G H H I l J J K K L L M M
N N O o P P Q Q R R S S T T U u V v W w X x Y y
Z z 0 1 2 3 4 5 6 7 8 9 ! ? @ # & : ; " "

THE QUICK BROWN FOX JUMPS OVER THE LAZY DOG.

A a B b C c D d E e F f G g H h I i J j K k L l M m Nn
O o P p Q q R r S s T t U u V v W w X x Y y Z z 0 1 2 3 4
5 6 7 8 9 ! ? @ # & : ; " "

The quick brown fox jumps over the lazy dog.

A a B b C c D d E e F f G g H h I i J j K k L l M m
N n O o P p Q q R r S s T t U u V v W w X x Y y
Z z 0 1 2 3 4 5 6 7 8 9 ! ? & @ # $ % * : ; "

The quick brown fox jumps over the lazy dog.

D

P22 Vienna Regular
*Stylized Sans Serif |
Pronounced Contrast | All Caps
with Selected Alternates |*

P22 Type Foundry
www.p22.com
p22@p22.com
800.P22.5080

D

P22 Salon Full
*Stylized Semi-Serif | Flared
Stems | Medium Weight |
Condensed |*

P22 Type Foundry
www.p22.com
p22@p22.com
800.P22.5080

D t

Auriol™ Roman
*Graphic Serif | Medium
Weight | Script and Swash
Detail | Detached Strokes |*

Linotype Library GmbH
www.linotype.com
info@linotype.com
+49 (0) 6172 484.418

D

P22 Eaglefeather Bold
*Stylized Sans Serif |
Uniform Medium Weight |
Erratic Posture |*

P22 Type Foundry
www.p22.com
p22@p22.com
800.P22.5080

D T

P22 Founders
*Stylized Serif | Medieval
Details | Pronounced
Contrast | Medium Weight |*

P22 Type Foundry
www.p22.com
p22@p22.com
800.P22.5080

D t

**Toulouse Lautrec:
Le Petit Trottin**
*Stylized Semi-Serif | Slight
Modulation | Condensed |
Erratic Posture |*

T.26 Digital Type Foundry
www.t26.com
info@t26.com
888.T26.FONT

Art Nouveau Color

The hues that evoke Art Nouveau are a noticeable departure from the Victorian era's rich, deep tones. Medium-value earth tones and desaturated blue, aqua, mauve, and green predominate, offset by deep rust, brown, and ochre. Lavender offers a cool, nostalgic counterpart to the base palette. The color of parchment, often associated with pamphlets and lithographic posters from the Art Nouveau period, often forms a backdrop against which more dramatic hues interact. A hot orange red, evoking title treatments from posters by Charet and Toulouse-Lautrec, offers a dynamic counterpoint to the more sedate hues of the palette.

Sample Color Combinations

0	C	
5	M	
24	Y	
9	K	

0	C
28	M
67	Y
50	K

57	C
23	M
25	Y
0	K

72	C
30	M
0	Y
32	K

42	C
60	M
25	Y
12	K

45	C
0	M
55	Y
33	K

0	C
68	M
84	Y
52	K

0	C
25	M
87	Y
42	K

31	C
35	M
0	Y
14	K

25	C
88	M
100	Y
0	K

Imagine the metallic roar of the twentieth century rolling in: architecture, art, design, and industry collaborating on a new aesthetic embracing speed, power, travel, and science. From Mondrian and De Stijl to the Futurists and the Bauhaus, geometry, abstraction, and streamlined forms rule the Machine Age vision in type and color.

Machine Age

Type that recalls the early twentieth century—and indeed, many currently popular typefaces were designed during this time—varies from strong, geometric sans serifs to elegant hybrids and even some serifs, all conveying a particular sense of strength, durability, and power. Sans serif faces with pronounced geometric qualities, such as Futura (which is constructed on a base of square, circle, and triangle), carry the category, referencing not only the machinelike qualities of math and science but also the avant-garde, abstract art of the period. Some sans-serif faces of the period show extremes of proportion as well: they are often condensed and rhythmic, with topheavy counters in which the upper portions of letters such as capital E and R are forced downward, and often feature stylistic accents such as diagonal-cut terminals and cross-strokes that overlap their surrounding stems to bring a decorative, Art Moderne quality. Serif faces with geometric proportions—but with small x-heights, exaggerated height in their ascenders, and quirky modulation in their strokes—show a transition from the nineteenth century to the twentieth and reference European cabaret culture and its origins in Art Nouveau.

Event Poster
top, and detail, bottom

Momentum
Brent Wilson, designer
Paul Rodgers, illustrator
Saint Louis [MO] *USA*

AaBbCcDdEeFfGgHhIiJjKkLlMmNnOoPp
QqRrSsTtUuVvWwXxYyZz012345678
9!?@#✎%&*(){}::""
The quick brown fox jumps over the lazy dog.

D

Quaint Notions NF
Stylized Sans Serif | Pronounced Contrast | Black Weight |

Nick's Fonts
www.nicksfonts.com

ABCDEFGHIJKLMNOPQRSTUVWX
YZ0123456789!?$%&*():;""
THE QUICK BROWN FOX JUMPS OVER THE LAZY DOG.

D

Sinaloa™
Graphic | Black Weight | Linear Abstract Detail |

Linotype Library GmbH
www.linotype.com
info@linotype.com
+49 (0) 6172 484.418

AaBbCcDdEeFfGgHhIiJjKkLlMm
NnOoPpQqRrSsTtUuVvWwXxYy
Zz0123456789!?@#$%&*(){}:;""
The quick brown fox jumps over the lazy dog.

D *t*

Windsor™ Bold
Serif | Bold Weight | Reduced Contrast | Pronounced Oblique Axis |

Linotype Library GmbH
www.linotype.com
info@linotype.com
+49 (0) 6172 484.418

ABCDEFGHIJKLMNOP
QRSTUVWXYZ012345
6789!?&FI%*()[]:;""©$¥
THE QUICK BROWN FOX JUMPS OVER THE LAZY DOG.

D

Brazos
Sans Serif | Extended | Black Weight |

Nick's Fonts
www.nicksfonts.com

AaBbCcDdEeFfGgHhIiJjKkLlMmNn
OoPpQqRrSsTtUuVvWwXxYyZz01234
56789!?&fi%*()[]:;'"©$¥
The quick brown fox jumps over the lazy dog.

D *t*

McKenna Handletter Bold
Serif | Lesser Contrast | Semibold Weight | Pronounced Serifs |

Nick's Fonts
www.nicksfonts.com

AaBbCcDdEeFfGgHhIiJjKkLlMmNnOo
PpQqRrSsTtUuVvWwXxYyZz01234567
89!?&fi%*()[]:;'"©$¥
The quick brown fox jumps over the lazy dog.

D *t*

McKenna Handletter Regular
Serif | Lesser Contrast | Medium Weight | Pronounced Serifs |

Nick's Fonts
www.nicksfonts.com

AaBbCcDd Ee FfGg Hh Ii Jj Kk Ll Mm
Nn Oo Pp Qq Rr Ss Tt Uu Vv Ww X x Yy Zz
0123456789!?& fi%()[]:;*©$""

The quick brown fox jumps over the lazy dog.

Slam Bang Theater
*Stylized Serif | Pronounced
Contrast | Black Weight |*

Nick's Fonts
www.nicksfonts.com

A A B B C C D D E F F G G H H I I J J K K L L M M
N N O O P P Q Q R R S / T T U U V V W W X X Y Y
Z Z O 1 2 3 4 5 6 7 8 9 ! ? Σ @ # $ % · ∴ ˇ

THE QUICK BROWN FOX JUMPS OVER THE LAZY DOG.

P22 Il Futurismo
*Stylized Sans Serif |
Bold Weight | All Caps
with Alternates |*

P22 Type Foundry
www.p22.com
p22@p22.com
800.P22.5080

A A B B C C D D E E F F G G H H I I J J K K L L
M M N N O O P P Q Q R R S S T T U U V V W W
X X Y Y Z Z O 1 2 3 4 5 6 7 8 9 ! ? & @ $:;""

THE QUICK BROWN FOX JUMPS OVER THE LAZY DOG.

P22 Koch Neuland
*Stylized Serif |
Bold Weight | All Caps
with Alternates |*

P22 Type Foundry
www.p22.com
p22@p22.com
800.P22.5080

AaBbCcDdEeFfGgHhIiJjKkLlMmN
nOoPpQqRrSsTtUuVvWwXxYyZz
0123456789!?@№$%&*(){}:;""
The quick brown fox jumps over the lazy dog.

English Grotesk Light
*Sans Serif | Sharp Terminals |
Uniform Medium Weight |*

Device
www.devicefonts.co.uk
rianhughes@aol.com
44 (0) 7979.602.272

AaBbCcDdEeFfGgHhIiJjKkLlMm
NnOoPpQqRrSsTtUuVvWwXxYyZz
0123456789!?&@#$%*:;"

The quick brown fox jumps over the lazy dog.

P22 Pan Am
*Serif | Medium Weight |
Slightly Extended |*

P22 Type Foundry
www.p22.com
p22@p22.com
800.P22.5080

A B B C D E F G H I J K K L M N O P Q R
S T U U W X Y Y 2 0 1 2 3 4 5 6 7 8 9 !
? & 回 S :; " "

THE QUICK BROWN FOX JUMPS OVER THE LAZY DOG.

P22 De Stijl Regular
*Stylized Sans Serif | Uniform
Medium Weight | All Caps
with Selected Alternates |*

P22 Type Foundry
www.p22.com
p22@p22.com
800.P22.5080

A a B b C c D d E e F f G g H h I i J j K k L l M m
N n O o P p Q q R r S s T t U u V v W w X x Y y
Z z 0 1 2 3 4 5 6 7 8 9 ! ? & @ # % * : ; "

The quick brown fox jumps over the lazy dog.

D

P22 Bifur A
Graphic | Extreme Contrast |
Linear Detail |

P22 Type Foundry
www.p22.com
p22@p22.com
800.P22.5080

A a B b C c D d E e F f G g H h I i J j K k L l M m
N n O o P p Q q R r S s T t U u V v W w X x Y y Z z
0 1 2 3 4 5 6 7 8 9 ! ? & @ # $ % * : ; "

The quick brown fox jumps over the lazy dog.

D **T**

LTC Deepdene
Serif | Medium Weight |

P22 Type Foundry
www.p22.com
p22@p22.com
800.P22.5080

A a B b C c D d E e F f G g H h I i J j K k L l M m
N n O o P p Q q R r S s T t U u V v W w X x
Y y Z z 0 1 2 3 4 5 6 7 8 9 ! ? @ # $ % & * ( )
{ } : ; " "
The quick brown fox jumps over the lazy dog.

D **t**

Futura® Bold
Sans Serif | Geometric
Construction | Uniform Strokes |

Linotype Library GmbH
www.linotype.com
info@linotype.com
+49 (0) 6172 484.418

A A B C D E F G H I J K K L M M N N O P Q R R S T U V W W
X Y Z 0 1 2 3 4 5 6 7 8 9 ! ? & @ # $ % * : ; "

THE QUICK BROWN FOX JUMPS OVER THE LAZY DOG.

D

LTC Jefferson Gothic
Sans Serif | Uniform Light
Weight | Extra Condensed |
Caps with Selected Alternates |

P22 Type Foundry
www.p22.com
p22@p22.com
800.P22.5080

A Å A A A B B B C Ç C D D E E E E Ē F F G G H H I I J j
K K L L M M N N O Ó O P P Q Q R R S S S S T T U Ü U
V V W W W W X X Y Y Z Z 0 1 2 3 4 5 6 7 8 9 & ? ! $
THE QUICK BROWN FOX JUMPS OVER THE LAZY DOG.

D

Katwalk
Sans Serif | Medium Weight |
All Caps with Alternates |

The Chank Company
www.chank.com
friendlyfolks@chank.com
877.GO.CHANK

A B C D E F G H I J K L M N O P Q R S T U V
W X Y Z 0 1 2 3 4 5 6 7 8 9 ! ? & @ # $ % * : ; "

THE QUICK BROWN FOX JUMPS OVER THE LAZY DOG.

D

MVB Magnesium Regular
Sans Serif | Pronounced
Contrast | Black Weight |
All Caps |

MVB Fonts
www.mvbfonts.com
info@mvbfonts.com
510.525.4288

AaBbCcDdEeFfGgHhIiJjKkLl
MmNnOoPpQqRrSsTtUuVvWw
XxYyZz0123456789!?R$%&'(
):;" "

The quick brown fox jumps over the lazy dog.

D

Dolmen™
*Sans Serif | Black Weight |
Extreme Contrast |*

Linotype Library GmbH
www.linotype.com
info@linotype.com
+49 (0) 6172 484.418

AaBbCcDdEeFfGgHhIiJjKkLlMm
NnOoPpQqRrSsTtUuVvWwXxYyZz
0123456789!?&@#$%*:;"

The quick brown fox jumps over the lazy dog.

D **t**

Rosemary Serif
*Pronounced Contrast |
Bold Weight |*

The Chank Company
www.chank.com
friendlyfolks@chank.com
877.GO.CHANK

AaBbCcDdEeFfGgHhIiJjKkLlMmNnOoPpQqRrSsTt
UuVvWwXxYyZz0123456789!?Wa$%&'()YN::" "

The quick brown fox jumps over the lazy dog.

D

Heliotype™
*Serif | Medium Weight |
Ultra Condensed |*

Linotype Library GmbH
www.linotype.com
info@linotype.com
+49 (0) 6172 484.418

AaBbCcDdEeFfGgHhIiJjKkLlMmNnOoPpQqR
SsTtUuVvWwXxYyZz0123456789!?WAs%&'():;
" "

The quick brown fox jumps over the lazy dog.

D

Rundfunk™
*Serif | Bold Weight |
Pronounced Contrast |
Condensed |*

Linotype Library GmbH
www.linotype.com
info@linotype.com
+49 (0) 6172 484.418

AaBbCcDdEeFfGgHhIiJjKkLl
MmNnOoPpQqRrSsTtUuVvWw
XxYyZz0123456789!?& @#$%

The quick brown fox jumps over the lazy dog.

D **t**

LTC Goudy Heavyface
*Serif | Pronounced Contrast |
Black Weight |*

P22 Type Foundry
www.p22.com
p22@p22.com
800.P22.5080

AABBCcDDEeFFGGHhIIJJKkLLMmNN
OoPpQqRRSsTtUuVvWwXxYyZz0123
456789!?&@$:;""

THE QUICK BROWN FOX JUMPS OVER THE LAZY DOG.

D

Venis Small Caps Bold
*Stylized Sans Serif | Slightly
Extended | Moderate Contrast |
Caps and Small Caps |*

The Chank Company
www.chank.com
friendlyfolks@chank.com
877.GO.CHANK

Machine Age Color

Perhaps the single most defining color of the Machine Age palette is red: a bright, slightly cool red of medium value and intense saturation. In combination with black, cool gray, white, light cream, and parchment, red immediately references the aesthetic of the period, appearing in countless posters, advertisements, publications, and interiors. A complementary cobalt blue—edging toward violet but still clearly retaining its identity—augments the palette. Because of early offset printing technology, the surprint—in which ink colors are printed directly on top of one another for the sake of simplicity— colors made from such direct overlaps of the base colors are also prominent in the palette. The surprint of red on top of a neutral gray, for example, creates a color that is commonly seen in printed ephemera from the time.

Sample Color Combinations

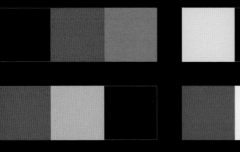

>	0 C
	100 M
	80 Y
	20 K

>	20 C
	20 M
	20 Y
	100 K

>	12 C
	0 M
	0 Y
	54 K

>	4 C
	3 M
	14 Y
	2 K

>	4 C
	5 M
	17 Y
	8 K

>	100 C
	70 M
	0 Y
	0 K

>	0 C
	62 M
	75 Y
	63 K

>	29 C
	14 M
	0 Y
	41 K

>	0 C
	10 M
	20 Y
	25 K

>	0 C
	0 M
	0 Y
	70 K

The glamour and style of the film industry's golden era—embodied in the films of Fairbanks, Garbo, and Astaire—are complemented and countered by the harsh realities of the Great Depression and World Wars. In type and color, a range of elegant and drab aspects comes together to encapsulate this contradictory time.

Hollywood Heyday

Typefaces from Hollywood's heyday, for the most part, are stylized and decorative. They include condensed sans-serif and serif forms with a great deal of stroke contrast and abrupt junctures, as well as a host of script faces that are elegant and highly refined—the kind of typefaces commonly used for film posters and advertising. Many of these faces are holdovers from Deco and Moderne, with a streamlined quality that carries some aspects of the Machine Age forward and evolves them into less austere forms with greater character and panache. Geometric sans serifs give way to more humanistic versions that incorporate serif details in the lowercase, as in Franklin Gothic. Gothic/serif hybrids, such as Copperplate—uniform-weight, all-capital sans serifs with truncated, almost vestigial, serifs—are also common, especially in the context of industry and municipal design work.

Print Collateral
top, and detail, bottom

Studio Flux (Now ODO)
John Moes, Holly Robbins
Minneapolis *USA*

ABCDEFGHIJKLMNOPQRSTUV
WXYZ0123456789!?&@#$%

THE QUICK BROWN FOX JUMPS OVER THE LAZY DOG.

D

Laureate Three
Stylized Sans Serif |
Extra Light Weight | All Caps

T.26 Digital Type Foundry
www.t26.com
info@t26.com
888.T26.FONT

ABCDEFGHIJKLMNOPQRST
UVWXYZ0123456789!?&@$
%[]()*:;""

THE QUICK BROWN FOX JUMPS OVER THE LAZY DOG.

D

Keester Black
Stylized Sans Serif | Heavy
Bold Weight |
Pronounced Contrast |

The Chank Company
www.chank.com
friendlyfolks@chank.com
877.GO.CHANK

AaBbCcDdEeFfGgHhIiJjKkLlMmNn
OoPpQqRrSsTtUuVvWwXxYyZz0123
456789!?@#$%&*(){}:;""
The quick brown fox jumps over the lazy dog.

D **T**

Bernhard Modern™ Roman
Serif | Medium Weight |
Modulation | Abrupt Joints |

Linotype Library GmbH
www.linotype.com
info@linotype.com
+49 (0) 6172 484.418

AaBbCcDdEeFfGgHhIiJjKkLlMmNnOo
PpQqRrSsTtUuVvWwXxYyZz01234567
89!?@#$%&*(){}:;""
The quick brown fox jumps over the lazy dog.

D

Bernhard Fashion
Sans Serif | Ultra Light
Weight | Uniform Strokes |
Exaggerated Proportions |

Linotype Library GmbH
www.linotype.com
info@linotype.com
+49 (0) 6172 484.418

AaBbCcDdEeFfGgHhIiJjKkLlMm
NnOoPpQqRrSsTtUuVvWwXxYyZz
0123456789!?&@#$%*:;"
The quick brown fox jumps over the lazy dog.

D

Laundrette
Stylized Geometric Serif |
Mixed Width | Pronounced
Contrast | Bold Weight |

The Chank Company
www.chank.com
friendlyfolks@chank.com
877.GO.CHANK

AaBbCcDdEeFfGgHhIiJjKkLlMm
NnOoPpQqRrSsTtUuVvWwXxYy
Zz0123456789!?&fl©%*:;()$""
The quick brown fox jumps over the lazy dog.

D **t**

Artemisia
Script–Sans Serif Hybrid |
Uniform Light Weight |

Nick's Fonts
www.nicksfonts.com

A a B b C c D d E e F f G g H h I i J j K k L l M m N n
O o P p Q q R r S s T t U u V v W w X x Y y Z z 0 1 2 3
4 5 6 7 8 9   ! ? & fi % * ( ) [ ] : ; " " © $ ¥
The quick brown fox jumps over the lazy dog.

De Rigueur
Stylized Sans Serif |
Dislocated Joints |
Black Weight |

Nick's Fonts
www.nicksfonts.com

A a B b C c D d E e F f G g H h I i J j K k L l M m N n O o P p
Q q R r S s T t U u V v W w X x Y y Z z 0 1 2 3 4 5 6 7 8 9 ! ? &
% : ; ( ) [ ] * $ " "
The quick brown fox jumps over the lazy dog.

Londonderry Air
Script–Sans Serif Hybrid |
Uniform Light Weight |

Nick's Fonts
www.nicksfonts.com

A a B b C c D d E e F f G g H h I i J j K k
L l M m N n O o P p Q q R r S s T t U u
V v W w X x Y y Z z 0 1 2 3 4 5 6 7 8 9
! ? @ # $ % & * ( ) { } : ; " "
The quick brown fox jumps over the lazy dog.

ITC Hornpype™
Graphic Serif | Black Weight |
Moderate Contrast | Inline
Detail | Modulated Contours |

Linotype Library GmbH
www.linotype.com
info@linotype.com
+49 (0) 6172 484.418

A B C D E F G H I J K L M N O P Q R S T U V W X
Z 0 1 2 3 4 5 6 7 8 9 ! ? @ # $ % & " ( ) { } : ; " "

THE QUICK BROWN FOX JUMPS OVER THE LAZY DOG.

Nord Express
Graphic | Extended |
Solid-Outline Hybrid |

Nick's Fonts
www.nicksfonts.com

A A B C D E F G H I J K K L M M N O P Q R S T U U
V W W X Y Z 0 1 2 3 4 5 6 7 8 9 ! ? & @ # $ % * : ; "

THE QUICK BROWN FOX JUMPS OVER THE LAZY DOG.

LTC Spire
Serif | Extreme Contrast |
Extra Condensed |

P22 Type Foundry
www.p22.com
p22@p22.com
800.P22.5080

A a B b C c D d E e F f G g H h I i J J K L M m N n O o P p Q q R r
S S T t U u V w X Y Z 0 1 2 3 4 5 6 7 8 9 ! ? ¢ @ # $ % * : ;

The quick brown fox jumps over the lazy dog.

Industrie No. 35
Stylized Sans Serif | Extra
Condensed | Mixed Case with
Selected Alternates |

The Chank Company
www.chank.com
friendlyfolks@chank.com
877.GO.CHANK

A a B b C c D d E e F f G g H h I i J j K k L l M m N n O o P p Q q R r S s T t U u V v W w X x Y y Z z 0 1 2 3 4 5 6 7 8 9 ! ? & @ # $ % * : ; "

The quick brown fox jumps over the lazy dog.

D *t*

Cocaine
Stylized Slab Serif | Erratic Proportions | Pronounced Serifs |

The Chank Company
www.chank.com
friendlyfolks@chank.com
877.GO.CHANK

A a B b C c D d E e F f G g H h I i J j K k L l M m N n O o P p Q q R r S s T t U u V v W w X x Y y Z z 0 1 2 3 4 5 6 7 8 9 !? @ # $ % & * ( ) { } : ; " "

The quick brown fox jumps over the lazy dog.

D

Radiogram Regular
Stylized Sans Serif | Pronounced Contrast | Extra Condensed |

Device
www.devicefonts.co.uk
rianhughes@aol.com
44 (0) 7979.602.272

A a B b C c D d E e F f G g H h I i J j K k L l M m N n O o P p Q q R r S s T t U u V v W w X x Y y Z z 0 1 2 3 4 5 6 7 8 9 !? @ # $ % & * ( ) { } : ; " "

The quick brown fox jumps over the lazy dog.

D

Bernhard Bold Condensed
Serif | Bold Weight | Pronounced Contrast | Condensed |

Linotype Library GmbH
www.linotype.com
info@linotype.com
+49 (0) 6172 484.418

A a B b C c D d E e F f G g H h I i J j K k L l M m N n O o P p Q q R r S s T t U u V v W w X x Y y Z z 0 1 2 3 4 5 6 7 8 9 ! ? @ # $ % & * ( ) { } : ; " "

The quick brown fox jumps over the lazy dog.

D T

Univers™ 57 Condensed
Sans Serif | Medium Weight | Uniform Strokes | Condensed |

Linotype Library GmbH
www.linotype.com
info@linotype.com
+49 (0) 6172 484.418

A a B b C c D d E e F f G g H h I i J j K k L l M m N n O o P p Q q R r S s T t U u V v W w X x Y y Z z 0 1 2 3 4 5 6 7 8 9 !? $ % & * ( ) : ; " "

The quick brown fox jumps over the lazy dog.

D

Burlington™
Serif | Medium Weight | Pronounced Contrast | Two-Weight-Stroke Inline | Condensed |

Linotype Library GmbH
www.linotype.com
info@linotype.com
+49 (0) 6172 484.418

A a B b C c D d E e F f G g H h I i J j K k L l M m N n O o P p Q q R r S s T t U u V v W w X x Y y Z z 0 1 2 3 4 5 6 7 8 9 ! ? & @ # $ % * : ; "

The quick brown fox jumps over the lazy dog.

D

Jawbox
Graphic Sans Serif | Pronounced Upper Emphasis | Medium Weight |

The Chank Company
www.chank.com
friendlyfolks@chank.com
877.GO.CHANK

A a B b C c D d E e F f G g H h I i J j K k L l M m
N n O o P p Q q R r S s T t U u V v W w X x Y y Z z
0 1 2 3 4 5 6 7 8 9 ! ? @ # $ % & * ( ) { } : ; " "
The quick brown fox jumps over the lazy dog.

D T

Metromedium #2 Roman
Sans Serif | Medium Weight | Abrupt Joints |

Linotype Library GmbH
www.linotype.com
info@linotype.com
+49 (0) 6172 484.418

*A a B b C c D d E e F f G g H h I i J j K k L l M m
N n O o P p Q q R r S s T t U u V v W w X x Y y Z z
0 1 2 3 4 5 6 7 8 9 ! ? & @ # $ % * : ; "*

The quick brown fox jumps over the lazy dog.

D

LTC Flash
Stylized Sans Serif | Brush Detail | Medium Weight | Acute Posture |

P22 Type Foundry
www.p22.com
p22@p22.com
800.P22.5080

A a B b C c D d E e F f G g H h I i J j K k L l M m
N n O o P p Q q R r S s T t U u V v W w X x Y y Z z
0 1 2 3 4 5 6 7 8 9 ! ? @ # $ % & * ( ) { } : ; " "
THE QUICK BROWN FOX JUMPS OVER THE LAZY DOG.

D

ITC Vintage™
Sans Serif | Medium Weight | Notable Contrast | Caps and Small Caps |

Linotype Library GmbH
www.linotype.com
info@linotype.com
+49 (0) 6172 484.418

**A a B b C c D d E e F f G g H h I i J j K k L l M m N n O o
P p Q q R r S s T t U u V v W w X x Y y Z z 0 1 2 3 4 5 6 7
8 9 ! ? @ # $ % & * ( ) { } : ; " "**

The quick brown fox jumps over the lazy dog.

D t

Egyptian Bold Condensed
Slab Serif | Black Weight | Condensed |

Linotype Library GmbH
www.linotype.com
info@linotype.com
+49 (0) 6172 484.418

A a B b C c D d E e F f G g H h I i J j K k L l M m N n O o P p
Q q R r S s T t U u V v W w X x Y y Z z 0 1 2 3 4 5 6 7 8 9 ! ? & @
$ % * : ; "

The quick brown fox jumps over the lazy dog.

D

Peccadillo 24
Slab Serif | Extra Condensed | Light Weight |

MVB Fonts
www.mvbfonts.com
info@mvbfonts.com
510.525.4288

A a B b C c D d E e F f G g H h I i J j K k L l M m
N n O o P p Q q R r S s T t U u V v W w X x Y y Z
0 1 2 3 4 5 6 7 8 9 ! ? & @ # $ % * : ; "

The quick brown fox jumps over the lazy dog.

D

Zephyr Openface
Serif | Light Weight | Moderate Contrast | Inline and Swash Details |

P22 Type Foundry
www.p22.com
p22@p22.com
800.P22.5080

Hollywood Heyday Color

The color palette of this time frame is subtle and varied, mixing neutrals and desaturated hues of the late 1920s and early 1930s with neutrals, metallics, and bolder hues prevalent toward the end of World War II. Elegant mauves, pinks, and lavenders; cool, almost-colored grays; white, cream, and ivory; and neutral gray, black, and white, are characteristic of photography and film-industry fashions and interiors. Cherry and walnut wood tones evoke the sumptuous offices of Hollywood moguls, as does a deep green that is almost black—a reference to marcasite and marble used for interior detailing. Copper, silver, bronze, and a sultry, lipstick red—even cooler than the red of the Machine Age—bring a darker and more vivid range of neutral and warm color to the palette.

Sample Color Combinations

❯
0 C
43 M
0 Y
15 K

❯
21 C
38 M
0 Y
13 K

❯
35 C
35 M
0 Y
0 K

❯
8 C
0 M
0 Y
30 K

❯
0 C
3 M
12 Y
4 K

❯
0 C
10 M
10 Y
50 K

❯
0 C
65 M
45 Y
69 K

❯
5 C
0 M
0 Y
70 K

❯
68 C
68 M
0 Y
25 K

❯
0 C
35 M
77 Y
57 K

An unbridled optimism and an explosion of consumer culture inform the styles of the period after the Great Depression and World War II and on into the early 1960s. The beginnings of rock n' roll, TV dinners, and suburban living are evoked in a range of playful typefaces and a cartoonlike palette of colors.

Baby Boomer

Baby boomer type styles run the gamut from the neutral and professional-looking—owing to the proliferation of corporations, the burgeoning "identity" industry, the International Style of typography, and general social conformity—to the remarkably quirky and stylized, created in large part by the advertising industry to promote the exciting new consumer products and automobiles flooding the market. In the former category, neutral faces such as Univers, introduced by Monotype in 1958, exemplify the International Style's goal of systematizing and objectifying visual language across the world. In the latter category, many typefaces are exaggerated script faces with angular, geometric construction—rather than round and fluid. Squared curve forms, angular and tapered strokes joined abruptly in quasi-italic or script presentation, are common, as are cartoonish sans serifs that are exceptionally bold and extended and show a disconnect between outer and inner contours, as though the counters have been shifted out of their usual position. Some of these faces combine upper- and lowercase characters in one set—a popular stylistic conceit of the late 1950s and 1960s.

Poster *top, and detail, bottom*

Johnny V. Design
Johnny Vitorovich
Alexandria [VA] *USA*

AaBbCcDdEeFfGgHhIiJjKkLlMmNnOoPpQqRrSsTtUuVvWwXxYyZz
0123456789!?@#$%&*[]{}·:;""
The quick brown fox jumps over the lazy dog.

D

Slack Casual Medium
Stylized Sans Serif |
Extra Condensed |
Erratic Baseline |

Device
www.devicefonts.co.uk
rianhughes@aol.com
44 (0) 7979.602.272

AaBbCcDdEeFfGgHhIiJjKkLlMm
NnOoPpQqRrSsTtUuVvWwXxYyZz
0123456789!?&@#$%*:;"
The quick brown fox jumps over the lazy dog.

D *t*

Bello Script
Moderate Contrast | Bold
Weight | Moderate Slope |

Underware
www.underware.nl
info@underware.nl
31 (0) 70 42 78 117

AaBb Cc Dd Ee Ff Gg Hh Ii Jj Kk Ll
Mm Nn Oo Pp Qq Rr Ss Tt Uu Vv Ww
Xx Yy Zz 0123456789! ? & @ $:;""
The quick brown fox jumps over the lazy dog.

D

P22 Daddy-O Hip
Stylized Serif | Pronounced
Contrast | Erratic Weight |
Erratic Posture |

P22 Type Foundry
www.p22.com
p22@p22.com
800.P22.5080

AaBbCcDdEeFfGgHhIiJjKkLlMmNnOoPp
QqRrSsTtUuVvWwXxYyZz0123456789
!?@#$%&*(){}:;""
The quick brown fox jumps over the lazy dog.

D *t*

Bordello Bold
Modified Wedge Serif |
Uniform Bold Weight |
Erratic Posture |

Device
www.devicefonts.co.uk
rianhughes@aol.com
44 (0) 7979.602.272

aaBbCcDdEeFfGgHhIiJjKkLlMM
NNOOPPQQRRSSTTUUVVWWXXYY
ZZ0123456789!?&@#$%★:;"
THE QUICK BROWN FOX JUMPS OVER THE LAZY DOG.

D

P22 Sniplash
Stylized Sans Serif | Mixed
Case | Moderate Contrast |
Erratic Posture |

P22 Type Foundry
www.p22.com
p22@p22.com
800.P22.5080

AaBbCcDdEeFfGgHhIiJjKkLlMmNn
OoPpQqRrSsTtUuVvWwXxYyZz01234
56789!?&@#$%*:;"
The quick brown fox jumps over the lazy dog.

D **T**

MVB Pedestria Regular
Stylized Sans Serif | Lighter
Medium Weight |

MVB Fonts
www.mvbfonts.com
info@mvbfonts.com
510.525.4288

A a B b C c D d E e F f G g H h I i J j K k L l M m N n
O o P p Q q R r S s T t U u V v W w X x Y y Z z 0 1 2 3
4 5 6 7 8 9 ! ? & @ # $ % * : ; "

The quick brown fox jumps over the lazy dog.

D T

MVB Pedestria Bold
*Stylized Sans Serif |
Bold Weight |*

MVB Fonts
www.mvbfonts.com
info@mvbfonts.com
510.525.4288

A a B b C c D d E e F f G g H h I i J j K k L l M m N n
O o P p Q q R r S s T t U u V v W w X x Y y Z z 0 1 2
3 4 5 6 7 8 9 ! ? & @ $: ; " "

The quick brown fox jumps over the lazy dog.

D *t*

P22 Sparrow
*Stylized Serif | Lesser
Contrast | Light Weight |
Pronounced Serifs |*

P22 Type Foundry
www.p22.com
p22@p22.com
800.P22.5080

A a B b c c D d E e F f G g H h I i J j K k L l
M m N n O o P p Q q R r S s T t U u V v W w
X x Y y Z z 0 1 2 3 4 5 6 7 8 9 ! ? & @ # $ % * : ;

The quick brown fox jumps over the lazy dog.

D

Elevator Boy
*Stylized Sans Serif | Erratic
Bold Weight | Erratic Posture |*

The Chank Company
www.chank.com
friendlyfolks@chank.com
877.GO.CHANK

A A B B C C D D E E F F G G H H I I J J K K L L M M
N N O O P P Q Q R R S S T T U U V V W W X X Y Y Z Z
0 1 2 3 4 5 6 7 8 9 ! ? @ # $ % & * ( ) { } : ; " "

the quick brown fox jumps over the lazy dog.

D

Bingo
*Graphic | All Caps with
Alternates | Black Weight |*

Device
www.devicefonts.co.uk
rianhughes@aol.com
44 (0) 7979.602.272

A a B b C c D d E e F f G g H h I i J j K k L l M m
N n O o P p Q q R r S s T t U u V v W w X x Y y Z z
0 1 2 3 4 5 6 7 8 9 ! ? & @ # $ % * : ; "

The quick brown fox jumps over the lazy dog.

D

Parkway Motel
*Stylized Sans Serif |
Script Ligatures | Uniform
Medium Weight |*

The Chank Company
www.chank.com
friendlyfolks@chank.com
877.GO.CHANK

A a B b C c D d E e F f G g H h I i J j K k L l M m
N n O o P p 2 q R r S s T t U u V v W w X x Y y Z z
0 1 2 3 4 5 6 7 8 9 ! ? & @ # $ % * : ; "

The quick brown fox jumps over the lazy dog.

D

LTC Swing Bold
*Script | Uniform Medium
Weight | Moderate Posture |*

P22 Type Foundry
www.p22.com
p22@p22.com
800.P22.5080

Baby Boomer Color

The postwar, baby-boomer consumer culture is embodied in a color palette that is at once stylish, uplifting, and cartoonish. Candy apple red, bright orange, sea foam green, chartreuse, pale lemon yellow, pink, mauve, and sky blue are the predominant colors in the baby-boomer scheme. Pink, in particular—in the form of toned-down fuchsia and very pale cotton candy hues—is an important player in the baby-boomer palette. Though black and most neutrals are notably absent, a number of cool grays in different values form a neutral backdrop for these happy colors. Toward the later part of the period, into the 1960s, desaturated versions of these colors, as well as the introduction of olive and ochre, mark a shift in outlook and a more sophisticated aesthetic in development.

Sample Color Combinations

15 C **100 M** **71 Y** **0 K**	
0 C **70 M** **100 Y** **0 K**	
30 C **0 M** **38 Y** **0 K**	
22 C **0 M** **56 Y** **5 K**	
55 C **0 M** **0 Y** **0 K**	
0 C **40 M** **0 Y** **5 K**	
0 C **15 M** **0 Y** **0 K**	
5 C **0 M** **0 Y** **20 K**	
0 C **4 M** **43 Y** **25 K**	
0 C **32 M** **64 Y** **27 K**	

From the mods of the 1960s and the flower children of the 1970s to
the punks and ravers of the 1980s and 1990s, the counterculture has
had a profound impact on the visual language of recent times. Subversive,
outrageous, young, and energetic—antiestablishment design for the
street drives popular design in type and color.

Counterculture

Each phase of the counterculture is marked by its own styles of type, but
all the faces that evoke the counterculture genre have one thing in common:
they're anything but plain. For the most part, counterculture type styles
tend to be distressed, a reflection of social unrest that drives antiestablishment style. Mod typefaces of the 1960s show quirky, unbalanced distortions of more common faces, often extended sans serifs. The influence of
science fiction shows itself in geometric faces with graphic linear detailing,
hybrid upper- and lowercase character sets, futuristic, glyphic inclusions,
and so on. The mod street style is exuberant and sometimes comical,
reflected in typefaces in which the letters are canted at various angles
along the baseline or change in overall height or width from character to
character. Late 1960s and 1970s psychedelia introduces organic, rounded,
amorphous shapes in typefaces that carry Art Nouveau fluidity to an extreme
and often test the limits of legibility. 1970s and 1980s punk and new wave
are represented by jagged, dirty distortions from poor photocopying, cutting,
and pasting, usually performed on a sans-serif base, as well as highly
stylized fonts that sometimes refer back to the 1920s and 1930s—often
very condensed or very extended, with decorative geometric details or
inclusions. Rave culture of the 1990s finds expression in typefaces with
futuristic, experimental, almost techno digital structures and shifting,
rhythmic proportional changes among the characters.

Event Poster *top, and detail*

Kenzo Izutani Office Corp.
Tokyo *Japan*

AaBbCcDdEeFfGgHhIiJjKkLlMm
NnOoPpQqRrSsTtUuVvWwXxYyZz
0123456789!?■❊♥❧&✳()·;" "
THE QUICK BROWN FOX JUMPS OVER THE LAZY DOG.

D

F2F Poison Flowers™
*Graphic Sans Serif | Bold
Weight | Erratic Contrast |*

Linotype Library GmbH
www.linotype.com
info@linotype.com
+49 (0) 6172 484.418

AABBCCDD EE FFGG HH IIJJKK LL MM NN
OOPPQQ RRSSTT UUVVWWXXYYZZ
‹1234567890›!?*@□■■

THE QUICK BROWN FOX JUMPS OVER THE LAZY DOG.

D

P22 Blanco Neg
*Graphic | Medium Weight |
All Caps with Alternates |*

P22 Type Foundry
www.p22.com
p22@p22.com
800.P22.5080

*AaBbCcDdEeFfGgHhIiJjKkLlMm
NnOoPpQqRrSsTtUuVvWwXxYyZz
0123456789!?@#$%&*(){}:;" "
The quick brown fox jumps over the lazy dog.*

D

Lazybones™
*Graphic Serif | Bold Weight |
Reduced Contrast |
Swash Detail | Italic Posture |*

Linotype Library GmbH
www.linotype.com
info@linotype.com
+49 (0) 6172 484.418

AaBbCcDdEeFfGgHhIiJjKkLlMmNnOo
PpQqRrSsTtUuVvWwXxYyZz012345
6789!?$%&*[]:;" "
The quick brown fox jumps over the lazy dog.

D *t*

Data Seventy™
*Graphic | Medium Weight |
Squared Bowls and Shoulders |*

Linotype Library GmbH
www.linotype.com
info@linotype.com
+49 (0) 6172 484.418

AaBbCcDdEeFfGgHhIiJjKkLlMm
NnOoPpQqRrSsTtUuVvWwXxYyZz
0123456789!?@#$%&*(){}:;" "
The quick brown fox jumps over the lazy dog.

D *t*

F2F MadZine™ Dirt
*Graphic Serif | Medium Weight |
Textural Inclusions | Erratic
Posture | Slight Distortion |*

Linotype Library GmbH
www.linotype.com
info@linotype.com
+49 (0) 6172 484.418

AABBCCDDEEFFGGHHIIJJKKLL
MMNNOOPPQQRRSSTTUUVVWW
XXYYZZ0123456789!?&@$:;" "
THE QUICK BROWN FOX JUMPS OVER THE LAZY DOG.

D

P22 Pop Art Comic
*Stylized Sans Serif | Lighter
Medium Weight | Moderate
Italic Posture |*

P22 Type Foundry
www.p22.com
p22@p22.com
800.P22.5080

A A B B C C D D E E F F G G H H I I J J K K L L M M
N N O O P P Q Q R R S S T T U U V V W W X X Y Y Z Z
0 1 2 3 4 5 6 7 8 9 ! ? & ℗ # $ % * : ; "
THE QUICK BROWN FOX JUMPS OVER THE LAZY DOG.

D

Bollocks
Stylized Sans Serif | Bold Weight |
Pronounced Contrast |
Pronounced Lower Emphasis |

Garage Fonts Type Foundry
www.garagefonts.com
info@garagefonts.com
800.681.9375

A a B b C c D d E e F F G g H h I i J K K L L M m N
n O O P p Q q R p S s T T U u V v W w X x y y z z
0 1 2 3 4 5 6 7 8 9 ! ? @ # $ % & * ( ) [ ] ß ß " "
The quick brown fox jumps over the lazy dog.

D

Novak Spring
Graphic | Black Weight |
Swash and Illustrative Details |

Device
www.devicefonts.co.uk
rianhughes@aol.com
44 (0) 7979.602.272

A A B B C c D D E E F F G G H h I i J J K k L L M M
N N O O P P Q q R R S S T T U u V v W w X x Y Y Z z
0 1 2 3 4 5 6 7 8 9 ! ? AT No $ % & * ( ) [ ] : ; " "
THE QUICK BROWN FOX JUMPS OVER THE LAZY DOG.

D t

Reasonist Medium
Stylized Sans Serif |
Bold Weight | Pronounced
Upper Emphasis |

Device
www.devicefonts.co.uk
rianhughes@aol.com
44 (0) 7979.602.272

A a B b C c D d E e F f G g H h I i J j K K L l
M m N n O o P p Q q R r S s T t U u V v W w
X x Y y Z z 0 1 2 3 4 5 6 7 8 9 ! ? & @ # $ % * : ; "
The quick brown fox jumps over the lazy dog.

D t

Cabourg Regular
Sans Serif | Medium Weight |

T.26 Digital Type Foundry
www.t26.com
info@t26.com
888.T26.FONT

A a B b C c D d E e F f G g H h I i J j K k L l M m
N n O o P p Q q R r S s T t U u V v W w X x Y y Z z
0 1 2 3 4 5 6 7 8 9 ! ? @ # & : ; " "
The quick brown fox jumps over the lazy dog.

D

P22 Gothic Gothic
Stylized Sans Serif |
Uniform Medium Weight |
Gothic Fraktur Detail |

P22 Type Foundry
www.p22.com
p22@p22.com
800.P22.5080

A a B C C D D E e F F G H I i J K L M M N N
O P P Q R S T U V V W W X Y Z 0 1 2 3 4 5
6 7 8 9 ! ? & @ # $ % * : ; "
THE QUICK BROWN FOX JUMPS OVER THE LAZY DOG.

D

Jacks BV
Stylized Sans Serif | Mixed Case |
Bolder Medium Weight |

The Chank Company
www.chank.com
friendlyfolks@chank.com
877.GO.CHANK

AaBbCcDdEeFfGgHhIiJjKkLlMmNnOoPpQqRr
SsTtUuVvWwXxYyZz0123456789!?@#$%&*
[]{}:;" "

The quick brown fox jumps over the lazy dog.

D

ITC Black Tulip™
Sans Serif | Black Weight | Compressed Counters | Condensed |

Linotype Library GmbH
www.linotype.com
info@linotype.com
+49 (0) 6172 484.418

AaBbCcDdEeFfGgHhIiJjKkLlMmNnOo
PpQqRrSsTtUuVvWwXxYyZz0123456789
!?@#$%&*(){}:;" "

The quick brown fox jumps over the lazy dog.

D

Bottleneck™
Graphic Slab Serif | Black Weight | Pronounced Lower Horizontal Emphasis |

Linotype Library GmbH
www.linotype.com
info@linotype.com
+49 (0) 6172 484.418

AaBbCcDdEeFfGgHhIiJjKkLlMmNnOo
PpQqRrSsTtUuVvWwXxYyZz012345
6789!?$%&*():;" "

The quick brown fox jumps over the lazy dog.

D

Dalcora™
Sans Serif | Bold Weight | Erratic Contrast | Italic Posture |

Linotype Library GmbH
www.linotype.com
info@linotype.com
+49 (0) 6172 484.418

AABBCCDDEEFFGGHHIIJJKKLLMMNN
OOPPQQRRSSTTUUVVWWXXYYZZ0123
456789!?@#$%&*(){}:;""

THE QUICK BROWN FOX JUMPS OVER THE LAZY DOG.

D

Dauphine
Stylized Sans Serif | Uniform Light Weight | Caps and Small Caps |

Device
www.devicefonts.co.uk
rianhughes@aol.com
44 (0) 7979.602.272

AaBbCcDdEeFfGgHhIiJjKkLlMmNnOoPpQqRr
SsTtUuVvWwXxYyZz0123456789!?@#$%&*
(){}:;" "

The quick brown fox jumps over the lazy dog.

D

Zipper™
Sans Serif | Bold Weight | Condensed | Reversed Contrast |

Linotype Library GmbH
www.linotype.com
info@linotype.com
+49 (0) 6172 484.418

AaBbCcDdEeFfGgHhIiJjKkLlMmNn
ooPpQqRrSsTtUuVvWwXxYyZz0123
456789!?@#$%&*(){}:;" "

The quick brown fox jumps over the lazy dog.

D

Linotype Down Town™
Graphic | Erratic Weight and Contrast | Erratic Baseline |

Linotype Library GmbH
www.linotype.com
info@linotype.com
+49 (0) 6172 484.418

A B C D E F G H I J K L M N O P Q R
S T U V W X Y Z 0 1 2 3 4 5 6 7 8 9
! ? & @ Š : ; "

THE QUICK BROWN FOX JUMPS OVER THE LAZY DOG.

P22 Pop Art Stencil
Serif | All Caps | Bold Weight | Broken Joints |

P22 Type Foundry
www.p22.com
p22@p22.com
800.P22.5080

A a B b C c D d E e F f G g H h I i J j K k L l M m
N n O o P p Q q R r S s T t U u V v W w X x Y y Z z
0 1 2 3 4 5 6 7 8 9 ! ? @ # $ % & * ( ) { } : ; " "
The quick brown fox jumps over the lazy dog.

Linotype Fehrle Display™
Sans Serif | Black Weight | Compressed counters | Uniform Strokes | Extended |

Linotype Library GmbH
www.linotype.com
info@linotype.com
+49 (0) 6172 484.418

A B C D E F G H I J K L
M N O P Q R S T U V
W X Y Z 0 1 2 3 4 5 6 7 8 9 ! ? : ; "

THE QUICK BROWN FOX JUMPS OVER THE

P22 Stanyan Eros
Stylized Serif | All Caps with Illustrative Alternates | Pronounced Contrast |

P22 Type Foundry
www.p22.com
p22@p22.com
800.P22.5080

A a B b C c D d E e F f G g H h I i J j K k L l M m N n O o
P p Q q R r S s T t U u V v W w X x Y y Z z 0 1 2 3 4 5 6 7
8 9 ! ? % & * ( ) { } : ; " "
The quick brown fox jumps over the lazy dog.

Reporter™ #2
Graphic | Bold Weight | Brush Detail |

Linotype Library GmbH
www.linotype.com
info@linotype.com
+49 (0) 6172 484.418

A a B b C c D d E e F f G g H h I i J j K k L l M m
N n O o P p Q q R r S s T t U u V v W w X x Y y
Z z 0 1 2 3 4 5 6 7 8 9 ! ? $ % & * ( ) : ; " "
The quick brown fox jumps over the lazy dog.

Woodstock™
Slab Serif | Bold Weight | Rounded Terminals |

Linotype Library GmbH
www.linotype.com
info@linotype.com
+49 (0) 6172 484.418

A a B B C G D D E e F f G G H H I i J j K R L l
M M N N O O P P Q Q R r S S T t U U V V W W
X x Y y Z Z 0 1 2 3 4 5 6 7 8 9 ! ? & @ # $ % * : ; "

THE QUICK BROWN FOX JUMPS OVER THE LAZY DOG.

Perla
Stylized Serif | Pronounced Contrast | Uniform Cap and Lowercase Height |

T.26 Digital Type Foundry
www.t26.com
info@t26.com
888.T26.FONT

Counterculture Color

With its focus in urban areas, the counterculture is often represented by black, especially with regard to more recent phases—punk, new wave, and rave. With the addition of a variety of cool grays, in several values, the cool affectation of these neutrals acts as a backdrop to a number of other sub-schemes in color that distinguish the various periods. The exceptions to this black/gray color base are 1960s mod and 1970s psychedelia, both periods evoked by a riot of color—mod by violet, a more yellow version of Kelly green, and pink; psychedelia by bright orange, rust, brown, green, red, and blue, usually in combinations that involve all of these simultaneously. The new wave color scheme adds brighter versions of 1950s pink, blue, and sea foam green, along with chartreuse and hot red, to the black and gray backdrop; rave culture pushes the saturation of these colors into the acid and fluorescent realm, adding fluorescent orange, lime green, and aqua to the mix.

Sample Color Combinations

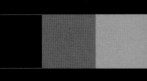

>	20 C / 0 M / 0 Y / 70 K
>	10 C / 0 M / 0 Y / 50 K
>	10 C / 0 M / 0 Y / 30 K
>	20 C / 20 M / 20 Y / 100 K
>	71 C / 85 M / 0 Y / 0 K
>	64 C / 0 M / 100 Y / 0 K
>	5 C / 80 M / 0 Y / 5 K
>	0 C / 66 M / 100 Y / 10 K
>	0 C / 64 M / 94 Y / 66 K
>	64 C / 0 M / 24 Y / 0 K

The late 1990s and early twenty-first century find a return to naturalism, spirituality, and concern for the future expressed in popular culture. Clashing to some degree with styles from heavy commercialism and exploding technology, the type and color of this period looks somewhat to the past as well as to the potential of upcoming generations.

New Age

The New Age is pluralistic in style, a reflection of conflicting outlooks; this dichotomy is mirrored in the typography of the present. At one end of the spectrum, historically derivative typefaces abound, with a concentration in humanistic serifs and strong display faces that hark back somewhat nostalgically to the 1930s, 1940s, and 1950s. Bold slab serifs and highly refined serif text faces abound, along with a resurfacing of organic script faces. These type styles seem to explore tried and true formal ideas, but evolved and influenced by technology—often showing joint and terminal detailing that are indicative of digital drawing. Hybrid forms, mixing details from various styles, come together in a search for something new while honoring the past—possibly an attempt to blend the simplicity and familiarity of yesteryear with the advances of the sometimes scary present day. Sans serifs in New Age style follow this trend as well, incorporating traditionally serif forms, especially in their lowercase characters, while exhibiting proportional shifts and peculiar terminal detailing that speaks to the potential of unexplored future design territory. Notably lighter serifs and sans serifs hint at quiet contemplation and some trepidation.

Packaging

STIM Visual Communication
Timothy Samara
New York City *USA*

A a β b C c D d E e F ₣ G g H h I i J j K K L l
M n N n O o P p Q q R r S s T t U u V v W ω X x
Y y Z z σ 1 2 3 4 5 6 7 8 9 ! ? @ # $ % & * ( ) { }
: ; " "

The quick brown fox jumps over the lazy dog.

**A a B b C c D d E e F f G g H h I i J j K k L l M m
N n O o P p Q q R r S s T t U u V v W w X x Y y
Z z 0 1 2 3 4 5 6 7 8 9 ! ? & @ # $ % * : ; "**

The quick brown fox jumps over the lazy dog.

A a B b C c D d E e F f G g H h I i J j K k L l M m N n
O o P p Q q R r S s T t U u V v W w X x Y y Z z 0 1 2 3
4 5 6 7 8 9 ! ? @ # $ % & * ( ) { } : ; " "

The quick brown fox jumps over the lazy dog.

A a B b c c D d E e F f G g H h I i J j K k L l M m N n O o P p
Q q R r S s T t U u V v W w X x Y y Z z 0 1 2 3 4 5 6 7 8 9
! ? a l $ % & * ( ) e i : ; " "

The quick brown fox jumps over the lazy dog.

A a B b C c D d E e F f G g H h I i J j K k L l M m N n
O o P p Q q R r S s T t U u V v W w X x Y y Z z 0 1 2 3
4 5 6 7 8 9 ! ? @ # $ % & * ( ) { } : ; " "

The quick brown fox jumps over the lazy dog.

A a B b C c D d E e F f G g H h I i J j K k L l M m N n O o
P p Q q R r S s T t U u V v W w X x Y y Z z 0 1 2 3 4 5 6 7
8 9 ! ? @ # $ % & * ( ) { } : ; " "

The quick brown fox jumps over the lazy dog.

D *t*

Elementis™ Std Regular
*Sans Serif | Light Weight |
Script Details | Rounded
Terminals |*

Linotype Library GmbH
www.linotype.com
info@linotype.com
+49 (0) 6172 484.418

D *t*

Yan Series 333 JY
Black Lining
*Semi-Serif | Lesser Contrast |
Bold Weight |
Brushform Details |*

JY&A Fonts
www.jyanet.com/fonts

D **T**

Joanna™
*Serif | Lighter Medium Weight |
Moderate Contrast |*

Linotype Library GmbH
www.linotype.com
info@linotype.com
+49 (0) 6172 484.418

D

Flight™
*Graphic Script | Ultra Light
Weight | Joint Contrast |
Erratic Posture and Baseline |*

Linotype Library GmbH
www.linotype.com
info@linotype.com
+49 (0) 6172 484.418

D *t*

ITC Tempus™ Sans Italic
*Sans Serif | Light Weight |
Slight Contrast |
Textured Contour |*

Linotype Library GmbH
www.linotype.com
info@linotype.com
+49 (0) 6172 484.418

D *t*

Linotype Nautilus™ Roman
*Sans Serif | Notable Contrast |
Condensed |*

Linotype Library GmbH
www.linotype.com
info@linotype.com
+49 (0) 6172 484.418

A a B b C c D d E e F f G g H h I i J j K k L l M m N n
O o P p Q q R r S s T t U u V v W w X x Y y Z z 0 1 2 3
4 5 6 7 8 9 ! ? $ % & * ( ) : ; " "

The quick brown fox jumps over the lazy dog.

D

Fling™
Script | Medium Weight |
Upright Posture |

Linotype Library GmbH
www.linotype.com
info@linotype.com
+49 (0) 6172 484.418

A a B b C c D d E e F f G g H h I i J j K k L l M m N n O o P p Q q R r
S s T t U u V v W w X x Y y Z z 0 1 2 3 4 5 6 7 8 9 ! ? @ # $ % & * ( )
{ } : ; " "

The quick brown fox jumps over the lazy dog.

D

Linotype Go Tekk™ Medium
Serif | Uniform Weight |
Angled Curves and Joints |
Condensed |

Linotype Library GmbH
www.linotype.com
info@linotype.com
+49 (0) 6172 484.418

A a B b C c D d E e F f G g H h I i J j K k L l M m N n
O o P p Q q R r S s T t U u V v W w X x Y y Z z 0 1 2 3
4 5 6 7 8 9 ! ? & @ # $ % * : ; "

The quick brown fox jumps over the lazy dog.

D t

JY Integrity Lining
Serif | Lesser Contrast |
Condensed | Light Weight |

JY&A Fonts
www.jyanet.com/fonts

A A B B C C D D E E F F G G H H I I J J K K L L M M
N N O O P P Q Q R R S S T T U U V V W W X X Y Y
Z Z 0 1 2 3 4 5 6 7 8 9 ! ? & @ # $ % * : ; "

THE QUICK BROWN FOX JUMPS OVER THE LAZY DOG.

D

Yan Series 333 JY SCOSF
Semi-Serif | Brush Details |
Uniform Light Weight |

JY&A Fonts
www.jyanet.com/fonts

A a B b C c D d E e F f G g H h I i J j K k L l M m N n O o P p
Q q R r S s T t U u V v W w X x Y y Z z 0 1 2 3 4 5 6 7 8 9 ! ?
@ # $ % & * ( ) { } : ; " "

The quick brown fox jumps over the lazy dog.

D t

ITC Nora™
Sans Serif | Notable Contrast |
Modulation | Curved Stems |
Script Detail |

Linotype Library GmbH
www.linotype.com
info@linotype.com
+49 (0) 6172 484.418

A a B b C c D d E e F f G g H h I i J j K k L l M m
N n O o P p Q q R r S s T t U u V v W w X x Y y Z z
0 1 2 3 4 5 6 7 8 9 ! ? & @ # $ % * : ; "

The quick brown fox jumps over the lazy dog.

D T

Auto 3 Italic
Script–Sans Serif Hybrid |
Moderately Condensed | Swash
Details | Uniform Light Weight |

Underware
ww.underware.nl
info@underware.nl
31 (0)70 42 78 117

New Age Color

A return to the familiarity of the natural and sometimes nostalgic coloring of the past mixes with unexpectedly vivid colors in the New Age palette. A series of muted beiges, ochres, warm and cool grays, subdued blue-green and lavender, and smoky ivory is supported by deep brown-black umber, mahogany, and olive to form a quiet, elegant, and decisive palette of naturalistic, even spiritual, hues. In contrast, saturated red-orange, black, blue violet and lime green—the influence of commercial popular culture and technology—present vivid foils to the calming aspects of the other colors in the New Age scheme. In combination, the two subpalettes present a sophisticated, albeit somewhat conflicted, color feeling that evokes the evolved yet anxious outlook of the age.

Sample Color Combinations

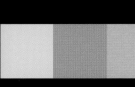

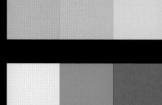

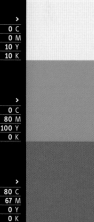

15 C	
15 M	
31 Y	
0 K	

0 C	
28 M	
67 Y	
50 K	

0 C	
68 M	
75 Y	
73 K	

10 C	
6 M	
0 Y	
30 K	

32 C	
0 M	
13 Y	
17 K	

28 C	
17 M	
0 Y	
13 K	

0 C	
0 M	
10 Y	
10 K	

0 C	
80 M	
100 Y	
0 K	

80 C	
67 M	
0 Y	
0 K	

0 C	
0 M	
75 Y	
62 K	

Soft and tiny, inspiring the nurturing instinct, babies have fresh, new minds waiting to learn about the world. Their newness and innocence inform the type styles and color choices used to communicate about— and with—newborns.

Babies

Of course, because babies don't read, typographic style in this category involves communicating to adults about babies, more than to babies directly. Typefaces that are simple in construction, with optically even widths among characters and a minimum of detailing, communicate the simple, pre-educated world of babies. Sans serifs, especially those with large x-heights, rounded terminals, and slight modulation in their strokes, allude to a baby's softness; slightly extended sans serifs with these qualities effect a slower cadence in reading, creating a calming sensation. Some serif faces that have smaller, more rounded serifs and larger x-heights—meaning open counters that feel bright and perky— also feel appropriate in conveying a newborn quality in a type style.

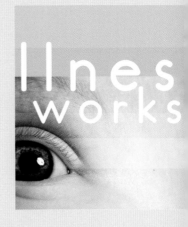

Program Cover
top, and detail, bottom

STIM Visual Communication
Timothy Samara
New York City *USA*

A a B b C c D d E e F f G g H h I i J j K k L l M m N n
O o P p Q q R r S s T t U u V v W w X x Y y Z z 0 1
2 3 4 5 6 7 8 9 ! ? & @ # $ % * : ; "

The quick brown fox jumps over the lazy dog.

P22 Platten Regular
Stylized Sans Serif | Medium Weight | Erratic Width |

P22 Type Foundry
www.p22.com
p22@p22.com
800.P22.5080

**A a B b C c D d E e F f G g H h I i J j K k L l
M m N n O o P p Q q R r S s T t U u V v W w
X x Y y Z z 0 1 2 3 4 5 6 7 8 9 ! ? & @ # $ % * : ;**

The quick brown fox jumps over the lazy dog.

Slippy Black Italic
Sans Serif | Moderate Posture | Slightly Extended |

T.26 Digital Type Foundry
www.t26.com
info@t26.com
888.T26.FONT

A a B b C c D d E e F f G g H h I i J j K k L l M m
N n O o P p Q q R r S s T t U u V v W w X x Y y Z z
0 1 2 3 4 5 6 7 8 9 ! ? @ # $ % & * ( ) { } : ; " "

The quick brown fox jumps over the lazy dog.

ITC Avant Garde Gothic®
Sans Serif | Medium Weight | Geometric Construction |

Linotype Library GmbH
www.linotype.com
info@linotype.com
+49 (0) 6172 484.418

A B C D E F G H I J K L M N O P Q R S
T U V W X Y Z 0 1 2 3 4 5 6 7 8 9 ! ? @ # $ % &
( ) { } * : ; " "

THE QUICK BROWN FOX JUMPS OVER THE LAZY DOG.

Critter™
Graphic | Black Weight | Illustrative Inclusions |

Linotype Library GmbH
www.linotype.com
info@linotype.com
+49 (0) 6172 484.418

A a B b C c D d E e F f G g H h I i J j K k L l M m N n
O o P p Q q R r S s T t U u V v W w X x Y y Z z 0 1 2 3
4 5 6 7 8 9 ! ? @ # $ % & * ( ) { } : ; " "

The quick brown fox jumps over the lazy dog.

Cronos™ Pro Bold
Sans Serif | Bold Weight | Slight Contrast | Canted and Rounded Terminals |

Linotype Library GmbH
www.linotype.com
info@linotype.com
+49 (0) 6172 484.418

A a B b C c D d E e F f G g H h I i J j K k L l M m N n
O o P p Q q R r S s T t U u V v W w X x Y y Z z 0 1
2 3 4 5 6 7 8 9 ! ? $ % & * ( ) : ; " "

The quick brown fox jumps over the lazy dog.

Frankfurter™ Medium
Sans Serif | Bold Weight | Uniform Strokes | Rounded Terminals |

Linotype Library GmbH
www.linotype.com
info@linotype.com
+49 (0) 6172 484.418

A B C D E F G H I J K L M N O P Q R S T U V W X
Y Z 0 1 2 3 4 5 6 7 8 9 ! ? $ % & * ( ) : ; " "

THE QUICK BROWN FOX JUMPS OVER THE LAZY DOG.

D

Frankfurter™ Normal
Sans Serif | Black Weight |
Uniform Strokes | Rounded
Terminals |

Linotype Library GmbH
www.linotype.com
info@linotype.com
+49 (0) 6172 484.418

A a B b C c D d E e F f G g H h I i J j K k
L l M m N n O o P p Q q R r S s T t U u V v
W w X x Y y Z z 0 1 2 3 4 5 6 7 8 9 ! ? @ # $ %
& * ( ) { } : ; " "

The quick brown fox jumps over the lazy dog.

D *t*

Memphis™ Extra Bold
Slab Serif | Black Weight |
Slight Contrast |

Linotype Library GmbH
www.linotype.com
info@linotype.com
+49 (0) 6172 484.418

A a B b C c D d E e F f G g H h I i J j K k L l M m N n
O o P p Q q R r S s T t U u V v W w X x Y y Z z 0 1 2 3
4 5 6 7 8 9 ! ? @ # $ % & * ( ) { } : ; " "

The quick brown fox jumps over the lazy dog.

D T

Sassoon® Infant Regular
Sans Serif | Light Weight |
Uniform Strokes | Script Details|

Linotype Library GmbH
www.linotype.com
info@linotype.com
+49 (0) 6172 484.418

A a B b C c D d E e F f G g H h I i J j K k L l M m N n
O o P p Q q R r S s T t U u V v W w X x Y y Z z 0 1 2 3
4 5 6 7 8 9 ! ? @ # $ % & * ( ) { } : ; " "

The quick brown fox jumps over the lazy dog.

D *t*

ITC Stylus™
Sans Serif | Light Weight |
Soft Joints | Rounded Terminals |

Linotype Library GmbH
www.linotype.com
info@linotype.com
+49 (0) 6172 484.418

A a B b C c D d E e F f G g H h I i J j K k L l M m N n
O o P p Q q R r S s T t U u V v W w X x Y y Z z 0 1 2 3
4 5 6 7 8 9 ! ? @ # $ % & * ( ) { } : ; " "

The quick brown fox jumps over the lazy dog.

D T

Stymie Medium
Slab Serif | Medium Weight |
Uniform Strokes |

Linotype Library GmbH
www.linotype.com
info@linotype.com
+49 (0) 6172 484.418

A a B b C c D d E e F f G g H h I i J j K k L l M m N n
O o P p Q q R r S s T t U u V v W w X x Y y Z z 0 1
2 3 4 5 6 7 8 9 ! ? @ # $ % & * ( ) { } : ; " "

The quick brown fox jumps over the lazy dog.

D T

VAG Rounded Bold
Sans Serif | Bold Weight |
Uniform Strokes | Rounded
Terminals |

Linotype Library GmbH
www.linotype.com
info@linotype.com
+49 (0) 6172 484.418

Baby Color

The palette for design related to babies is split into two parts—one for design work that will actually be used by babies, the other for communicating to adults about babies. In the former palette are saturated primaries and secondaries—red, yellow, blue, orange, green, violet—that are as pure as possible help babies begin to distinguish colors. Newborns and infants have still-developing optical systems and are able to distinguish only very vivid colors that are clearly unrelated. In communicating with adults about babies, however, the color palette is soft, pale, and muted, conveying the softness and freshness of babies. Pale pink and powder blue have traditionally been reserved for girls and boys, respectively, but as times change, a wider range of colors for both sexes is possible and may be intermixed. Soft lavender, mauve, yellow, light green-blue, sea foam or mint green, beige, taupe, and ivory are all part of the soft palette that conveys the idea of babies.

Sample Color Combinations

0 C	100 M	100 Y	0 K
0 C	10 M	100 Y	0 K
100 C	45 M	0 Y	0 K
81 C	0 M	100 Y	0 K
0 C	54 M	100 Y	0 K
44 C	92 M	0 Y	0 K
22 C	24 M	0 Y	0 K
24 C	0 M	15 Y	0 K
17 C	15 M	32 Y	0 K
0 C	3 M	13 Y	0 K

Out of the crib, onto the floor—and out the door! Toddlers are active and excited about exploring the world, especially now that they're mobile. Toddler style in typography and color is vibrant and fun.

Toddlers

The conventionally rounded approach to typefaces aimed at describing or communicating with babies is still valid for toddlers. Faces that are constructed simply and offer a minimum of confusing detail, especially sans serifs, dominate the category for this age group. Consider that toddlers of three—and even two—years of age will begin reading during this time; the simpler the letterforms, the easier it will be for them. Typefaces used to convey the idea of toddlers to adults may be more stylized. Sans serifs, in their simplicity, continue to convey the idea of childhood's early stages, but condensed, heavier weights, along with italics, convey the toddler's mobility. More decorative faces—ones that show different heights among characters, shifts above and below the baseline, or create disconnects between interior and exterior contours—present the quality of movement and new sense of self associated with these young explorers.

Book Pages *top, and detail*

STIM Visual Communication
Timothy Samara
New York City [NY] *USA*

A a B b C c D d E e F f G g H h I i J j K k L l M m N n
O o P p Q q R r S s T t U u V v W w X x Y y Z z 0 1
2 3 4 5 6 7 8 9 ! ? @ # $ % & * ( ) { } : ; " "
The quick brown fox jumps over the lazy dog.

Fontoon™
Graphic Sans Serif | Medium Weight | Hand-Drawn Detail | Condensed |

Linotype Library GmbH
www.linotype.com
info@linotype.com
+49 (0) 6172 484.418

A a B b C c D d E e F f G g H h I i J j K k L l M m
N n O o P p Q q R r S s T t U u V v W w X x Y y
Z z 0 1 2 3 4 5 6 7 8 9 ! ? & @ # $ % ✻ : ; "
The quick brown fox jumps over the lazy dog.

Sauna Black
Semi-Serif | Moderate Contrast | Slightly Extended |

Underware
www.underware.nl
info@underware.nl
31 (0)70 42 78 117

A a B b C c D d E e F f G g H h I i J j K K L l M m
N n O o P p Q q R r S s T t U u V v W w X x Y y Z z
0 1 2 3 4 5 6 7 8 9 ! ? & @ # $ % * : ; "
The quick brown fox jumps over the lazy dog.

P22 Toybox Regular
Graphic | Uniform Medium Weight | Erratic Baseline |

P22 Type Foundry
www.p22.com
p22@p22.com
800.P22.5080

A a B b C c D d E e F f G g H h I i J j K k L l
M m N n O o P p Q q R r S s T t U u V v W w
X x Y y Z z 0 1 2 3 4 5 6 7 8 9 ! ? & @ # $ % * : ; "
The quick brown fox jumps over the lazy dog.

MVB Grenadine
Sans Serif | Medium Weight |

MVB Fonts
www.mvbfonts.com
info@mvbfonts.com
510.525.4288

A a B b C c D d E e F f G g H h I i J j K k L l M m
N n O o P p Q q R r S s T t U u V v W w X x Y y
Z z 0 1 2 3 4 5 6 7 8 9 ! ? @ # $ % & * ( ) { }
: ; " "
The quick brown fox jumps over the lazy dog.

Carousel™
Serif | Black Weight | Extreme Contrast |

Linotype Library GmbH
www.linotype.com
info@linotype.com
+49 (0) 6172 484.418

A a B b C c D d E e F f G g H h I i J j K k L l
M m N n O o P p Q q R r S s T t U u V v W w
X x Y y Z z 0 1 2 3 4 5 6 7 8 9 ! ? @ # $ % & *
The quick brown fox jumps over the lazy dog.

ITC Freddo™
Sans serif | Black Weight | Pronounced Contrast | Soft Terminals |

Linotype Library GmbH
www.linotype.com
info@linotype.com
+49 (0) 6172 484.418

A a B b C c D d E e F f G g H h I i J j K K L l
M m N n O o P p Q q R r S s T t U u V v W w X x
Y y Z z 0 1 2 3 4 5 6 7 8 9 ! ? & @ # $ % * : ; "

The quick brown fox jumps over the lazy dog.

Nice Weekend Bold
Modified Slab Serif | Slightly Condensed | Medium Weight |

Garage Fonts Type Foundry
www.garagefonts.com
info@garagefonts.com
800.681.9375

A a B b C c D d E e F f G g H h I i J j K k L l M m
N n O o P p Q q R r S s T t U u V v W w X x Y y
Z z 0 1 2 3 4 5 6 7 8 9 ! ? & @ № $ % * : ; "

The quick brown fox jumps over the lazy dog.

Slappy Inline
Graphic | Uniform Medium Weight | Erratic Baseline |

T.26 Digital Type Foundry
www.t26.com
info@t26.com
888.T26.FONT

A a B b C c D d E e F f G g H h I i J j K k L l
M m N n O o P p Q q R r S s T t U u V v W w
X x Y y Z z 0 1 2 3 4 5 6 7 8 9 ! ? & @ # $ % * : ; "

The quick brown fox jumps over the lazy dog.

Arbuckle Black
Stylized Sans Serif | Small Counters |

Garage Fonts Type Foundry
www.garagefonts.com
info@garagefonts.com
800.681.9375

A a B b C c D d E e F f G g H h I i J j K K L l M m
N n O o P p Q q R r S s T t U u V v W w X x Y y Z z
0 1 2 3 4 5 6 7 8 9 ! ? ¢ @ # $ % * : ; "

The quick brown fox jumps over the lazy dog.

Chaloops
Graphic | Uniform Medium Weight | Erratic Baseline |

The Chank Company
www.chank.com
friendlyfolks@chank.com
877.GO.CHANK

A a B b C c D d E e F f G g H h I i J j K k L l M m N n
O o P p Q q R r S s T t U u V v W w X x Y y Z z 0 1 2 3
4 5 6 7 8 9 ! ? @ # $ % & * ( ) { } : ; " "

The quick brown fox jumps over the lazy dog.

Tekton™ Regular
Sans Serif | Light Weight | Uniform Strokes | Rounded Terminals |

Linotype Library GmbH
www.linotype.com
info@linotype.com
+49 (0) 6172 484.418

A a B b C c D d E e F f G g H h I i J j K K L l M m
N n O o P p Q q R r S s T t U u V v W w X x Y y Z z
0 1 2 3 4 5 6 7 8 9 ! ? ¢ @ # $ % . * : ; "

The quick brown fox jumps over the lazy dog.

Chumley Medium
Graphic | Uniform Medium Weight | Erratic Baseline |

The Chank Company
www.chank.com
friendlyfolks@chank.com
877.GO.CHANK

Toddler Color

Building on toddlers' newfound ability to distinguish more complex colors, the toddler palette expands on the baby palette of primaries. Tertiary colors—aqua, yellow-orange, fuchsia—and slightly desaturated primaries, along with basic neutrals, such as brown and beige, enter the palette. Combinations of these colors may be more analogous, meaning that colors that are related to one another may be combined—orange and yellow-orange, for example, or green and aqua. Neutrals, while sometimes appropriate, should be considered secondary with regard to the brighter hues of the color scheme and therefore used sparingly.

Sample Color Combinations

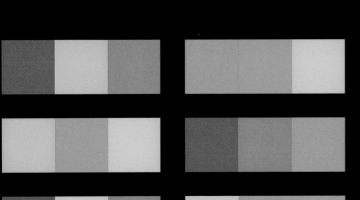

> 80 C
> 0 M
> 28 Y
> 0 K

> 15 C
> 92 M
> 0 Y
> 0 K

> 0 C
> 35 M
> 84 Y
> 0 K

> 0 C
> 77 M
> 65 Y
> 0 K

> 68 C
> 25 M
> 0 Y
> 0 K

> 54 C
> 11 M
> 49 Y
> 0 K

> 0 C
> 50 M
> 60 Y
> 52 K

> 20 C
> 20 M
> 25 Y
> 0 K

> 0 C
> 35 M
> 50 Y
> 0 K

> 68 C
> 0 M
> 5 Y
> 0 K

Playful, experimental, light hearted, direct, and a little independent—typefaces and color that capture these aspects and appeal to kids between four and ten years of age show movement and simplicity. They also convey the effortlessness and energy of games and toys, exploration, and kids' growing sense of themselves as entities separate from their parents.

Kids

An aspect of gaming or fun is the most common quality among typefaces that are directed toward a youthful audience or that try to evoke this group in communications. This fun element is rarely contrived in appearance, however, as simplicity and artlessness are equally important. Often, an extra-bold or black sans serif with geometric construction gives the appearance of smiling or cute eyes in the apertures of the lowercase; indeed, relying more on the lowercase tends to give the type a more childlike character. But soft, oldstyle serifs, with less contrast, especially in semibold or bold weights—in which their curves become more pronounced and rhythmic—take on a cherubic quality. Similarly, rounded-terminal sans serifs achieve this same formal quality. Typefaces from educational textbooks—slab serifs and serif gothics found in nursery rhyme or storybooks—connote school and education. For slightly older kids in this group who are reading and participating in activities such as sports and computer games, and who have been introduced to popular culture and entertainment, typefaces with abstract details, geometric construction, and illustrative inclusions resonate.

Beverage Packaging

Smith Design
Laura Markley, design
Jim Olson, lettering
Mike Wepplo, illustration
Glenn Ridge [NJ] *USA*

ⓇⓐℬⓑℭⓒⅅⓓℰℱⓕⓖℊℋℌⓗℐⓘⅉⓙℐⓀⓚℒⓛⓂⓜⓃⓝ
ⓄⓄℙℙℚⓠℛℱⓢ℠ⓉℰℰℐⅅℴⓦℐⓧⓎⓎℤℤⓄⅈ
②③④⑤⑥⑦⑧⑨!?@#$%℥⁕()﹛﹜﹕﹒"'"

The quick brown fox jumps over the lazy dog.

D

Strumpf™ Open
Graphic | Bold Weight |
Outline with Filled Counters |
Erratic Proportions |

Linotype Library GmbH
www.linotype.com
info@linotype.com
+49 (0) 6172 484.418

A A B B C c D D E e F F G G H H I i J J K K L L M m
N N O O P P Q Q R R S s T T U U V V W W X X Y Y
Z Z 0 1 2 3 4 5 6 7 8 9 ! ? ‡ @ # $ % ⌗ : ; "

The quick brown fox jumps over the lazy dog.

D

Brubeck's Cube
Graphic | Light Weight |
Outline | Extruded |

The Chank Company
www.chank.com
friendlyfolks@chank.com
877.GO.CHANK

A A B B C C D D E E F F G G H H I I J J K K L L
M M N N O O P P Q Q R R S S T T U U V V W W
X X Y Y Z Z 0 1 2 3 4 5 6 7 8 9 ! ? @ # $ % & * ( )
{ } : ; " "

THE QUICK BROWN FOX JUMPS OVER THE LAZY DOG.

D

ITC Static™
Graphic Slab Serif | Medium
Weight | Textured Contour |
Caps with Alternates |

Linotype Library GmbH
www.linotype.com
info@linotype.com
+49 (0) 6172 484.418

AaBbCcDdEeFfGgHhIiJjKkLlMmNn
OoPpQqRrSsTtUuVvWwXxYyZz
0123456789!?@▣$%&*(){}:;""

The quick brown fox jumps over the lazy dog.

D *t*

Foonky Starred
Graphic | Bold Weight |

Device
www.devicefonts.co.uk
rianhughes@aol.com
44 (0) 7979.602.272

A a B b C c D d E e F f G g H h I i J j K k L l M m
N n O o P p Q q R r S s T t U u V v W w X x Y y
Z z 0 1 2 3 4 5 6 7 8 9 ! ? @ # $ % & * ( ) { } : ; " "

The quick brown fox jumps over the lazy dog.

D **T**

ITC Tyfa™ Medium
Serif | Notable Contrast |
Slight Modulation |

Linotype Library GmbH
www.linotype.com
info@linotype.com
+49 (0) 6172 484.418

A a B b C c D d E e F f G g H h I i J j K k L l M m
N n O o P p Q q R r S s T t U u V v W w X x Y y
Z z 0 1 2 3 4 5 6 7 8 9 ! ? & @ # $ % * : ; "

The quick brown fox jumps over the lazy dog.

D

P22 Relax Regular
Stylized Sans Serif | Erratic
Weight | Pronounced Contrast |

P22 Type Foundry
www.p22.com
p22@p22.com
800.P22.5080

AABBCCDDEEFFGGHHIIJJKKLLMMN
NOOPPQQRRSSTTUUVVWWXXYYZZ
0123456789!?@#$%&*(){}:;""

THE QUICK BROWN FOX JUMPS OVER THE LAZY DOG.

D

Chantal Bold Italic
Stylized Sans Serif | Uniform Weights | Erratic Baseline | Caps and Small Caps |

Device
www.devicefonts.co.uk
rianhughes@aol.com
44 (0) 7979.602.272

AaBbCcDdEeFfGgHhIiJj KkLlMmNn
OoPpQqRrSsTtUuVvWwXxYyZz01
23456789!?&@$:;""

The quick brown fox jumps over the lazy dog.

D

P22 Vidro Regular
Graphic | Pronounced Contrast | Erratic Weight |

P22 Type Foundry
www.p22.com
p22@p22.com
800.P22.5080

AABBCCDDEEFFGGHHIIJJKKLL
MMNNOOPPQQRRSSTTUUVVWW
XXYYZZ0123456789!?&@#$%*:;

THE QUICK BROWN FOX JUMPS OVER THE LAZY DOG.

D

JY Comic Pro
Stylized Sans Serif | Uniform Weights | All Caps with Bold Alternates |

JY&A Fonts
www.jyanet.com/fonts

AaBbCcDdEeFfGgHhIiJjKkLlMmNn
OoPpQqRrSsTtUuVvWwXxYyZz012
3456789!?&@#$%*:;"

The quick brown fox jumps over the lazy dog.

D t

August Regular
Script–Sans Serif Hybrid | Moderate Contrast |

T.26 Digital Type Foundry
www.t26.com
info@t26.com
888.T26.FONT

AaBbCcDdEeFfGgHhIiJjKkLlMmNnOo
PpQqRrSsTtUuVvWwXxYyZz0123456
789!?@#$%&*(){}:;""

The quick brown fox jumps over the lazy dog.

D

Chascarillo
Graphic Script | Bold Weight | Erratic Proportions |

Device
www.devicefonts.co.uk
rianhughes@aol.com
44 (0) 7979.602.272

AaBbCcDdEeFfGgHhIiJjKkLl
MmNnOoPpQqRrSsTtUuVvWw
XxYyZz0123456789!?&@$:;""

The quick brown fox jumps over the lazy dog.

D

Yellabelly
Script | Uniform Medium Weight | Moderate Posture |

The Chank Company
www.chank.com
friendlyfolks@chank.com
877.GO.CHANK

aaBbCcDdEeFfGgHhIiJjKKLl
mmnnooPpQqRrSsEtUuVvwWW
xXYYZZ0123456789!?&@#§%*:;

the quick brown fox jumps over the lazy dog.

Marshmallow Superpuff
Stylized Sans Serif | Unicase with Alternates | Medium Weight |

T.26 Digital Type Foundry
www.t26.com
info@t26.com
888.T26.FONT

AaBbCcDdEeFfGgHhIiJjKkLlMmNnOo
PpQqRrSsTtUuVvWwXxYyZz01234567
89!?@#$%&*(){}:;" "

The quick brown fox jumps over the lazy dog.

Linotype Leggodt™ One
Graphic Sans Serif | Medium Weight | Grid Construction |

Linotype Library GmbH
www.linotype.com
info@linotype.com
+49 (0) 6172 484.418

AaBbCcDdEeFfGgHhIiJjKkLlMm
NnOoPpQqRrSsTtUuVvWwXxYyZz
0123456789!?@#$%&°(){}::" "

The quick brown fox jumps over the lazy dog.

Chwast Buffalo™ Black Condensed
Sans Serif | Black Weight | Serif Detail | Condensed |

Linotype Library GmbH
www.linotype.com
info@linotype.com
+49 (0) 6172 484.418

AaBbCcDdEeFfGgHhIiJjKkLlMmNn
OoPpQqRrSsTtUuVvWwXxYyZz01
23456789!?@#$%&*(){}:;" "

The quick brown fox jumps over the lazy dog.

Linotype Conrad™ Regular
Slab Serif | Medium Weight | Modulation | Slight Italic Posture

Linotype Library GmbH
www.linotype.com
info@linotype.com
+49 (0) 6172 484.418

AaBbCcDdEeFfGgHhIiJjKkLlMmNn
OoPpQqRrSsTtUuVvWwXxYyZz0123
456789!?@#$%&*(){}:;""

The quick brown fox jumps over the lazy dog.

F2F MadZine™ Fear
Graphic | Bold Weight | Stroke Distortion | Condensed |

Linotype Library GmbH
www.linotype.com
info@linotype.com
+49 (0) 6172 484.418

AaBbCcDdEeFfGgHhIiJjKkLlMmNn
OoPpQqRrSsTtUuVvWwXxYyZz0123
456789!?&@#$%*:;"

THE QUICK BROWN FOX JUMPS OVER THE LAZY DOG.

Megan
Graphic | Bold Weight | Pronounced Contrast | Erratic Baseline |

The Chank Company
www.chank.com
friendlyfolks@chank.com
877.GO.CHANK

A a B b C c D d E e F f G g H h I i J j K k L l M m
N n O o P p Q q R r S s T t U u V v W w X x Y y
Z z 0 1 2 3 4 5 6 7 8 9 ! ? @ # $ % & * ( ) { } : ; " "
The quick brown fox jumps over the lazy dog.

D T

**New Century Schoolbook™
Roman**
*Serif | Medium Weight |
Moderate Contrast |*

Linotype Library GmbH
www.linotype.com
info@linotype.com
+49 (0) 6172 484.418

A a B b C c D d E e F f G g H h I i J j
K k L l M m N n O o P p Q q R r S s T t
U u V v W w X x Y y Z z 0 1 2 3 4 5 6 7
8 9 ! ? @ # $ % & * ( ) { } : ; " "
The quick brown fox jumps over the lazy dog.

D

Postino™
*Slab Serif | Bold Weight |
Erratic Modulation |*

Linotype Library GmbH
www.linotype.com
info@linotype.com
+49 (0) 6172 484.418

A a B b C c D d E e F f G g H h I i J j Kk Ll Mm
N n O o P p Q q R r S s T t U u V v W w X x Y y
Z 3 0 1 2 3 4 5 6 7 8 9 ! ? & @ $: ; " "

The quick brown fox jumps over the lazy dog.

D *t*

P22 Stanyan Autumn Bold
*Graphic | Light Weight |
Exaggerated Descenders |*

P22 Type Foundry
www.p22.com
p22@p22.com
800.P22.5080

A a B b C c D d E e F f G g H h I i J j K k L l M m
N n O o P p Q q R r S s T t U u V v W w X x Y y Z z
0 1 2 3 4 5 6 7 8 9 ! ? & @ # $ % * : ; "

The quick brown fox jumps over the lazy dog.

D T

Bawdy Bold
*Stylized Sans Serif |
Bold Weight |*

The Chank Company
www.chank.com
friendlyfolks@chank.com
877.GO.CHANK

A A B B C C D D E E F F G G H H I I J J K K L L M M
N N O O P P Q Q R R S S T T U U V V W W X X
Y Y Z Z 0 1 2 3 4 5 6 7 8 9 ! ? @ # $ % & * ( ) { }
: ; " "

THE QUICK BROWN FOX JUMPS OVER THE LAZY DOG.

D

ITC Surfboard™
*Graphic | Bold Weight | Stroke
Distortion | Sharp Terminals |*

Linotype Library GmbH
www.linotype.com
info@linotype.com
+49 (0) 6172 484.418

A a B b C c D d E e F f G g H h I i J j K k L l M m N n O o
P p Q q R r S s T t U u V v W w X x Y y Z z 0 1 2 3 4
5 6 7 8 9 ! ? ¢ @ # $ % * : ; "

The quick brown fox jumps over the lazy dog.

D

Chauncy Decaf Medium
*Graphic | Uniform Medium
Weight | Erratic Baseline |*

The Chank Company
www.chank.com
friendlyfolks@chank.com
877.GO.CHANK

Kid Color

Variations on the additive primaries—red, blue, and yellow—are the base scheme in a color palette for kids. Their "basic" quality connotes simplicity and even a naïve character. Shifting the primaries as a set left and right toward analogous color sets increases the complexity and sophistication of the color mix, mirroring the increasingly sophisticated age group represented or targeted by the colors. Generally, intense colors in combination that are near complementary, or at least very separate, on the color wheel—orange, cyan, hot pink, leafy green—promote the same association as primaries. As the age of the audience increases, so too does their taste for more complex colors and combinations. Black and gray are introduced as neutrals, and triadic or systematic color relationships also come into play—using two or three analogous colors and a complementary accent, for example.

Sample Color Combinations

> 0 C
> 84 M
> 100 Y
> 0 K

> 0 C
> 39 M
> 100 Y
> 0 K

> 31 C
> 0 M
> 80 Y
> 0 K

> 79 C
> 42 M
> 0 Y
> 0 K

> 65 C
> 88 M
> 0 Y
> 12 K

> 100 C
> 0 M
> 0 Y
> 0 K

> 0 C
> 100 M
> 0 Y
> 0 K

> 69 C
> 0 M
> 68 Y
> 0 K

> 75 C
> 18 M
> 29 Y
> 0 K

> 0 C
> 0 M
> 0 Y
> 40 K

Yo, that's cool, dawg! Young adults, from early teenagers to pre-college age, are increasingly independent and looking to establish their identities as adults, experimenting and rebelling. Typography and color targeted at adolescents is expressive, irreverent, and always cool.

Young Adults

Stylistically, typefaces that appeal to young adults are all over the place—much like the age group itself. One defining attribute that binds them together, however, is their pronounced difference from styles that are plain, austere, or conventional in any way. Younger teens respond to faces with dramatic proportional changes, bold weights, abstract detailing—such as patterns, geometric shape inclusions, curlicues, oddly shaped slab serifs, and so on—and faces that appear unstable. Within this category, type styles that are appear drawn or manipulated by hand mirror young adults' search for identity and convey a sense of impropriety or non-schoolishness. Older teens, as they evolve into maturity, respond to faces of slightly more conventional structure but with sharper and somewhat less pronounced detailing than those associated with younger teens. Faces that are derived from classical type but that have been distorted or otherwise visually compromised, as well as those that are extremely experimental in structure, appeal to young adults' sense of rebellion, and their efforts to separate their identities from those of their parents.

Event Poster *top,*
and detail, bottom

Modern Dog Design Co.
Junichi Tsuneoka
Seattle *USA*

ᎪₐᏴᏏᏟ🜂ᎠᏇᎬ➾ᎦᎦᎶᎶᎻᎻᏂᏓᎥᎥᏗᎥᏥ🜂
ᏞᎥᎷᏔᏁᏁᎣᎣᎣᏢᏢᏗᎶᏒᏒᏕᏕᏖᏖᏔᏔ
ᏌᎥᏔᏔᏐᎯᎯᏙᏙᏕᏕᎣᎥᎶᎶᏔᏎᏮᏮᎴᏝᏝ
ᎥᎮᏕᏕᎪᏕᎰᎴᎴᎴᏗᏗᎴᏗᏗᏗᏗᏗ " "

the quick brown fox jumps over the lazy dog.

D

Linotype GlassFlag™ Regular
Graphic Sans Serif |
Medium Weight | Extended |
Stroke Distortion

Linotype Library GmbH
www.linotype.com
info@linotype.com
+49 (0) 6172 484.418

A B C D E F G H I J K L M N O P Q R S T U V W X Y Z
0 1 2 3 4 5 6 7 8 9 ! ? $ % & ° ( ) : ; " "

THE QUICK BROWN FOX JUMPS OVER THE LAZY DOG.

D

Princetown™
Slab Serif | Bold Weight |
Heavy Outline Detail | Angled
Curve Structure |

Linotype Library GmbH
www.linotype.com
info@linotype.com
+49 (0) 6172 484.418

**A a B b C c D d E e F f G g H h I i J j K k L l M m
N n O o P p Q q R r S s T t U u V v W w X x Y y
Z z 0 1 2 3 4 5 6 7 8 9 ! ? & @ # $ % * : ; "**

The quick brown fox jumps over the lazy dog.

D **T**

JY Raj Extra Bold
Sans Serif | Bold Weight |

JY&A Fonts
www.jyanet.com/fonts

A a B b C c D d E e F f G g H h I i J j K k L l M m N n O o P p Q q
R r S s T t U u V v W w X x Y y Z z 0 1 2 3 4 5 6 7 8 9 ! ? @ # $ %
& * ( ) { } : ; " "

The quick brown fox jumps over the lazy dog.

D *t*

DIN 1451 EngSchrift
Sans Serif | Medium Weight |
Condensed |
Squared Shoulders |

Linotype Library GmbH
www.linotype.com
info@linotype.com
+49 (0) 6172 484.418

*A a B b C c D d E e F f G g H h I i J j K k L l M m
N n O o P p Q q R r S s T t U u V v W w X x Y y Z z
0 1 2 3 4 5 6 7 8 9 ! ? @ # $ % & * ( ) { } : ; " "
The quick brown fox jumps over the lazy dog.*

D

F2F BoneR™ Book
Graphic | Erratic Weight and
Contrast | Extreme Italic
Posture | Stroke Distortion |

Linotype Library GmbH
www.linotype.com
info@linotype.com
+49 (0) 6172 484.418

A a B b C c D d E e F f G g H h I i J j K k L l M m N n O o
P p Q q R r S s T t U u V v W w X x Y y Z z 0 1 2 3 4 5
6 7 8 9 ! ? & @ # $ % * : ; "

The quick brown fox jumps over the lazy dog.

D **T**

Domestos Serif
Serif | Moderate Contrast |
Medium Weight |

T.26 Digital Type Foundry
www.t26.com
info@t26.com
888.T26.FONT

AaBbCcDdEeFfGgHhIiJjKkLlMmNnOoPp
QqRrSsTtUuVvWwXxYyZz0123456789
!?@#$%&*[]{}:;""

The quick brown fox jumps over the lazy dog.

Linotype Rezident™ One
*Sans Serif | Light Weight |
Condensed | Abrupt Joints and
Angles | Slight Italic Posture |*

Linotype Library GmbH
www.linotype.com
info@linotype.com
+49 (0) 6172 484.418

ABCDEFGHIJKLMNOPQRSTUVW
XYZ0123456789!?&@#$%*:;"

THE QUICK BROWN FOX JUMPS OVER THE LAZY DOG.

Metropolitan
*Stylized Sans Serif | Lesser
Contrast | Condensed |
Medium Weight |*

T.26 Digital Type Foundry
www.t26.com
info@t26.com
888.T26.FONT

AaBbCcDdEeFfGgHhIiJjKkLlMm
NnOoPpQqRrSsTtUuVvWwXxYy
Zz0123456789!?@#$%&*(){}:;

The quick brown fox jumps over the lazy dog.

**Linotype Authentic™
Small Serif Medium**
*Serif | Bold Weight |
Condensed |*

Linotype Library GmbH
www.linotype.com
info@linotype.com
+49 (0) 6172 484.418

AaBbCcDdEeFfGgHhIiJjKkLlMmNnOo
PpQqRrSsTtUuVvWwXxYyZz0123456
789!?&@#$%*:;"

The quick brown fox jumps over the lazy dog.

Napier Regular
*Stylized Sans Serif | Moderate
Contrast | Condensed |
Medium Weight |*

T.26 Digital Type Foundry
www.t26.com
info@t26.com
888.T26.FONT

AaBbCcDdEeFfGgHhIiJjKkLlMm
NnOoPpQqRrSsTtUuVvWwXxYy
Zz0123456789!?@#$%&*(){}:;

The quick brown fox jumps over the lazy dog.

**Linotype Authentic™
Serif Medium**
*Slab Serif | Bold Weight |
Condensed |*

Linotype Library GmbH
www.linotype.com
info@linotype.com
+49 (0) 6172 484.418

AaBbCcDdEeFfGgHhIiJjKkLlMmNn
OoPpQqRrSsTtUuVvWwXxYyZz012
3456789!?&@#$%*:;"

The quick brown fox jumps over the lazy dog.

Metamorphosis Regular
*Stylized Serif | Moderate
Contrast | Medium Weight |*

T.26 Digital Type Foundry
www.t26.com
info@t26.com
888.T26.FONT

A a B b C c D d E e F f G g H h I i J j K k L l M m N n O o P p Q q R r S s T t U u
V v W w X x Y y Z z 0 1 2 3 4 5 6 7 8 9 ! ? @ # $ % & * | | { } : ; " "

The quick brown fox jumps over the lazy dog.

D

Compacta™ Light
*Sans Serif | Bold Weight |
Ultra-Condensed |*

Linotype Library GmbH
www.linotype.com
info@linotype.com
+49 (0) 6172 484.418

a B C D E F G H I J K L M N O P Q R S T U V W
X Y Z 0 1 2 3 4 5 6 7 8 9 ! ? & @ # $ % ∗ : ; "

THE QUICK BROWN FOX JUMPS OVER THE LAZY DOG.

D

Idyll
*Sans Serif | Uniform
Medium Weight | Unicase
with Alternates |*

The Chank Company
www.chank.com
friendlyfolks@chank.com
877.GO.CHANK

A a B b C c D d E e F f G g H h I i J j K k L l M m
N n O o P p Q q R r S s T t U u V v W w X x Y y
Z z 0 1 2 3 4 5 6 7 8 9 ! ? & AV № $ % ⊙ : ; "

THE QUICK BROWN FOX JUMPS OVER THE LAZY DOG.

D

Behaviour Good
*Stylized Sans Serif | Moderate
Contrast | Pronounced Cross-
Strokes | Medium Weight |*

T.26 Digital Type Foundry
www.t26.com
info@t26.com
888.T26.FONT

A a B b C c D d E e F f G g H h I i J j K k L l M m
N n O o P p Q q R r S s T t U u V v W w X x Y y
Z z 0 1 2 3 4 5 6 7 8 9 ! ? @ # $ % & * ( ) ⊠ ⌫
. ; " "

The quick brown fox jumps over the lazy dog.

D t

F2F Czykago™ Semi Serif
*Slab Serif | Bold Weight |
Moderate Contrast |*

Linotype Library GmbH
www.linotype.com
info@linotype.com
+49 (0) 6172 484.418

A a B b C c D d E e F f G g H h I i J j K k L l M m N n
O o P p Q q R r S s T t U u V v W w X x Y y Z z 0 1 2 3
4 5 6 7 8 9 ! ? @ # $ % & * ( ) { } : ; " "
The quick brown fox jumps over the lazy dog.

D

F2F MadZine™ Script
*Serif-Script Hybrid |
Bold Weight | Erratic Weight |
Modulation |*

Linotype Library GmbH
www.linotype.com
info@linotype.com
+49 (0) 6172 484.418

A a B b C c D d E e F f G g H h I i J j K k L l M m
N n O o P p Q q R r S s T t U u V v W w X x Y y Z z
0 1 2 3 4 5 6 7 8 9 ! ? & @ # $ % * . ; "

The quick brown fox jumps over the lazy dog.

D t

Basic
*Stylized Sans Serif | Uniform
Light Weight | Condensed |*

The Chank Company
www.chank.com
friendlyfolks@chank.com
877.GO.CHANK

AaBbCcDdEeFfGgHhIiJjKkLlMmNnOo
PpQqRrSsTtUuVvWwXxYyZz012345
6789!?@#$%&*[]{}:;" "

The quick brown fox jumps over the lazy dog.

D *t*

Linotype Kaliber™ Bold
Sans Serif | Bold Weight |
Squared Curves | Condensed |

Linotype Library GmbH
www.linotype.com
info@linotype.com
+49 (0) 6172 484.418

AaBbCcDdEeFfGgHhIiJjKkLlMm
NnOoPpQqRrSsTtUuVvWwXxYyZz
0123456789!?&@#$%*:;"

The quick brown fox jumps over the lazy dog.

D *t*

Mechanic Gothic
Stylized Sans Serif |
Bold Weight | Condensed |
Moderate Contrast |

T.26 Digital Type Foundry
www.t26.com
info@t26.com
888.T26.FONT

---

aBCDDeFFGHIiJjKKMNOPQRr
STtUVWXYZ0123456789!?@#$%
&*(){}:;" "

THE QUICK BROWN FOX JUMPS OVER THE LAZY DOG.

D

Quartan™ Std Book
Sans Serif | Medium Weight |
Unicase | Slightly Extended |

Linotype Library GmbH
www.linotype.com
info@linotype.com
+49 (0) 6172 484.418

AaBbCcDdEeFfGgHhIiJjKkLl
MmNnOoPpQqRrSsTtUuVvWwXx
YyZz0123456789!?&@#$%*:;"

The quick brown fox jumps over the lazy dog.

D **T**

Betabet Sans
Stylized Sans Serif | Moderate
Contrast | Medium Weight |

T.26 Digital Type Foundry
www.t26.com
info@t26.com
888.T26.FONT

AaBbCcDdEeFfGgHhIiJjKkLlMmNnOo
PpQqRrSsTtUuVvWwXxYyZz012345
6789!?$%&*():;" "

The quick brown fox jumps over the lazy dog.

D *t*

Green™
Sans Serif | Semibold Weight |
Erratic Contrast and Modulation

Linotype Library GmbH
www.linotype.com
info@linotype.com
+49 (0) 6172 484.418

ABCDEFGHIJKLMNOPQRSTUVW
XYZ0123456789!?&@№$¢*:;"

THE QUICK BROWN FOX JUMPS OVER THE LAZY DOG.

D

F-Groove 76
Graphic | Bold Weight |
Multiple Inline |

T.26 Digital Type Foundry
www.t26.com
info@t26.com
888.T26.FONT

Young Adult Color

As kids grow into young adulthood, their color sense becomes more complex, but vivid, saturated colors still rule. Hot pink, orange, yellow, acid green, red, violet, cobalt blue, black, and gray form the basic palette for young adults. More complex tertiary colors, however, become part of the scheme: warmer burgundies, olive green, deep ochre, and grays that are clearly warm or cool—almost showing color, but not quite. The saturated hues, in combination, allude to the emotional intensity of adolescence yet are also holdovers from earlier childhood, still very much a part of the young adult psyche. Gaming, sports, and popular culture—especially music—make their influence known through these colors as well. Jarring combinations of these vibrant hues, and combinations with the more neutral ones of the palette—for example, orange with olive, intense aqua with brown—convey the rebelliousness and experimental nature of young adults. Gender identity becomes especially important for young adults, and groupings of these colors can be appropriate in resonating with audiences that are either predominantly male or predominantly female: orange, red, blue, acid green, and black for boys; burgundies, violet, colored grays, and olive for girls.

Sample Color Combinations

10 C	
100 M	
0 Y	
0 K	

0 C
70 M
100 Y
0 K

31 C
0 M
100 Y
0 K

100 C
68 M
0 Y
0 K

78 C
100 M
0 Y
26 K

30 C
95 M
0 Y
53 K

0 C
0 M
72 Y
60 K

100 C
0 M
33 Y
0 K

12 C
0 M
0 Y
38 K

0 C
45 M
100 Y
34 K

With allusions to simplicity and poise, a mature quality in design work—
and of design directed toward an adult audience—may encompass
typefaces and color with characteristics that could also be described as
"conservative," "elegant," or "professional"—for example, a classic serif.
The differences among options at this level of specificity become minute,
but there are typefaces, as well as color schemes, that push toward
a relaxed state, a kind of authority in repose, that more closely charac-
terizes the evolved adult over the strictly corporate or elegant.

Adults

Maturity is a state of being fully developed, and transitional serifs, rather
than oldstyle or archaic ones, communicate this in their sharper serifs,
increased contrast, and precise details. Similarly, a script typeface, which
might initially seem romantic or elegant, may feel more mature if it is less
decorative and shows a more pronounced handwritten quality. Moreover,
script faces that are more upright—rather than those with a steep, cursive
posture—may exhibit some qualities associated with sans-serif types and,
thus, may connote not only the confidence of strong handwriting but also
the sober, objective, and reasoned nature of an adult. Typefaces of one
class—sans serifs, for example—that include details obviously derived from
older, serif styles, may also be said to feel "mature" in that they transmit a
sense of the historical continuum through their forms. Pronounced details
of form, such as exaggerated ductus from stem to branch, overly shapely
counters, and more rigid—almost geometric or abrupt—modulation, also
allude to a sense of extra development in their studied presentation.

Magazine Page Spread
top, and detail, bottom

Code **Magazine**
Beverly Hills [CA] *USA*

A a B b C c D d E e F f G g H h I i J j K k L l M m N n
O o P p Q q R r S s T t U u V v W w X x Y y Z z 0 1 2 3
4 5 6 7 8 9 ! ? & @ # $ % * : ; "

The quick brown fox jumps over the lazy dog.

JY Klin
Stylized Sans Serif | Condensed |
Uniform Medium Weight |

JY&A Fonts
www.jyanet.com/fonts

A a B b C c D d E e F f G g H h I i J j K k L l M m N n
O o P p Q q R r S s T t U u V v W w X x Y y Z z 0 1 2 3
4 5 6 7 8 9 ! ? & @ # $ % * : ; "

The quick brown fox jumps over the lazy dog.

D t

JY Klin Alternatives
Stylized Sans Serif | Condensed |
Uniform Medium Weight |

JY&A Fonts
www.jyanet.com/fonts

A a B b C c D d E e F f G g H h I i J j K k L l M m
N n O o P p Q q R r S s T t U u V v W w X x Y y Z z
0 1 2 3 4 5 6 7 8 9 ! ? & @ # $ % * : ; "

The quick brown fox jumps over the lazy dog.

D T

Dolly Roman
Serif | Lesser Contrast |
Medium Weight |

Underware
www.underware.nl
info@underware.nl
31 (0)70 42 78 117

**A a B b C c D d E e F f G g H h I i J j K k L l M m
N n O o P p Q q R r S s T t U u V v W w X x Y y Z z
0 1 2 3 4 5 6 7 8 9 ! ? & @ # $ % * : ; "**

The quick brown fox jumps over the lazy dog.

D T

Dolly Bold
Serif | Pronounced Contrast |
Bold Weight |

Underware
www.underware.nl
info@underware.nl
31 (0)70 42 78 117

A a B b C c D d E e F f G g H h I i J j K k L l M m N n
O o P p Q q R r S s T t U u V v W w X x Y y Z z 0 1 2 3
4 5 6 7 8 9 ! ? @ # $ % & * ( ) ( ) : ; " "
The quick brown fox jumps over the lazy dog.

D T

Linotype Textra™ Medium
Sans serif | Medium Weight |
Canted Terminals |

Linotype Library GmbH
www.linotype.com
info@linotype.com
+49 (0) 6172 484.418

A a B b C c D d E e F f G g H h I i J j K k L l M m
N n O o P p Q q R r S s T t U u V v W w X x Y y
Z z 0 1 2 3 4 5 6 7 8 9 ! ? & @ # $ % * : ; "

The quick brown fox jumps over the lazy dog.

D T

Tempelhof Medium
Sans Serif | Uniform Medium
Weight | Condensed |

T.26 Digital Type Foundry
www.t26.com
info@t26.com
888.T26.FONT

A a B b C c D d E e F f G g H h I i J j K k L l M m
N n O o P p Q q R r S s T t U u V v W w X x Y y
Z z 0 1 2 3 4 5 6 7 8 9 ! ? & @ # $ % * : ; "

The quick brown fox jumps over the lazy dog.

D T

Tainted Regular
*Semi-Serif | Uniform Medium
Weight | Slightly Condensed |*

T.26 Digital Type Foundry
www.t26.com
info@t26.com
888.T26.FONT

**A a B b C c D d E e F f G g H h I i J j K k L l M m N n
O o P p Q q R r S s T t U u V v W w X x Y y Z z 0 1
2 3 4 5 6 7 8 9 ! ? @ # $ % & * ( ) { } : ; " "
The quick brown fox jumps over the lazy dog.**

D T

Linotype Finnegan™ Bold
*Sans Serif | Notable Contrast |
Modulation | Soft Terminals |*

Linotype Library GmbH
www.linotype.com
info@linotype.com
+49 (0) 6172 484.418

A a B b C c D d E e F f G g H h I i J j K k L l M m N n
O o P p Q q R r S s T t U u V v W w X x Y y Z z 0 1
2 3 4 5 6 7 8 9 ! ? & @ # $ % * : ; "

The quick brown fox jumps over the lazy dog.

D T

RTF Dokument Gothic
*Sans Serif | Uniform
Medium Weight |*

P22 Type Foundry
www.p22.com
p22@p22.com
800.P22.5080

A a B b C c D d E e F f G g H h I i J j K k L l M m N n
O o P p Q q R r S s T t U u V v W w X x Y y Z z 0 1
2 3 4 5 6 7 8 9 ! ? @ # $ % & * ( ) { } : ; " "
The quick brown fox jumps over the lazy dog.

D T

Linotype Aroma™ Regular
*Sans Serif | Medium Weight |
Sharp Terminals |*

Linotype Library GmbH
www.linotype.com
info@linotype.com
+49 (0) 6172 484.418

A a B b C c D d E e F f G g H h I i J j K k L l M m
N n O o P p Q q R r S s T t U u V v W w X x Y y
Z z 0 1 2 3 4 5 6 7 8 9 ! ? @ # $ % & * ( ) { } : ; " "
The quick brown fox jumps over the lazy dog.

D T

Berling™ Roman
*Serif | Medium Weight |
Sharp Serifs |
Noticeable Contrast |*

Linotype Library GmbH
www.linotype.com
info@linotype.com
+49 (0) 6172 484.418

A a B b C c D d E e F f G g H h I i J j K k L l M m
N n O o P p Q q R r S s T t U u V v W w X x Y y Z z
0 1 2 3 4 5 6 7 8 9 ! ? @ # $ % & * ( ) { } : ; " "
The quick brown fox jumps over the lazy dog.

D T

Caslon 540 Roman
*Serif | Medium Weight |
Pronounced Contrast |*

Linotype Library GmbH
www.linotype.com
info@linotype.com
+49 (0) 6172 484.418

A a B b C c D d E e F f G g H h I i J j K k L l M m N n
O o P p Q q R r S s T t U u V v W w X x Y y Z z 0 1
2 3 4 5 6 7 8 9 ! ? @ # $ % & * ( ) { } : ; " "
The quick brown fox jumps over the lazy dog.

D T

ITC Charter™ Regular
Serif | Moderate Contrast |
Abrupt Joints | Slab Influence |

Linotype Library GmbH
www.linotype.com
info@linotype.com
+49 (0) 6172 484.418

A a B b C c D d E e F f G g H h I i J j K k L l M m N n
O o P p Q q R r S s T t U u V v W w X x Y y Z z 0 1 2 3
4 5 6 7 8 9 ! ? @ # $ % & * ( ) { } : ; " "
The quick brown fox jumps over the lazy dog.

D t

Ellington™ Light
Serif | Pronounced Contrast |
Modulation | Condensed

Linotype Library GmbH
www.linotype.com
info@linotype.com
+49 (0) 6172 484.418

A a B b C c D d E e F f G g H h I i J j K k L l M m N n O o
P p Q q R r S s T t U u V v W w X x Y y Z z 0 1 2 3 4 5
6 7 8 9 ! ? @ # $ % & * ( ) { } : ; " "
The quick brown fox jumps over the lazy dog.

D T

Linotype Ergo™ Regular
Sans Serif | Medium Weight |
Slightly Squared Curves |
Abrupt Terminals |

Linotype Library GmbH
www.linotype.com
info@linotype.com
+49 (0) 6172 484.418

A a B b C c D d E e F f G g H h I i J j K k L l M m N n
O o P p Q q R r S s T t U u V v W w X x Y y Z z 0 1
2 3 4 5 6 7 8 9 ! ? @ # $ % & * ( ) { } : ; " "
The quick brown fox jumps over the lazy dog.

D T

Esperanto™ Roman
Serif | Medium Weight |
Moderate Contrast | Sharp
Terminals |

Linotype Library GmbH
www.linotype.com
info@linotype.com
+49 (0) 6172 484.418

A a B b C c D d E e F f G g H h I i J j K k L l M m
N n O o P p Q q R r S s T t U u V v W w X x Y y Z z
0 1 2 3 4 5 6 7 8 9 ! ? @ # $ % & * ( ) { } : ; " "
The quick brown fox jumps over the lazy dog.

D T

ITC Mendoza Roman® Book
Serif | Medium Weight |
Moderate Contrast | Slight
Angularity |

Linotype Library GmbH
www.linotype.com
info@linotype.com
+49 (0) 6172 484.418

A a B b C c D d E e F f G g H h I i J j K k L l M m N n
O o P p Q q R r S s T t U u V v W w X x Y y Z z 0 1 2 3
4 5 6 7 8 9 ! ? @ # $ % & * ( ) { } : ; " "
The quick brown fox jumps over the lazy dog.

D t

Linotype Pisa™ Regular
Sans serif | Medium Weight |
Slight Italic Posture | Condensed

Linotype Library GmbH
www.linotype.com
info@linotype.com
+49 (0) 6172 484.418

A a B b C c D d E e F f G g H h I i J j K k L l M m
N n O o P p Q q R r S s T t U u V v W w X x Y y
Z z 0 1 2 3 4 5 6 7 8 9 ! ? @ # $ % & * ( ) { } : ; " "
The quick brown fox jumps over the lazy dog.

D T

Walbaum Roman
Serif | Noticeable Contrast |
Slightly Squared Curves |

Linotype Library GmbH
www.linotype.com
info@linotype.com
+49 (0) 6172 484.418

A a B b C c D d E e F f G g H h I i J j K k L l M m N n
O o P p Q q R r S s T t U u V v W w X x Y y Z z 0 1 2 3
4 5 6 7 8 9 ! ? & @ # $ % * : ; "
The quick brown fox jumps over the lazy dog.

D T

Revalo Classic Regular
Sans Serif | Uniform Medium
Weight | Condensed |

T.26 Digital Type Foundry
www.t26.com
info@t26.com
888.T26.FONT

A a B b C c D d E e F f G g H h I i J j K k L l M m N n
O o P p Q q R r S s T t U u V v W w X x Y y Z z 0 1
2 3 4 5 6 7 8 9 ! ? @ # $ % & * ( ) { } : ; " "
The quick brown fox jumps over the lazy dog.

D T

Photina™ Roman
Serif | Medium Weight |
Pronounced Contrast |
Sharp Serifs |

Linotype Library GmbH
www.linotype.com
info@linotype.com
+49 (0) 6172 484.418

A a B b C c D d E e F f G g H h I i J j K k L l M m
N n O o P p Q q R r S s T t U u V v W w X x Y y Z z
0 1 2 3 4 5 6 7 8 9 ! ? @ # $ % & * ( ) { } : ; " "
The quick brown fox jumps over the lazy dog.

D T

Swift™ Pro Regular
Serif | Moderate Contrast |
Pronounced Wedge Serifs |

Linotype Library GmbH
www.linotype.com
info@linotype.com
+49 (0) 6172 484.418

A a B b C c D d E e F f G g H h I i J j K k L l M m
N n O o P p Q q R r S s T t U u V v W w X x Y y
Z z 0 1 2 3 4 5 6 7 8 9 ! ? & @ # $ % * : ; "
The quick brown fox jumps over the lazy dog.

D T

Slappy Regular
Sans Serif | Uniform
Medium Weight |

T.26 Digital Type Foundry
www.t26.com
info@t26.com
888.T26.FONT

A A B B C C D D E E F F G G H H I I J J K K L L M M
N N O O P P Q Q R R S S T T U U V V W W X X Y Y
Z Z 0 I 2 3 4 5 6 7 8 9 ! ? @ # $ % & * ( ) { } : ; " "
THE QUICK BROWN FOX JUMPS OVER THE LAZY DOG.

D

Koloss™ Regular
Slab Serif | Medium Weight |
Uniform Strokes | Caps with
Small Caps |

Linotype Library GmbH
www.linotype.com
info@linotype.com
+49 (0) 6172 484.418

Adult Color

Maturity is reflected in color as complexity and restraint—color that has become worldly and grown up. Generally, middle-value blue, blue-violet, teal-blue, and similar-value neutrals in equal combinations are mature in nature—the authority and stateliness of blue, the stability of green, the considerate quality of violet, tempered by desaturation and mixed with a bit of black, neither bright nor deep and rich. Adults between thirty and fifty years of age tend to respond to neutrals, especially in combinations that explore the richness of a single color family—monochromatic color schemes that center around wood and earth tones, metal and textiles. These colors speak to the adult's urge to nest and acquire comfort after the tumultuous period of youth.

Sample Color Combinations

100 C	
44 M	
0 Y	
30 K	

88 C	
59 M	
0 Y	
27 K	

74 C	
17 M	
27 Y	
0 K	

0 C	
19 M	
26 Y	
42 K	

44 C	
0 M	
32 Y	
41 K	

0 C	
25 M	
36 Y	
57 K	

0 C	
48 M	
57 Y	
67 K	

0 C	
10 M	
20 Y	
55 K	

56 C	
46 M	
0 Y	
57 K	

25 C	
25 M	
51 Y	
0 K	

Traditionally thought of as quiet, staid, and uninvolved, seniors today are active individuals enjoying the later years of their life after the kids have left and work has ended—albeit with a few more aches and pains than in their youth. Typography and color for the elder population are indeed relatively restrained, but still lively.

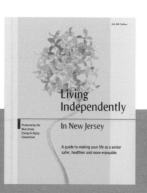

Seniors

Type styles geared toward seniors, while not necessarily oldstyle or academic-looking, eschew excessive detailing and present a straightforward message in their drawing. This directness responds to the senior's sense of the importance of their available time and a disregard for nonsense or childish things. Typefaces that are highly resolved, with optically uniform widths among characters, open counters, large x-heights, even stroke width—or minimal contrast and soft, fluid joints—not only present an even, unsyncopated rhythm that reflects this desire for simplicity but also accommodate the average senior's difficulty with reading small or condensed type. Serifs and sans serifs are equally appropriate stylistically, although older styles in each tend to feel more relevant to expressing the age of older people.

Book Jacket
top, and detail, bottom

STIM Visual Communication
Timothy Samara
New York City *USA*

A a B b C c D d E e F f G g H h I i J j K k L l M m N n
O o P p Q q R r S s T t U u V v W w X x Y y Z z 0 1 2
3 4 5 6 7 8 9 ! ? & @ # $ % * : ; "

The quick brown fox jumps over the lazy dog.

D T

JY Décennie Express
*Stylized Sans Serif | Slightly
Condensed | Moderate Contrast |
Light Weight |*

JY&A Fonts
www.jyanet.com/fonts

A a B b C c D d E e F f G g H h I i J j K k L l M m
N n O o P p Q q R r S s T t U u V v W w X x Y y Z z
0 1 2 3 4 5 6 7 8 9 ! ? & @ # $ % * : ; "

The quick brown fox jumps over the lazy dog.

D T

JY Tranquility Newstyle
*Serif | Uniform Medium Weight |
Slightly Condensed |*

JY&A Fonts
www.jyanet.com/fonts

A a B b C c D d E e F f G g H h I i J j K k L l M m N n
O o P p Q q R r S s T t U u V v W w X x Y y Z z 0 1
2 3 4 5 6 7 8 9 ! ? @ # $ % & * ( ) { } : ; " "
The quick brown fox jumps over the lazy dog.

D T

Cisalpin™ Std Regular
*Sans Serif | Medium Weight |
Large x-Height |
Abrupt Terminals |*

Linotype Library GmbH
www.linotype.com
info@linotype.com
+49 (0) 6172 484.418

A a B b C c D d E e F f G g H h I i J j K k L l M m N n
O o P p Q q R r S s T t U u V v W w X x Y y Z z 0 1 2 3
4 5 6 7 8 9 ! ? @ # $ % & * ( ) { } : ; " "
The quick brown fox jumps over the lazy dog.

D T

ITC Clearface® Regular
*Serif | Notable Contrast |
Softened Serifs |
Slightly Condensed |*

Linotype Library GmbH
www.linotype.com
info@linotype.com
+49 (0) 6172 484.418

A A B B C C D D E E F F G G H H I I J J K K L L M M
N N O O P P Q Q R R S S T T U U V V W W X X Y Y
Z Z 0 1 2 3 4 5 6 7 8 9 ! ? @ # $ % & * ( ) { } : ; " "
THE QUICK BROWN FOX JUMPS OVER THE LAZY DOG.

D

Copperplate Gothic 31 BC
*Serif | Bold Weight | Caps with
Small Caps | Sharp Serifs |*

Linotype Library GmbH
www.linotype.com
info@linotype.com
+49 (0) 6172 484.418

A a B b C c D d E e F f G g H h I i J j K k L l M m N n
O o P p Q q R r S s T t U u V v W w X x Y y Z z 0 1 2 3
4 5 6 7 8 9 ! ? @ # $ % & * ( ) { } : ; " "
The quick brown fox jumps over the lazy dog.

D T

Dialog™ Roman
*Sans Serif | Medium Weight |
Slight Modulation |
Noticeably Large x-Height |*

Linotype Library GmbH
www.linotype.com
info@linotype.com
+49 (0) 6172 484.418

A a B b C c D d E e F f G g H h I i J j K k L l M m N n
O o P p Q q R r S s T t U u V v W w X x Y y Z z 0 1 2 3
4 5 6 7 8 9 ! ? @ # $ % & * ( ) { } : ; " "
The quick brown fox jumps over the lazy dog.

D **T**

Linotype Finnegan™ Regular
*Sans serif | Medium Weight |
Modulation | Turned and Canted
Terminals |*

Linotype Library GmbH
www.linotype.com
info@linotype.com
+49 (0) 6172 484.418

A A B B C C D D E E F F G G H H I I J J K K L L M M N N
O O P P Q Q R R S S T T U U V V W W X X Y Y Z Z 0 1 2 3
4 5 6 7 8 9 ! ? @ # $ % & * ( ) { } : ; " "
THE QUICK BROWN FOX JUMPS OVER THE LAZY DOG.

D

Linotype Finnegan™ Regular
Small Caps
*Sans serif | Medium Weight |
Modulation | Turned and
Canted Terminals |*

Linotype Library GmbH
www.linotype.com
info@linotype.com
+49 (0) 6172 484.418

A a B b C c D d E e F f G g H h I i J j K k L l M m N n
O o P p Q q R r S s T t U u V v W w X x Y y Z z 0 1 2 3
4 5 6 7 8 9 ! ? @ # $ % & * ( ) { } : ; " "
The quick brown fox jumps over the lazy dog.

D **T**

ITC Franklin Gothic® Medium
*Sans serif | Medium Weight |
Uniform Strokes |
Noticeably Large x-Height |*

Linotype Library GmbH
www.linotype.com
info@linotype.com
+49 (0) 6172 484.418

A a B b C c D d E e F f G g H h I i J j K k L l M m
N n O o P p Q q R r S s T t U u V v W w X x Y y
Z z 0 1 2 3 4 5 6 7 8 9 ! ? @ # $ % & * ( ) { } : ; " "
The quick brown fox jumps over the lazy dog.

D **T**

ITC Leawood® Book
*Serif | Moderate Contrast |
Noticeably Large x-Height |*

Linotype Library GmbH
www.linotype.com
info@linotype.com
+49 (0) 6172 484.418

A a B b C c D d E e F f G g H h I i J j K k L l M m
N n O o P p Q q R r S s T t U u V v W w X x Y y
Z z 0 1 2 3 4 5 6 7 8 9 ! ? @ # $ % & * ( ) { } : ;
" "

The quick brown fox jumps over the lazy dog.

D **T**

Lucida® Serif Roman
*Serif | Moderate Contrast |
Slightly Condensed |
Slab Influence |*

Linotype Library GmbH
www.linotype.com
info@linotype.com
+49 (0) 6172 484.418

A a B b C c D d E e F f G g H h I i J j K k L l M m N n
O o P p Q q R r S s T t U u V v W w X x Y y Z z 0 1 2 3
4 5 6 7 8 9 ! ? @ # $ % & * ( ) { } : ; " "
The quick brown fox jumps over the lazy dog.

D **T**

Memento™ Roman
*Serif | Medium Weight |
Moderate Contrast | Minimal
Wedge Serifs | Slightly
Condensed |*

Linotype Library GmbH
www.linotype.com
info@linotype.com
+49 (0) 6172 484.418

Senior Color

As adults get older, they come to prefer cleaner, more pure colors, as their ability to distinguish between more complex shading decreases with age. Although pure primaries and secondary colors may be a bit jarring, desaturated versions of red, orange, yellow, blue, green, and violet maintain their chromatic identities while presenting a less intense visual experience. Older age is represented, however, as a continued desaturation of the core colors and a shift toward warmer neutrals—almost autumnal and then wintry in character. Graying these colors, as well as lightening their values, symbolizes the unavoidable frailty and wisdom of old age.

Sample Color Combinations

>	0 C
	82 M
	75 Y
	28 K
>	0 C
	27 M
	72 Y
	0 K
>	71 C
	30 M
	0 Y
	5 K
>	50 C
	68 M
	15 Y
	22 K
>	68 C
	0 M
	57 Y
	20 K
>	36 C
	0 M
	53 Y
	37 K
>	0 C
	26 M
	45 Y
	35 K
>	0 C
	23 M
	39 Y
	55 K
>	3 C
	16 M
	0 Y
	45 K
>	7 C
	0 M
	3 Y
	39 K

Brand Engine
80 Liberty Ship Way, Ste. 1
Sausalito, CA 94965 *USA*
www.brandengine.com

132

Christine Fent, Manja Uellpap, Gilmar Wendt
6 Salem Road
London W2 4BU *UK*

108

Code
8484 Wilshire Boulevard, Ste. 900
Beverly Hills, CA 90211 *USA*
www.code-magazine.com

244

Creuna Design
Stranden 3A
NO-0250 Oslo *Norway*
www.creunadesign.no

148

Crush
6 Gloucester Street
Brighton BN1 4EW *UK*
www.crushed.co.uk

56, 114

Fast Company
375 Lexington Avenue
New York, NY 10017 *USA*
www.fastcompany.com

50

Flat
391 Broadway, 3rd Floor
New York, NY 10013 *USA*
www.flat.com

170

Gorska Design
1277 8th Avenue, No. 105
San Francisco, CA 94122 *USA*
www.gorska.com

90

Joe Miller's Company
3080 Olcott Street, Ste. 105A
Santa Clara, CA 95054 *USA*
joecompany@aol.com

80

Johnny V. Design
2405 Wittington Boulevard
Alexandria, VA 22308 *USA*
www.funkfoto.com

210

Kenzo Izutani Office Corp.
1-24-19 Fukasawa, Setagaya-Ku
Tokyo 158-0081 *Japan*
www.izutanix.com

214

Loewy
147A Grosvenor Road
London SWIV 3NX *UK*
www.loewygroup.com

68

Love Communications
546 South 200 West
Salt Lake City, UT 84101 *USA*
www.lovecomm.net

164

LSD
San Andrés, 36, 2° 6
28004 Madrid *Spain*
www.lsdspace.com

138

Lure Design, Inc.
1009 Virginia Drive
Orlando, FL 32803 *USA*
www.luredesigninc.com

152

MAGMA Büro fur Gestaltung
Bachstrasse 43
D-76185 Karlsruhe *Germany*
www.magma-ka.de

74

Mires
2345 Kettner Boulevard
San Diego, CA 92103 *USA*
www.miresbrands.com

34

Mixer
Löwenplatz 5
CH 6005 Lucerne *Switzerland*
www.mixer.ch

96

Modern Dog Design Co.
7903 Greenwood Avenue North
Seattle, WA 98103 *USA*
www.moderndog.com

238

Momentum
6665 Delmar Boulevard
St. Louis, MO 63130 *USA*
www.momentumww.com

198

Motive Design Research
2028 Fifth Avenue, Ste. 204
Seattle, WA 98121 *USA*
www.altmotive.com

40

P22 Type Foundry
PO Box 770
Buffalo, NY 14213 *USA*
www.p22.com

28

Ph.D
1524A Clover Field Boulevard
Santa Monica, CA 90404 *USA*
www.phdla.com

180

Palozzolo™ Design
6410 Knapp Street NE
Ada, MI 49301 *USA*
www.palazzolodesign.com

186

The Pushpin Group
55 East 9th Street, #1G
New York, NY 10003 *USA*
www.pushpininc.com

192

Q
Sonnenberger Strasse 16
Wiesbaden 65193 *Germany*
www.q-home.de

142

Real Simple / Time, Inc.
1271 Avenue of the Americas
New York, NY 10020 *USA*
www.realsimple.com

16

Smith Design
205 Thomas Street | PO Box 8278
Glen Ridge, NJ 07028 *USA*
www.smithdesign.com

232

Starshot
Halsenstrasse 84
80638 Munich *Germany*
www.starshot.de

44

STIM Visual Communication
436 West 22nd Street, No. 4C
New York, NY 10011 *USA*
www.visual-stim.com

62, 102, 120, 158, 176, 220, 224, 228, 250

Studio Flux (now ODO)
4715 Pillsbury Avenue South
Minneapolis, MN 55419 *USA*
www.themightyodo.com

204

Underware
Schouwberg Straat 2
2511 VA Den Haag *Netherlands*
www.underware.nl

22

Untitled
Radar Studio, Coldblow Lane
Thurnham, Maidstone
Kent ME14 3LR *UK*
www.untitled.co.uk

126

Voice
217 Gilbert Street
Adelaide SA 5000 *Australia*
www.voicedesign.net

84